UNITS 41–50

The Gospels and Acts

Fourth Edition

Harry Wendt

CROSSWAYS INTERNATIONAL®
Minneapolis, MN

CROSSWAYS®—SECTION 5
was developed and written by
Harry Wendt, Minneapolis, MN

Illustrations by
Knarelle Beard, Adelaide, South Australia

The Bible text in this publication is from the New Revised Standard Version of the Bible, copyright 1989 by the Division of Christian Education of the National Council of Churches of Christ in the United States of America and used by permission.

CROSSWAYS®—SECTION 5
is published and distributed by
CROSSWAYS INTERNATIONAL®
7930 Computer Avenue South
Minneapolis, MN 55435
www.crossways.org

Printed in China

Nihil Obstat: Ms. Catherine Cory, Ph.D.
February 24, 2014

Imprimatur: The Most Reverend John C. Nienstedt, STD
March 31, 2014

Ecclesiastical approval is a declaration that a book or pamphlet is considered to be free from doctrinal or moral error. It is not implied that those who have granted the ecclesiastical approval agree with the contents, opinions, or statements expressed.

ISBN 978-1-891245-22-0

Fourth Edition

10 9 8 7 6 5 4 3

A Welcome from Crossways International®!

We at Crossways International (CI) are delighted that you are about to undertake a study of the entire sweep of the Old and New Testaments using our materials as your guide. May your journey be fruitful and rewarding, and draw you ever closer to the mind, manner, and meaning of Jesus, the Servant-Messiah.

CI is more than a publisher of Christian education and Bible study materials. We also offer hands-on training in the use of our materials, and we make our materials available to special ministries and missions all around the world. We would be happy to partner with you in *any way* that might help you to share the Good News of God's Kingdom with the people you reach.

The courses of Crossways International have been translated into dozens of languages and are used by all major Christian denominations in numerous countries around the world. We have trained tens of thousands of pastors, teachers, and lay-people to teach the Bible with joy and passion.

WHAT DISTINGUISHES CROSSWAYS INTERNATIONAL?

1 A Panoramic View of Scripture

CI's courses examine the meaning of the Bible by digging into the *complete story* that runs through it—from *Genesis to Revelation*. We believe you cannot fully grasp the enormity and profundity of Jesus the Messiah's mind and message without understanding what preceded Him and set the stage for His ministry and mission.

2 Visual Learning

All of CI's teaching materials make extensive use of specially designed *color graphics* to help people better understand and remember the written material. These make it easier to share God's Good News.

3 Focus on Jesus, the Servant-King

We are not about biblical study merely for study's sake. The core of every CI course is *Jesus*, the *King who washed feet*—the Messiah who invites us to follow Him by loving and serving others—as He did. These courses help to *transform hearts and lives.*

4 Tools for Faith Development

CI offers *survey courses of increasing depth* that lead people through the entire story of the Bible—plus *short courses* on specific biblical topics, such as Jesus' parables, Christian stewardship, prayer, the Passion and the Christmas stories.

5 Workshop Training for Teachers & Laity

For those interested in *revitalizing their ministries* using CI's courses, we offer workshops that train attendees, step-by-step, how to do it. We also offer workshops for lay-people who are eager to boost their biblical literacy and steep themselves in Scripture. Call us or visit our website.

6 Mission Around the World—and at Home

CI's dedication to the mission and message of Jesus goes beyond mere publishing and teacher-training. We make our materials available in the U.S. and all around the world in *prisons, hospitals, orphanages, street ministries*—anywhere the need is great but resources are scarce. CI is a *non-profit ministry* that relies on our modest sales and the benevolence of supporters in our efforts to heed the Great Commission to "go and make disciples of all nations."

Contact Crossways International® at 1-800-257-7308 or visit our website at www.crossways.org.

The Structure of the *Crossways*® Series

Crossways® is offered in six sections of ten units each. Although each section is available for separate purchase, would-be students of the Bible are encouraged to work through all six sections in sequence to gain an overview of the Bible's "big picture." If they choose not to do that, they should first work through a course that will give them an overview of the biblical story-line, such as Crossways International®'s *See Through the Scriptures*® or *The Divine Drama*®*—The Biblical Narrative*. The six sections of *Crossways* are:

From Creation to the Transjordan

Creation; the biblical overture; the patriarchal narratives; the Exodus from Egypt; the Sinai covenant and the Pentateuchal law-codes; the wilderness wanderings.

From the Conquest to the Babylonian Exile

The narratives in Joshua, Judges, 1 and 2 Samuel, 1 and 2 Kings; Worship and Holy War.

The Preexilic and Exilic Prophets

Introducing the Prophets; Amos; Hosea; Isaiah 1–39; Micah; Jeremiah; Nahum, Habakkuk, Zephaniah; Ezekiel.

The Postexilic Period and Judaism

The return from Babylon; the history of the intertestamental period; 1 and 2 Chronicles, Ezra, and Nehemiah; the postexilic prophets; Psalms; Wisdom literature; apocalyptic writings and Daniel, the Apocrypha and Pseudepigrapha; messianic expectations.

The Gospels and Acts

First-century Judaism; Mark; Matthew; Luke; John; Acts.

The Letters and Revelation

Paul and his letters; the Catholic letters; Revelation

UNITS 41–50

The Gospels and Acts

UNIT 41

First-Century Judaism

Religion and Politics in Judah at the Time of Jesus

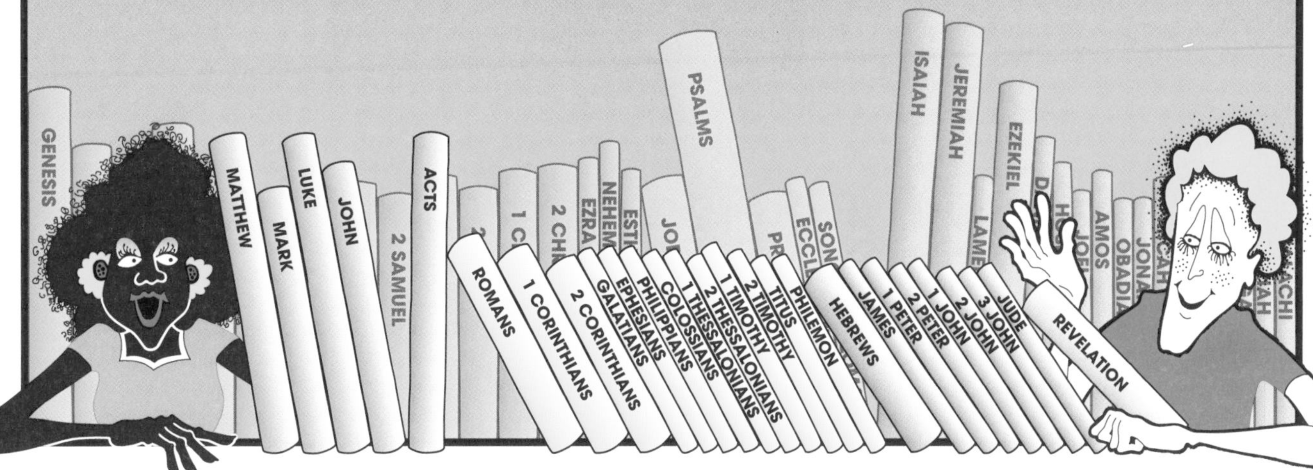

ILLUSTRATION

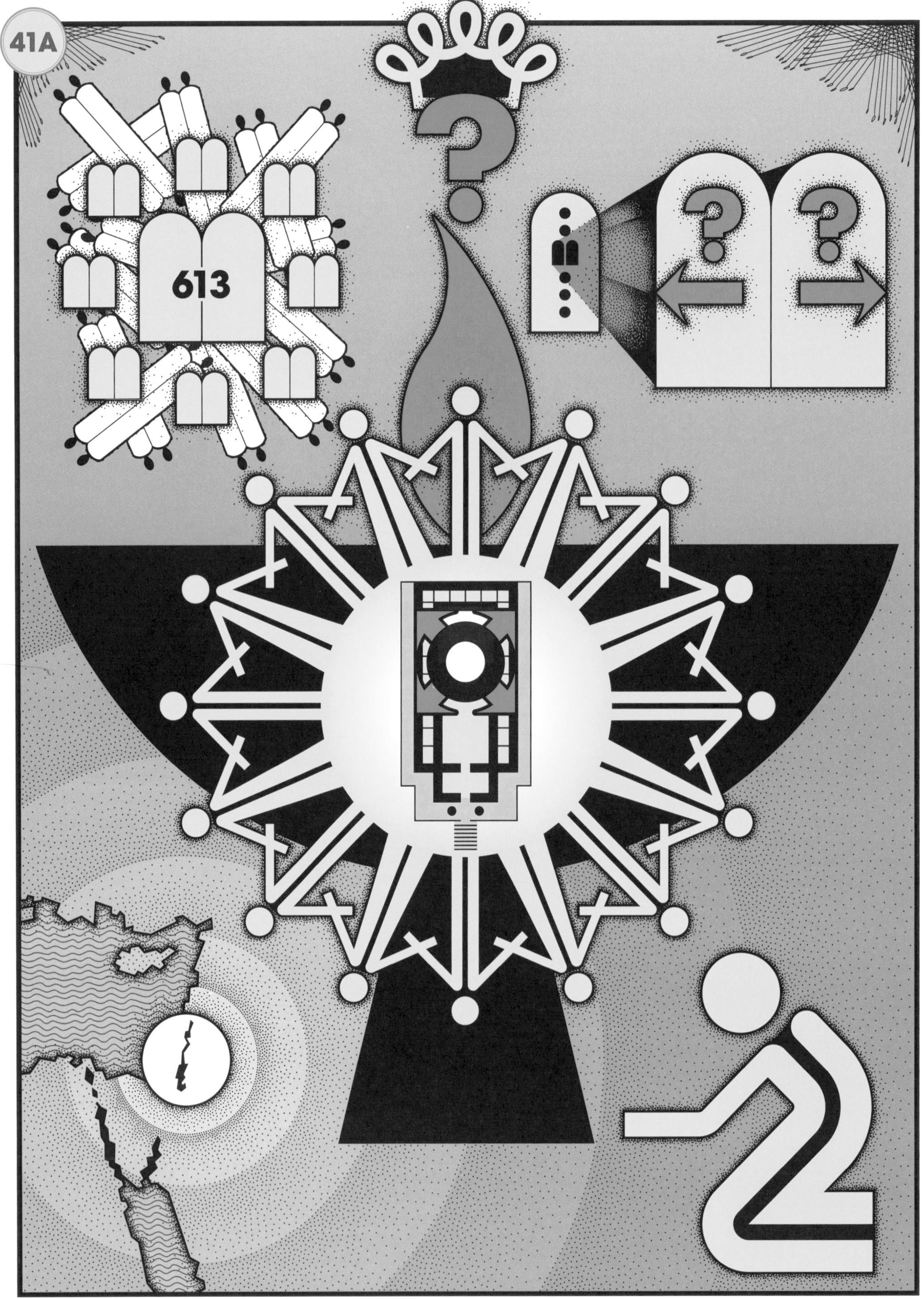

Key Issues in First-Century Judaism

ILLUSTRATIONS 41A–41E provide background material for the units that follow. **ILLUSTRATION 41A** depicts some of the major political and religious issues on which the postexilic community focused.

1 ***Crown, question mark:*** The Davidic dynasty was not reestablished after the return from Babylon. Judah remained under foreign control during most of the postexilic period.

2 ***Symbol for God; community around Temple:*** The High Priest and his associates played a central role in directing the life of the nation. They encouraged the people to think of themselves as an ecclesiastical community living in the presence of the one true God whose dwelling place on earth was the Jerusalem Temple. The people were to honor and worship that God through rituals, sacrifices, and obedience. In the years following the reign of the Syrian Seleucid, Antiochus IV "Epiphanes" (175–163 B.C.), the High Priests were not descendants of David's priest, Zadok—which angered many within the nation.

3 In the postexilic period, Aaron was seen as the ancestor of the Jerusalem priesthood who sacrificed and blessed and exercised supreme authority; he was held in high esteem, Sirach 45:20. The priesthood was divided among twenty-four families who each performed Temple duties for a week. Sixteen families claimed descent from Zadok (Eleazar's elder son; Eleazar was Aaron's oldest son) and eight from Ithamar (Aaron's youngest son), 1 Chronicles 24:1–19.

4 The Samaritan practice of worshiping God on Mt. Gerizim was disclaimed and attacked, and all other temples and worship sites were declared invalid.

5 Lamp, flame: In the postexilic period, Judah's religious leaders and rabbis (teachers) focused more on the concept of *divine wisdom* and less on the *nation's history.* To know wisdom was to possess the key to understanding creation and history. To know and practice wisdom was to be in harmony with God and creation, and with God's plan for humanity.

6 ***Scrolls*** (*top left*)***:*** Jewish rabbis analyzed the nation's holy writings in great detail. The *Pentateuch* was declared to be divine, sacred scripture about 500 B.C.; the *Prophets* about 200 B.C.; and the *Writings* about A.D. 70–100. Final decisions concerning which books were to be included in the Jewish scriptures were made in response to the appearance of numerous Christian documents. What was Jewish, and what was Christian? The apocryphal writings, written in Greek and included in the Septuagint (the Greek translation of Jewish sacred writings), were excluded from the Hebrew scriptures.

7 ***Large law-code surrounded by smaller law-codes*** (*top left*)***:*** The rabbis found ***613*** commandments in Exodus, Leviticus, Numbers, and Deuteronomy—writings which, together with Genesis, they said God dictated to Moses at Mt. Sinai. Many *oral* traditions (***smaller law-codes***) were developed to apply the *written* commandments to the daily life of later generations. According to the rabbis, God whispered these oral traditions to Moses—who memorized them and then whispered them to Joshua, whose successors memorized and whispered them to their successors—until they were finally written down about A.D. 200 in a collection of writings known as the *Mishnah.* The Mishnah is divided into six "Orders" (*Sedarim*): "Seeds" (*Zeraim*), "Festivals" (*Moed*), "Women" (*Nashim*), "Damages" (*Nezikin*), "Holy Things" (*Kodashim*), and "Purities" (*Tohorot*); each Order (*Seder*) was divided into different tractates.

8 ***Symbol for covenant, law-code, arrows and question marks*** (*top right*)***:*** The rabbis taught that obedience to the law-codes would ensure that a catastrophe such as the Babylonian exile (***arrow pointing backward***) would never take place again (Isaiah 40–55), and would hasten the coming of the Messiah (***arrow pointing forward***).

9 ***Concentric circles around Judah*** (*lower left*)***:*** Some rabbis taught that the Jewish people must make the God of Israel known to the nations. Some taught that the Gentile nations would eventually flock to Judah and Jerusalem to learn about the God of Israel. Others despised non-Jews, and taught that God would eventually crush the Gentile powers and make them servants of His people.

10 ***Servant figure*** (*lower right*)***:*** Although Isaiah's writings include numerous *servant songs* (42:1–4, 49:1–6, 50:4–11, 52:13–53:12), these received little attention during the latter part of the postexilic period.

41B
BALUSTRADE
To Bethany
Kidron Valley
Gethsemane
Mount of Olives
GENTILES
WOMEN
MEN
PRIESTS

The Jerusalem Temple

Solomon's Temple, completed about 945 B.C., was destroyed by the Babylonians in 587 B.C. The postexilic Temple was completed in 515 B.C. In 19 B.C., Herod the Great, with the approval of Judah's religious leaders, began replacing the postexilic Temple with a more magnificent structure set within a spacious court (**ILLUSTRATION 41B**). Work on the rebuilding project did not begin until all the materials needed for the Temple itself were prepared and ready. The overall structure took 82 years to build, and was completed in A.D. 63.

The central *Temple*, consisting of a *Holy of Holies* and a *Holy Place*, was built first. The two sections were separated by a curtain. Only the High Priest could enter the Holy of Holies, and did so once each year on the Day of Atonement. The priests were permitted to enter the *Court of the* ***PRIESTS*** and the Holy Place on a regular basis. Jewish men and Jewish women were allotted separate areas: the *Court of the* ***MEN*** and the *Court of the* ***WOMEN***. The Temple proper was surrounded by a ***BALUSTRADE*** (*soreq*), a low stone wall with ***thirteen entrances***. Non-Jews who visited the Temple were permitted access only to the *Court of the* ***GENTILES***. Any Gentile who dared pass beyond the balustrade was killed. Next to each entrance was a sign stating, "Any non-Jew who passes beyond this balustrade will have only himself to blame for the death that will follow as a consequence." Even Roman soldiers took this warning seriously.

The central section, to which only Jewish people had access, was built on a platform (*chel*) that rose nine feet (2.75 meters) above the Court of the Gentiles. The Court of the Women rose 11¼ feet (3.5 meters) above the *chel*. The Court of the Men rose 11¼ feet (3.5 meters) above the Court of the Women. The Court of the Priests rose 3¼ feet (1 meter) above the Court of the Men. The floor of the Temple itself was 9¾ feet (3 meters) higher than the Court of the Priests.

Those who built the Temple scraped away every trace of soil from beneath the platform area. They feared it might contain human remains or human waste—which would have rendered the entire structure ritually unclean. Although the central structure was built on and above a rock, the platform to the south and east was built on a series of supporting ***underground passageways*** (*lower section* of illustration).

The *eastern wall*, Solomon's Porch, was approximately 1,500 feet (460 meters) long. The *southern wall*, the Royal Porch, was approximately 1,000 feet (305 meters) long. Within the Royal Porch were a total of 162 columns in four rows; each column was 4.6 feet (1.5 meters) in diameter. No mortar or cement was used in the building process. All stones were cut to fit together perfectly, and were held in place through gravity. To date, the largest stone discovered by archaeologists measures 40 x 14 x 10 feet (12 x 4 x 3 meters), and weighs 500 tons (450 metric tons).

Located beneath the Royal Porch were the *Huldah Gates* (***five doors in southern wall***); Huldah was the prophetess who interpreted the Book of the Law to King Josiah in 621 B.C., 2 Kings 22:14. To enter the Temple area, people passed through the Huldah gates, walked through ornate underground passageways, and then climbed *stairs* (***upper sections*** shown in **ILLUSTRATION 41B**) to the Temple's platform. When entering and leaving the Temple complex, people had to face the central structure. There were also stairways at the platform's southeast and southwest corners, and in its western wall.

The ***Fortress of Antonia*** was located at the *northwest corner* of the Temple platform. Although many believe that Jesus' trial by Pilate took place within this fortress, others believe that it took place in Herod's palace to the west of the Jerusalem Temple—near what today is known as the Jaffa Gate.

In A.D. 70, the Romans destroyed the upper structures of the Temple complex, and pushed the rubble into the valleys to the east and south of the Temple platform.

ILLUSTRATION

41C

613

613

1 2

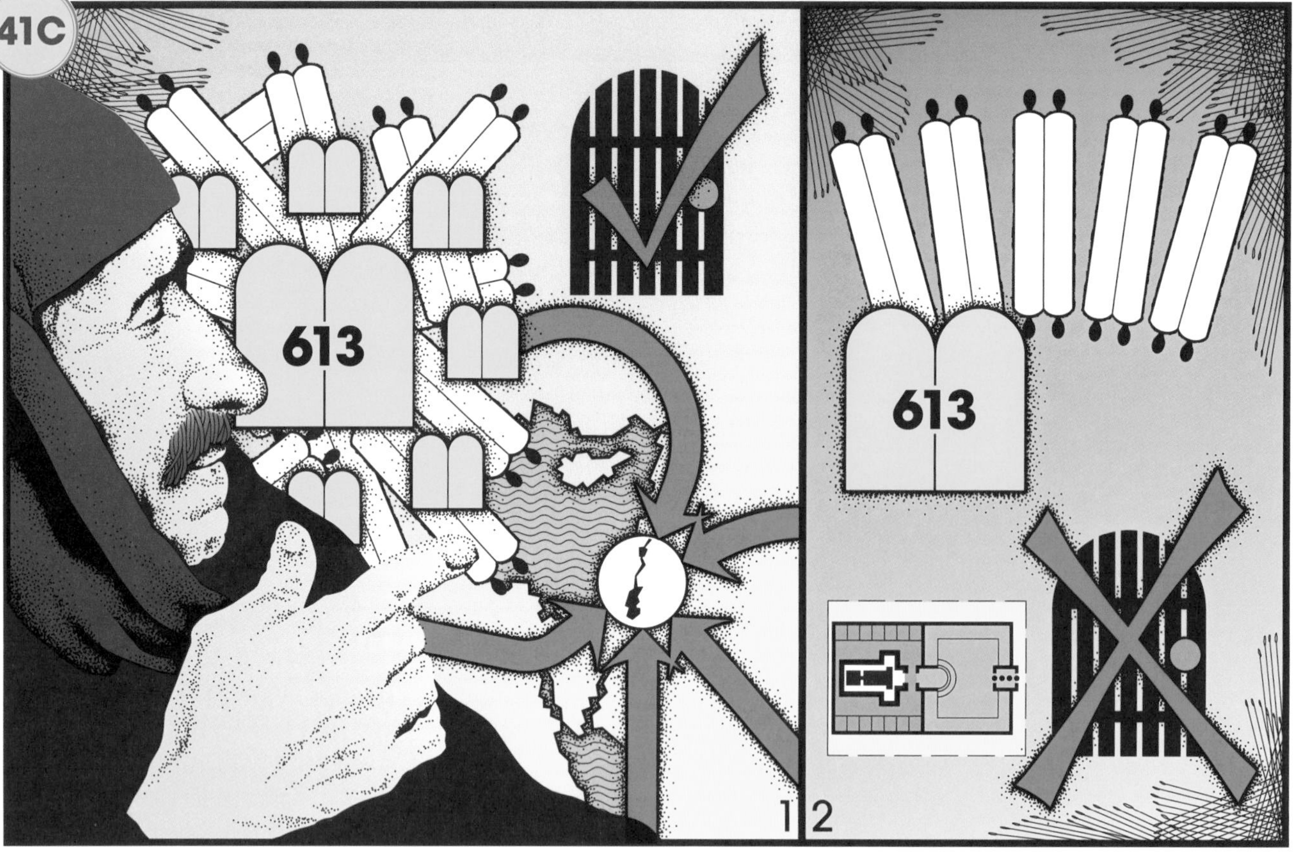

ONE GOD • NATIONALISM • TORAH(LAW)

3 4

Factions within Judaism

ONE GOD•NATIONALISM•TORAH/LAW *(center line)*

These three concepts lie at the heart of the belief system of postexilic Judaism.

- ***ONE GOD:*** The Jewish people believed that there was only one God—the God of creation, the patriarchs, the Exodus, the conquest, the judges and kings, the rescue from Babylon, etc.
- ***NATIONALISM:*** Only the Jewish people knew and belonged to that one true God.
- ***TORAH/LAW:*** The link between God and His people was the Torah, or Law (specifically, the five books attributed to Moses). The rabbis spoke of the Torah/Law as the *water of life*, the *bread of life*, and the *light of the world*.

Pharisees *(Upper left)*

1 Scholars link the origin of the Pharisees to the Hasidim who, in 168–165 B.C., cooperated with the Maccabees to bring to an end the persecution of the Jewish community by the Syrian Seleucid ruler, Antiochus IV "Epiphanes". (See Unit 37.)

- ***Scrolls:*** The Pharisees accepted the Law, Prophets, and Writings as their sacred scriptures.
- ***Large and small law-codes:*** The Pharisees accepted as authoritative both the written 613 laws within Exodus–Deuteronomy and the oral traditions that God whispered to Moses. They looked forward to the establishing of a kingdom in which they could keep the Jewish Law with total strictness.
- ***Circle around Judah; arrows pointing to Judah:*** The Pharisees looked forward to the coming of a Messianic Age, and said that when it came, all Jews scattered around the Mediterranean world would return to Judah to take part in it.
- ***Approval symbol on door with slats*** (symbol for resurrection)***:*** The Pharisees taught that those who died before the Messiah came would not miss out on the Messianic Age, but would rise from the dead to take part in it.

Saddducees *(Upper right)*

2 The Sadducees appeared on the scene at about the same time as did the Pharisees. They were a patrician party made up of members of the high priestly families, the landed aristocracy, and other wealthy individuals. Until the destruction of the Temple in A.D. 70, the majority of priests were Sadducees. The party died out when the Temple was destroyed.

- ***Five scrolls:*** The Sadducees accepted as authoritative only Genesis–Deuteronomy.
- ***Large law-code, 613; no smaller "oral traditions":*** They accepted as divine the law-codes listed in the Pentateuch, but not the oral traditions.
- ***Symbol for resurrection cancelled out:*** They rejected belief in the resurrection of the body, and belief in any coming Messiah or Messianic Age.
- ***Temple ground-plan:*** They focused on the Temple and its worship rituals.

Scribes *(Lower leftz)*

3 The scribes sought wisdom (***lamp***) by studying their sacred writings (***scroll***). The illustration depicts a ***section of sacred writing at center***, with ***scribal comments*** pointing to it.

Zealots *(Lower right)*

4 The Zealot movement began in A.D. 6 under the leadership of Judas the Galilean. It protested (***sword***) against the introduction of Roman procurators (***Roman helmet***) and the payment of taxes to Rome. The Romans responded by sending their Syrian legion south under the leadership of the legate, Quintilius Varus, and crucifying thousands of Jews. The movement persisted and played a leading role in stirring up revolts against Rome in A.D. 66–70, and again in A.D. 132–135 under Bar-Kochba.

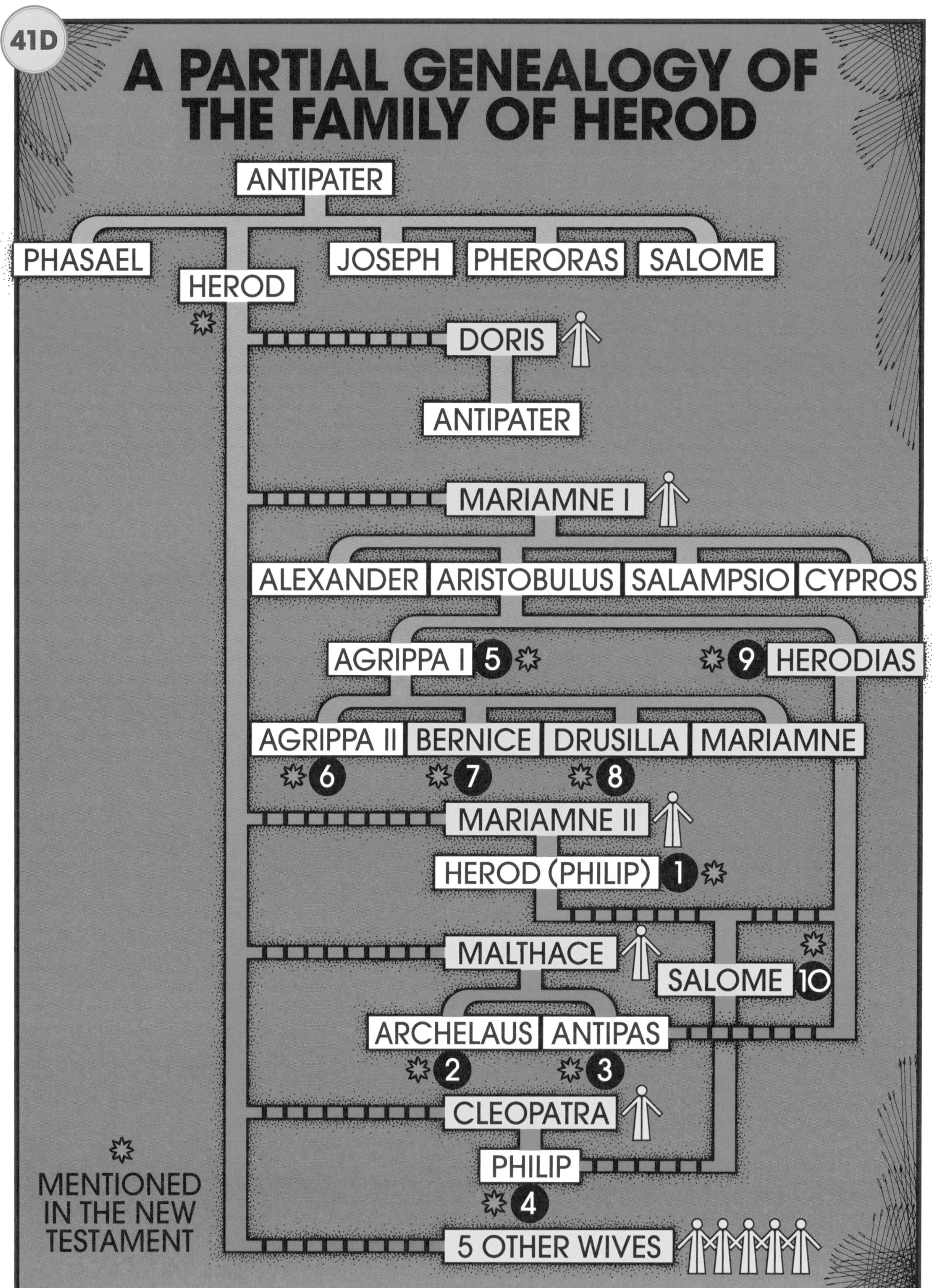
41D
A PARTIAL GENEALOGY OF THE FAMILY OF HEROD
ANTIPATER
PHASAEL
HEROD
JOSEPH
PHERORAS
SALOME
DORIS
ANTIPATER
MARIAMNE I
ALEXANDER
ARISTOBULUS
SALAMPSIO
CYPROS
AGRIPPA I 5
9 HERODIAS
AGRIPPA II 6
BERNICE 7
DRUSILLA 8
MARIAMNE
MARIAMNE II
HERODUS (PHILIP) 1
MALTHACE
SALOME 10
ARCHELAUS 2
ANTIPAS 3
CLEOPATRA
PHILIP 4
5 OTHER WIVES
MENTIONED IN THE NEW TESTAMENT

Herod the Great's Family Tree

Herod the Great was born about 73 B.C. His father, ***ANTIPATER*** (an Idumean—a descendant of Esau) was appointed governor of Judea in 47 B.C. by Julius Caesar. Antipater appointed his two sons to serve as military prefects—***HEROD*** of Galilee and ***PHASAEL*** of Judea. Several years later, the Roman governor of Syria made Antipater the military prefect of Coele-Syria. After the Parthians invaded Syria and Palestine, they set the Hasmonean Antigonus on the throne of Judea (40–37 B.C.). Although the Roman senate bestowed on Herod the title "King of the Jews," he had to wage war for three years against the Parthians and the Hasmonean, Antigonus, to capture Judea and Jerusalem to make the title effective. After achieving his goal, Herod governed for 33 years—as a loyal friend and ally of Rome.

ILLUSTRATION 41D provides information about Herod's offspring through five of his ten wives. The names below (*marked with an asterisk in the illustration*) are mentioned in the Gospels and Acts.

1. ***HEROD (PHILIP)***, a son of ***HEROD*** the Great and ***MARIAMNE II***, was the first husband of ***HERODIAS*** and the father of ***SALOME***.
2. ***ARCHELAUS***, a son of ***HEROD*** and ***MALTHACE***, ruled Judea after his father's death, Matthew 2:22. His repressive rule became so intolerable that a deputation of Judean and Samaritan leaders (who usually despised each other) went to Rome to warn of an impending revolt. After the Romans deposed and banished Archelaus in A.D. 6, Judea became a Roman province ruled by procurators (governors) appointed by the emperor.
3. ***HERODIAS*** eventually divorced her first husband and married (*Herod*) ***ANTIPAS***, tetrarch of Galilee. Herod Antipas, previously married to the daughter of the king of the Nabateans, inherited the Galilean and Perean portions of his father's realm. He is remembered chiefly for his part in the imprisonment and execution of John the Baptist (Mark 6:14–29) and for his brief encounter with Jesus while visiting Jerusalem when Pilate sent Jesus to him for judgment, Luke 23:6–12. In A.D. 39, Herod Antipas was denounced as a plotter to the Emperor Gaius by his nephew ***AGRIPPA II***. He was banished from his tetrarchy, and ended his days in exile. Herodias remained loyal to him after he was removed from office.
4. ***PHILIP*** (*the Tetrarch*) was a son of ***HEROD*** by his fifth wife, ***CLEOPATRA*** *of Jerusalem*. He ruled the territories east of Galilee (Gaulanitis, Trachonitis, and Iturea) from 4 B.C. until his death in A.D. 33/34. He married his niece ***SALOME***, the daughter of ***HEROD (PHILIP)*** and ***HERODIAS***. His rule was marked by moderation and justice.
5. (*Herod*) ***AGRIPPA I*** was a son of ***ARISTOBOLUS*** and a grandson of ***HEROD*** the Great and the Hasmonean, ***MARIAMNE I***. After Herod had ***ARISTOBOLUS*** and his brother, ***ALEXANDER***, strangled in 7 B.C., Agrippa was brought up in Rome in close association with the imperial family. The name *Agrippa* was assumed because of his friendship with Marcus Vispanius Agrippa, son-in-law of the emperor Augustus. During his reign, James, the son of Zebedee, was executed, Acts 12:2. In A.D. 37, Agrippa I was appointed by emperor Caligula (A.D. 37–41) to rule the former territories of Philip and Herod Antipas. In A.D. 41, the next emperor, Claudius, gave Agrippa the title of "king" and added Judea and Samaria to his realm. He now ruled a kingdom as large as that which his grandfather, Herod the Great, had ruled. His attack on the apostles, and his sudden death in Caesarea in A.D. 44 at the age of 54, is reported in Acts 12:20–24.
6. (*Herod*) ***AGRIPPA II***, a son of Herod ***AGRIPPA I*** and Cypros, succeeded his father at the age of 17, Acts 25:13–26:32. He had two sisters, ***BERNICE*** and ***DRUSILLA***, and lived in an incestuous relationship with Bernice after the death of her husband, Acts 25:13–23. From A.D. 50, he assumed increasing authority over territories in Palestine. The emperor Nero (A.D. 54–68) added parts of Galilee and Perea to his realm. Agrippa II expressed his gratitude to Nero by changing the name of his capital from Caesarea Philippi to Neronias. Agrippa tried to prevent the outbreak of the Jewish revolt against Rome in A.D. 66, and took the side of the invading Romans during the four years of warfare that followed—and was rewarded with a further increase in the size of his kingdom. He died in Rome in A.D. 93.
7. ***BERNICE*** eventually became the mistress of the Roman emperors Vespasian and Titus.
8. ***DRUSILLA*** became the third wife of the Roman governor Felix, Acts 24:24.
9. ***HERODIAS*** was first the wife of ***HEROD (PHILIP)***, and later the wife of Herod ***ANTIPAS***. (See 1 and 3.)
10. ***SALOME*** was the daughter of ***HEROD (PHILIP)*** and ***HERODIAS***, and the wife of ***PHILIP***. (See 1 and 4.)

41E

DA	EVENTS	HERODS	GOVERNORS OF JUDEA	EMPERORS
B.C.	JESUS born ca 4 B.C.	HEROD THE GREAT 37–4 B.C.		AUGUSTUS 27 B.C.–14 A.D.
A.D.		ARCHELAUS 4 B.C.–6 A.D.	COPONIUS 6–9	
10		PHILIP THE TETRARCH 4 B.C.–34 A.D.	MARCUS AMBIVIUS 9–12 ANNIUS RUFUS 12–15	
20	JOHN THE BAPTIST		VALERIUS GRATUS 15–26	TIBERIUS 14–37
30	JESUS' ministry PENTECOST PAUL'S conversion	HEROD ANTIPAS 4 B.C.–39 A.D.	PONTIUS PILATE 26–36 MARCELLUS 36–37	
40	PAUL—1st journey	HEROD AGRIPPA I 37–44	MARULLUS 37–41 CUSPIUS FADUS 44–46	CALIGULA 37–41 CLAUDIUS 41–54
50	2nd journey 3rd journey	HEROD AGRIPPA II 50–ca 100	TIBERIUS ALEX. 46–48 CUMANUS 48–52	
60	Arrest, voyage to Rome, & martyrdom		FELIX 52-60 FESTUS 60–62 ALBINUS 62–64 GESSIUS FLORUS 64–66	NERO 54–68
70	Destruction of JERUSALEM			GALBA, OTHO, & VITELLIUS 68–69 VESPASIAN 69–79
80				TITUS 79–81
90				DOMITIAN 81–96
100				NERVA 96 TRAJAN 98–117

Dates, Events, and Rulers

DATES AND EVENTS

Some of the key events referred to in the New Testament narrative are listed in the first column of **ILLUSTRATION 41E**. Debate continues concerning the dating of some of the events listed.

HERODS—see also ILLUSTRATION 41D.

- Herod the Great, Archelaus, Herod Antipas, Philip the Tetrarch: See 41D.1–4.
- Herod Agrippa I: See 41D.5.
- Herod Agrippa II: See 41D.6. Acts 25:13–26:32 describes Agrippa's meeting with Paul, with whom he bantered suggesting that Paul was trying to convert him to Christianity; see Acts 26:28.

GOVERNORS OF JUDEA

New Testament readers encounter the names of ***PONTIUS PILATE*** (in the Gospels), and ***FELIX*** and ***FESTUS*** (in Acts). Roman-appointed procurators had full control of Judea and the Roman army of occupation. The latter consisted of about 120 cavalry and 2,500–5,000 infantry stationed at Caesarea and a detachment of 600 soldiers stationed in the fortress of Antonia in Jerusalem. A procurator had the power of life and death over his subjects. He could reverse capital sentences passed by the Sanhedrin—all of which had to be submitted to him for ratification. He also appointed the High Priests, and exercised control over the Temple and its funds. The High Priest's vestments were in his custody and released only for festivals, at which time the procurator took up residence in Jerusalem and brought additional troops to patrol the city.

PONTIUS PILATE was appointed by Emperor ***TIBERIUS*** to serve as the fifth procurator of Judea. Early in his appointment, Pilate angered the Jews by setting up in Jerusalem Roman standards bearing images of the emperor. After six days, he yielded to Jewish anger and took the standards back to Caesarea. Josephus reports that he used money from the Temple treasury to build an aqueduct to carry water to Jerusalem from a spring about 25 miles (40 kilometers) away. When tens of thousands of Jews protested, Pilate sent his troops among them in disguise and slew large numbers of them.

There came the day when Pilate slaughtered a number of Samaritans who had assembled at Mt. Gerizim in response to a call from a deceiver who had promised to show them that Moses had hidden sacred vessels at Mt. Gerizim. When a Samaritan delegation protested to Vitellius, the governor of Syria, the latter replaced Pilate with ***MARCELLUS*** and ordered Pilate to answer the accusation of brutal rule before the emperor. Tiberius died while Pilate was on his way to Rome. ***CALIGULA*** (Gaius) replaced Tiberius as Emperor and, according to Greek historians, ordered Pilate to commit suicide.

Unrest increased under the rule of ***FELIX*** who was utterly merciless in crushing opposition. Tacitus reports that "with savagery and lust he exercised the powers of a king, with the disposition of a slave" (Tacitus, *Histories*, v. 9). After his arrest, Paul was taken to Caesarea, the Roman capital of Palestine, to be tried before Felix, Acts 23:31–24:27. The narrative reveals Felix's avarice and disregard for justice. Although there was ample evidence of Paul's innocence, Felix kept him in prison in the hope that Paul would offer him a bribe, Acts 24:26. When Felix was finally recalled by ***NERO***, he left Paul in prison to please the Jews (Acts 24:27) and possibly also Drusilla, his third wife and the daughter of ***HEROD ANTIPAS***.

FESTUS succeeded Felix as procurator of Judea in A.D. 60. Nothing is known of his life prior to his appointment, and he died in office after about two years. Although the Jewish historian, Josephus,

says that Festus was a wise and just official, Acts presents him in a less favorable light in that he was prepared to please the Jewish leaders in relation to Paul's trial, Acts 25:9. He later exploited his prisoner's presence to entertain ***HEROD AGRIPPA II*** and Bernice, 25:23–27. However, Agrippa stated that he was convinced that Paul was innocent of the charges being leveled against him, Acts 26:30–32.

4 The last procurator, ***GESSIUS FLORUS***, extracted a heavy payment of gold from the Temple treasury. The resulting civil war proved uncontrollable, and Florus was forced to abandon Jerusalem to the rebels. The revolt was also a popular uprising against Jerusalem's upper classes. Rebellion spread across the whole country. At first the Jews were successful in defeating an army sent by Cestius Gallus, the military governor of Syria. Eventually, the emperor ***NERO*** sent a general, ***VESPASIAN***, to deal with the revolt. Vespasian first gained control of Galilee, and by A.D. 68 was preparing to advance on Jerusalem. However, when Nero committed suicide, Vespasian left for Rome to assume the throne, leaving his son ***TITUS*** to take control of the military operation. In A.D. 70, after a long siege, Titus captured and destroyed Jerusalem and the Temple, and took the Temple's treasures as booty.

Resistance to Rome was now led by the Zealots, a fanatical nationalist party. They held out until A.D. 73 when their last stronghold, Masada, finally fell. Almost all of the 960 Jewish men, women, and children on Masada committed suicide rather than surrender. Only two women and five children remained alive when the Romans finally gained control of the fortress.

EMPERORS

The term "Caesar" derives from the name of a branch of the aristocratic family of the Julii that gained control over the Roman republic through the rise to power of Augustus; the family retained that control until Nero's death. The Caesars referred to in the Gospels are ***AUGUSTUS*** (Luke 2:1) and ***TIBERIUS***. In Acts they are ***CLAUDIUS*** (Acts 11:28, 18:2) and ***NERO***.

1 *Caesar Octavian* adopted the additional name of ***AUGUSTUS***—apparently to define the manner in which he proposed to rule his realm.

2 ***TIBERIUS*** was the stepson of ***AUGUSTUS***. After Augustus' death in A.D. 14, the Roman Senate transferred powers to Tiberius, who at 56 had a lifetime of government experience behind him. He continued Augustus' policies for another 23 years. His dour demeanor lost him the confidence of the people, and he finally retired to the island of Capri.

3 ***CLAUDIUS*** expelled Jews from Rome for rioting at the instigation of "Chrestus"—presumably the incident referred to in Acts 18:2.

4 ***NERO*** was ***AUGUSTUS'*** great-great-grandson; ***CLAUDIUS*** adopted him as his heir. His reign was marked by atrocities and feebleness of rule, and was driven by bloodthirsty paranoia during its latter stages. Many believed that Nero's mother had married Claudius to ensure that Nero would succeed him. Eventually, Nero had his mother put to death.

Nero was the emperor to whom Paul appealed, Acts 25:10,11. When much of Rome was destroyed by fire in A.D. 64, Nero undertook the mass arrest of Christians and, among other tortures, had some of them burnt alive in public. In the closing years of Nero's reign, his commanders in Judea were drawn into the war that ended with the destruction of Jerusalem in A.D. 70. Nero played no part in this final campaign and knew nothing about the issues involved. The critical year A.D. 67 found him engrossed in performing in literary festivals in theaters to satisfy his longing for recognition and prizes. Nero committed suicide in A.D. 68.

5 After Nero's death, ***GALBA***, the governor of Spain, was declared emperor. His reign was brief—he was murdered. Italy was in chaos. ***OTHO*** ascended to the throne, only to find that ***VITELLIUS***, the governor of Germany, had been declared emperor by his troops.

6 ***VESPASIAN*** joined the struggle for power—and eventually succeeded. He left it to his son ***TITUS***, to finish the task of crushing the Jewish revolt which began in A.D. 66. After the Romans destroyed Jerusalem and the Temple in A.D. 70, they set out to destroy the strongholds of the Herodium, Masada, and Machaerus. In A.D. 72, Roman forces led by Lucillius Bassus gained control of Machaerus and destroyed the Herodium. In A.D. 73, Flavius Silva, the commander of the Roman Tenth Legion, raised an enormous earthwork and succeeded in breaching the walls of the Masada fortress. However, when the Romans arrived at the summit of Masada, they found themselves "masters" of hundreds of bodies scattered around the smoldering ruins of what had been one of Masada's palaces. Of the 960 Jewish people who had sought refuge in the fortress, all but two women and five children had committed suicide.

7 ***TITUS*** succeeded his father, Vespasian, as emperor in A.D. 69, but ruled for only two years. He was succeeded by his brother, ***DOMITIAN***—who assumed despotic powers and demanded that he be worshiped as Lord and God (*Dominus et Deus*). At the end of his reign (A.D. 81–96), a persecution of Jews and Christians broke out. The reign of Domitian's successor, ***NERVA***, was short, A.D. 96–98.

8 Some of the most able and noble of Roman emperors were numbered among the persecutors of Christianity. Correspondence between ***TRAJAN*** and Pliny the Younger (who was serving as an imperial legate in Bithynia) indicates that the practice of Christianity was officially forbidden. If Christians recanted, they were to be spared. If they did not recant, they were subject to arrest, torture, imprisonment, seizure of property, forced labor on ships and in mines, and even death.

More About the Judaism of Jesus' Day 41F

Until a few decades ago, the prevailing belief was that Judaism *within* Israel kept itself pure from foreign influences, but Judaism *outside* Israel was influenced by Greek and Roman culture. This view has been abandoned. Archaeology has shown that many synagogues in Israel had Greek characteristics; the word "synagogue" is Greek. The writings of rabbis reveal that some who lived in the Holy Land had a taste for Greek culture, ideas, terms, and methods of interpretation. There was communication and travel between Israel and Jewish centers around the Mediterranean world. For example, each year emissaries were sent from Jerusalem to the Jews of the Dispersion who were expected to pay the annual half-shekel Temple tax. The result was a certain unity of thought among Jews everywhere, a unity that was expressed in the ubiquitous synagogue. Although the Judaism of Jesus' day was complex and contained a number of sects and movements, Judaism everywhere had much in common.

MONOTHEISM

1. The Greek mind sought God through reason. The Hebrew mind believed that God makes Himself known through revelation. God's existence posed no problems for the Hebrew mind; God was Lord over creation and life and Israel was God's "son," Exodus 4:22,23.

2. During the postexilic period, the Jews increasingly sought to preserve the *otherness* of God. From the third century B.C. onward, the name *Yahweh* (Lord) was excluded from the reading of Scriptures, and the name *Adonai* was used instead. The Greek translation of the Old Testament (*Septuagint*) translated *Yahweh* as *Kurios* (Lord). The *Targums* (Aramaic translations of the Hebrew text) used the word *Memra* (Word). In the liturgy of the Day of Atonement, the High Priest mumbled the name for God so that no one could understand it. To give a proper name to God was to suggest that He was merely a god among gods. By not using God's name, the Jews declared that God is above and beyond anything created.

3. Some might argue that this insistence on God's *otherness* removed Him from this world. Judaism answered by saying that one could experience God's presence on earth through His *Shekinah* (Presence) or *Doxa* (Glory). Although the Shekinah filled heaven and earth, it was located especially in the land of Israel. Furthermore, God made Himself present among the Jewish people through His Holy Spirit (which some persons possessed) and spoke to the nation through His own "voice" or "the daughter of a voice"; see Matthew 3:17; 17:5; John 12:28.

4. The Jewish attitude toward God was not one of fear. Although Proverbs 1:7 speaks of "the fear of the Lord" as "the beginning of knowledge," the term "the fear of the Lord" is roughly the equivalent of "religion." The verse might be translated, "The first principle of knowledge is to hold the Lord in awe." Israel emphasized God's love for the nation as much as its reverence for God.

NATIONALISM

1. In the mighty act of the Exodus from Egypt, God brought Israel into existence as a nation. Because Israel was God's supreme possession, a special relationship existed between them. God called the nation His first-born son, Exodus 4:22–23. Israel's cause was God's cause. Israel's affliction was God's affliction. Although God disciplined Israel, He would never abandon it. God was Israel's guardian and guide.

2. The rabbis said that God chose Israel to be His people, not because of merit, but out of sheer grace. At the same time, they said that God chose Israel because He knew that Israel alone, out of all the nations, would accept the Law and undertake to keep it. Israel was not chosen *because of* its deeds; it was chosen *to do* deeds. Although God had given the Law to Israel, this did not give Israel superiority over other nations; it placed on the nation's shoulders the responsibility of making God known to them by obeying His commandments, even to the point of death. The very reason for Israel's existence was to glorify God's name by studying and observing the Law.

3. From this it was but a short step to the conviction that Israel was a chosen people, and its history was idealized from this point of view. Excellence was ascribed, not only to the people, but also to the land of Israel. The *Shekinah* loved to dwell in Israel, for God had declared that land to be holy. According to some, those who lived in Israel would be the first to be raised from the dead when the Messianic Age finally broke in. There was, therefore, merit to living in Israel. As many saw it, to leave Israel was

a sin. At the center of Israel stood Jerusalem. Jerusalem became not only the geographic center of the Jewish nation, but also the expression of its faith.

4 What was the Jewish attitude toward the Gentiles? Many Jews stressed their superiority over the pagan world. God could not have acted otherwise than He did in choosing Israel. God had rejected the Gentiles, whom the Jews called "sinners." The Gentiles were enemies of God, and guilty of idolatry, immorality, and the oppression of Israel.

5 In contrast, some adopted a more kindly attitude toward the Gentiles. Some rabbis taught that the Gentiles, too, had been offered the Law, and it was therefore their own fault that they were not in the covenant. Attempts were made to excuse the Gentiles' failures and to give recognition to their virtues. When they sinned, they were not so much deliberately sinning as following national customs. Some Jews noted the good which Gentiles did. Regular prayers were said for the Emperor. Bulls were sacrificed at the Feast of Tabernacles to expiate the sins of the Gentile world. Some thought that in the Messianic Age many Gentiles would be converted. Some had an uneasy conscience about the Gentiles' fate and, as a result, a widespread missionary movement was undertaken to convert them to Judaism. However, conversion to Judaism meant naturalization into the nation of the Jewish people. To be a Jew was to belong to God. Any non-Jew wishing to belong to God had to become a Jew.

THE LAW

1 For the Jew, God was real. An eternal relationship existed between God and Israel. The link between them was *Torah*, usually translated into English with "Law." *Torah* is a much wider term than "Law" as it is traditionally understood in Christian circles. *Torah* means religious teaching, revelation, instruction. It is applied to the totality of revelation given at Sinai. Israel did not discover or invent the Law. God bestowed it on the nation as a gift. What does it contain?

a. The term *Torah* is most often applied to the *Pentateuch* (Genesis–Deuteronomy).

b. Some apply the term to the whole of the Old Testament. Nonetheless, primacy among the sacred writings belongs to the Pentateuch. Even if the rest of the Old Testament disappears, the belief is that the Pentateuch will persist into and throughout the Age to Come.

2 From an early date, Israel recognized the need to adapt the law-codes within the Pentateuch to changing circumstances. This practice led to the growth of the Oral Law, called "the traditions of the fathers" in the New Testament. It served as a protective hedge around the Written Law. To illustrate, the Written Law forbids work on the Sabbath, the most holy of days. What constitutes work? The rabbis eventually formulated 39 definitions that define the work to be avoided on the Sabbath. The concern is to avoid any infringement of the Written Law. The role of the Oral Law is to make the Written Law practicable. No regulation should be decreed that is beyond the power of the majority in the community to perform.

3 What importance was attached to the Oral Law? Although in principle it enjoyed the same authority as the Written Law, not all groups in Palestine accepted the Oral Law as binding. The Sadducees rejected it. Other groups accepted only some of its traditions. Even so, many rabbis accorded it an even higher authority than the Written law, and supported their position by asserting that the Oral Law had also been given to Moses at Sinai. All rabbinic decisions, all grammatical and other issues affecting the Law, were traced back to that awesome event. Although this belief was tradition rather than fact, it was the rabbis' way of establishing the value of the Oral Law. Historically, the Oral Law developed gradually. For a long time it was not written down. However, by the end of the second century A.D., it was codified, although not completely, in the *Mishnah* ("repetition")—a systematic collection of regulations derived from the oral traditions. What was not included in the *Mishnah* was preserved in the *Gemara* (Aramaic for "completion") and *Tosephta*—writings that are similar in content and form to the *Mishnah*.

4 Moses, as the mediator of the Law, dominated Jewish imagination like a colossus. The general view was that the Law given through him was eternally valid, although there was speculation about a "New Law" to be given in the Messianic Age. The Law is to be obeyed without question to the point of death, even if it is not understood, in both this age and the age to come.

Worship Activities

1 The Jews believed that God had called Israel to be His people and had given it the Law as a guide for life. On the basis of this, Judaism was to be a religion of gratitude to God for what He had done for the nation. That gratitude was to move Israel to observe what the Law demanded. What were those observances?

2 The Temple was the center for worship. It had played a central role in the life and thinking of Israel since the time of Solomon. The postexilic Temple, rebuilt by Herod the Great, stood out strikingly in gold and white above Jerusalem's skyline. Its glory was praised far and wide. A stream of sacrifices was offered within its inner courts.

3 The Temple was the place where the *Shekinah* loved to dwell. The "impure" were progressively excluded from the innermost shrine. Only the High Priest was permitted to enter the Holy of Holies, and only after the most elaborate preparations. Gentiles were allowed only into the Court of the Gentiles. The sacrificial system, centered in the Temple and controlled by the priests, was the means ordained by God for dealing with sin and for reconciling the people to God. When the High Priest stood before God on the Day of Atonement, he stood there on behalf of the people. The whole sacrificial system was a gift from God for the sake of the people. The sacrifices were to be performed properly with respect for the minutest detail. The intentions of both priest and those who offered the sacrifices had to be pure. Sacrifice had to be accompanied by prayer and confession. Restitution had to be made to any person wronged or injured.

4 The Temple was a symbol of God's perpetual presence among the Jewish people. Some of the observances within it served as reminders of the events in which God had intervened in the history of the Israelites. Although festivals such as Passover, Pentecost, and Tabernacles (or Booths) were originally connected with the agricultural year, each became linked to the commemoration of a great historical event. *Passover* recalled the Exodus event, the deliverance from Egypt. *Pentecost* recalled the giving of the Law on Sinai. *Tabernacles* recalled the wilderness wanderings and the formation of the nation. These festivals were to recreate the experiences of the fathers in the life of the contemporary Jew.

5 There were other observances. *The Feast of Dedication* (*Hanukkah*, or *The Feast of Lights*) celebrated the cleansing of the Temple after the abuses of Antiochus IV "Epiphanes" and the restoration of worship in 165 B.C. *The Feast of Purim* recalled the triumph of Esther over Haman. Both *Hanukkah* and *Purim* have nationalistic overtones.

The New Year Festival (*Rosh Hashanah*) recalled the creation of the world. The New Year was the day on which God judged people, and prayers were offered that God might judge Israel in kindness. *The Day of Atonement* (*Yom Kippur*) was not linked to the memory of an historical event; rather, it was observed with fasting, confession of sin, and sacrifice. Both of these latter festivals set out to create an awareness of sin and of the need of forgiveness.

6 How did the acceptance of the Law affect the life of a Jew? The importance of the Law, and the need to study it, brought the *synagogue* into existence. Already at the time of Jesus, each village had its own synagogue for prayer, worship, and study. There were Pharisees and teachers of the Law in every village of Galilee and Judea. The worship liturgy consisted of three main elements: prayer, the reading of Scripture, and a homily. Meetings were held on the Sabbath and on two other days of the week. Worship in the synagogue did not require the presence of a priest; this made the religious Jew a person of study and prayer.

7 The pious Jew began and ended the day with *prayer*. There was an appropriate prayer for every significant act of the day. The posture for prayer and the direction in which it was to be offered were closely defined. Many actions were to be consecrated and accompanied by prayer: rising, preparing for sleep, entering a house, washing hands, eating, the birth of a child, circumcision, betrothal, marriage, illness, death and its accompanying rituals.

8 The Jews were suspicious of *asceticism*, the practice of cutting one's self off from the supposedly sinful world and turning one's back on creation and the community. They believed that God had made all things good for Israel to enjoy. They were to be received and used with thanksgiving.

9 Jews were to engage in certain practices to denote that they were *different*. For instance, male Jews were to be *circumcised*; circumcision became the mark of the people of the covenant. Many Jews were prepared to give up their lives to retain the practice of circumcision; they felt almost a horror toward those who were not circumcised.

10 A Jewish man was not to wear *garments* made of mixed fabrics. He wore fringes on the corner of his cloak, *phylacteries* (small cubical boxes containing the text of Deuteronomy 6:4,5) on his forehead or arm, and fastened a *mezuzah* (a container with the same texts) to his doorpost. These things were thought to give divine protection, and served as reminders of the need to keep the Law.

11 Jews were to observe the *Sabbath*. In keeping the Sabbath, Israel bore witness to its Creator and participated in God's holiness. All activity resembling work was forbidden. The atmosphere of the day was joy. It was observed with special food and dress, and a liturgy in the home.

12 Certain functions were thought to be *polluting*. Contact with human corpses, lepers, and animals listed as impure in the Law resulted in one becoming ritually unclean. To recover purity, specific rites had to be observed. Certain dietary laws were also observed to maintain purity. Special precautions were to be taken in the slaughter of animals to avoid religious contamination. Blood could not be consumed.

13 It was not desirable to have *contact with Gentiles*, who were considered to be in a state of constant impurity; it was better to live in Israel than in other regions. This attitude fostered separation and segregation. There were often two standards: one for dealing with fellow Jews, and another for dealing with Gentiles. The Law could sometimes create in people a certain spiritual and intellectual snobbery. To be a good Jew, one had to know the Law. To know it, one had to study it. Hence, the life of study was idealized. The ignorant could not be religious. A contempt arose for "the people of the land," for "lesser breeds without the law."

Jewish Movements in Palestine

Pharisees

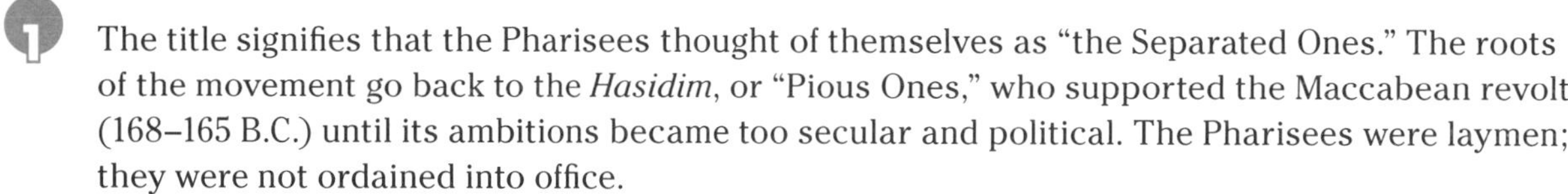

1 The title signifies that the Pharisees thought of themselves as "the Separated Ones." The roots of the movement go back to the *Hasidim*, or "Pious Ones," who supported the Maccabean revolt (168–165 B.C.) until its ambitions became too secular and political. The Pharisees were laymen; they were not ordained into office.

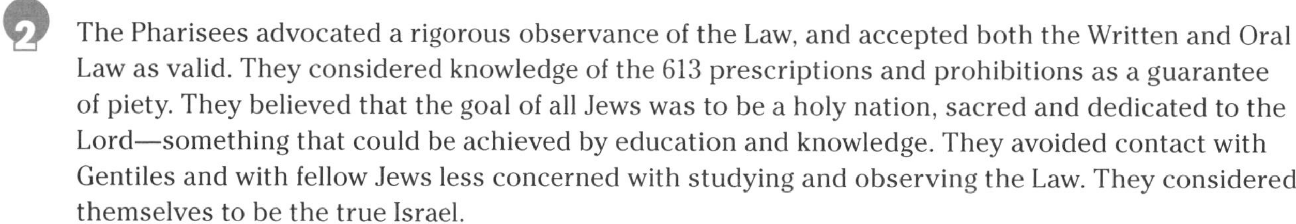

2 The Pharisees advocated a rigorous observance of the Law, and accepted both the Written and Oral Law as valid. They considered knowledge of the 613 prescriptions and prohibitions as a guarantee of piety. They believed that the goal of all Jews was to be a holy nation, sacred and dedicated to the Lord—something that could be achieved by education and knowledge. They avoided contact with Gentiles and with fellow Jews less concerned with studying and observing the Law. They considered themselves to be the true Israel.

3 They paid great attention to the observance of the Sabbath, ritual purity, tithing, and other external demonstrations of faith. Even so, their acceptance of the Oral Law made them flexible. They believed in human freedom under the control of divine providence, the resurrection of the body, the coming of a Messiah, and the in-gathering of Israel and its tribes at the end of time. Although they possibly never numbered more than six thousand, they exercised a great influence on other Jews.

Sadducees

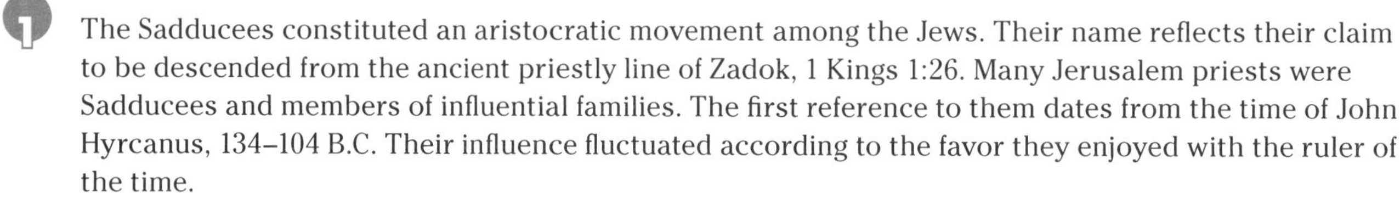

1 The Sadducees constituted an aristocratic movement among the Jews. Their name reflects their claim to be descended from the ancient priestly line of Zadok, 1 Kings 1:26. Many Jerusalem priests were Sadducees and members of influential families. The first reference to them dates from the time of John Hyrcanus, 134–104 B.C. Their influence fluctuated according to the favor they enjoyed with the ruler of the time.

2 The Sadducees opposed the Pharisees and their oral interpretations of the Law. Although they had their own interpretations, they resented any intrusion into what they considered a priestly privilege or prerogative. The first five books of the Old Testament were their guide in all religious matters. These books contain the basic regulations governing the Temple, the priesthood, and the sacrificial rites. They believed that the faithful and literal fulfillment of God's provision for sacrificial worship in the Temple was the crucial requirement for maintaining Israel's covenant relationship with the Lord.

3 The Sadducees showed a general lack of interest in religious questions. They saw people as being totally responsible for their actions. They denied the concept of divine providence, and rejected any belief in reward or punishment in the afterlife, angels and spirits, and the resurrection of the body—holding instead to traditional beliefs of Sheol. Some Sadducees were priests, others were wealthy land-owners who saw themselves as constituting the "upper class. Their manners were often boorish. They disappeared from history after the destruction of the Jerusalem Temple in A.D. 70.

Herodians

Little is known about the Herodians beyond what the New Testament reports. They were not a religious sect, but a party of friends and supporters of the Herod family—in particular of Herod Antipas. The fourth century church father, Epiphanius, says that they looked on Herod as the Messiah.

Galileans

The Jewish historian Josephus identifies these with a group of Pharisaic zealots. He says that their

love of liberty was unconquerable; God alone was to be the Ruler of the Jewish people. Possibly theirs was an extreme form of Pharisaism.

Zealots

The Zealots were an active group who regarded themselves as the zealous agents of the wrath of God and the instruments of deliverance of God's people. Phinehas (Numbers 25:1–13) was their ideal. They kept alive the spirit of the Maccabean resistance to foreign control—in Jesus' day, by the Romans.

Scribes

The Scribes were experts in the study of the Law. They performed a threefold function. They studied the Law in order to protect and defend it. They instructed others in the Law without charge and expected their students to share with others what they were taught. They served within the Sanhedrin as judges entrusted with the administration of the Law.

Essenes

1 The Essenes had their origins in the Hasidim movement at the time of the Maccabean campaigns. Some believe that their name derives from a Syrian word for "pious ones." Pliny the Elder located them on the northwestern shore of the Dead Sea between Jericho and En-gedi. Most likely, the area Pliny was referring to is the recently excavated site of Khirbet Qumran where the Dead Sea scrolls were discovered. According to Josephus, they also had houses throughout the country for the sake of providing hospitality. In Jesus' day, they numbered about 4,000.

2 Archaeological research indicates that, in earlier times, a fortress once existed on the Qumran site. It was built about the time of King Josiah (640–609 B.C.), but was destroyed by the Babylonians. It was resettled in the days of John Hyrcanus, 134–104 B.C., but destroyed by the Romans in A.D. 68 at the time of the Jewish revolt.

3 The Essenes believed that the final era in Israel's history would reflect its beginnings under Moses, Aaron, and Joshua. However, they insisted that wicked leaders now controlled the Holy Land, and that the nation was ignorant of the Scriptures and unfaithful to the Sinai covenant. God would soon act to introduce the new eternal covenant that He had promised. At that time, God's enemies within and beyond the borders of the Holy Land would be defeated, and the faithful would enter the Messianic Age. The Essenes claimed that they constituted the community of the New Covenant, and that they alone were the faithful remnant, the true Israel.

4 The Essenes opposed the Jerusalem Temple and its sacrificial system, both historically and on principle. They rejected the authority of the Jerusalem priesthood; it had Hasmonean rather than Zadokite roots.

5 An elaborate system of baptismal rites, a sacred meal, and a communal sharing of possessions played important roles in the life of their community. The Law of Moses was the object of much study. They observed the Sabbath so strictly that they refrained from any bowel movements on that day. They had secret doctrines about the angels, and took a vow not to divulge their names.

6 The Essenes waited for two Messiahs. The Messiah of Aaron would come from a *priestly* line. The Messiah of Israel would come from the *royal* line. The former would be instrumental in establishing the New Jerusalem and the New Temple. The latter would lead Israel to victory in the final battle against its foes.

7 The Dead Sea community is best remembered for the scrolls that bear its name. Most of the scrolls were made of animal skins with smooth sides written on with ink made from charcoal or iron. Some papyri fragments have also been found. One scroll consisted of copper sheets riveted together. About a quarter of all the manuscripts and fragments are biblical texts written about 250 B.C.–A.D. 50. These are about 1,000 years older than any other extant Old Testament manuscript. Scrolls containing apocryphal and pseudepigraphical writings have also been found.

8 Of all the sectarian writings, the most important is the "Manual of Discipline." The Essenes also produced numerous commentaries (e.g., Habakkuk) and elaborate paraphrases (e.g., Genesis). These provided contemporary applications of prophetic and poetic passages of the Bible. Because the Essenes believed they were living at the time when the Old Testament prophetic writings were being fulfilled, they interpreted them accordingly. The dominant figure in the community was the "Teacher of Righteousness," a person thought to be divinely empowered to interpret scripture and reveal the true meaning of the prophets.

9 Many believe that the "Damascus Document," found in 1896 in a Cairo synagogue, is really an Essene writing from Qumran. Among other things, this writing teaches that, although prophecy and direct revelation from on high had ceased, the Essenes (the elect) were blessed with a continuing revelation. This conviction gave the Essenes an enormous self-confidence and optimism, despite the sufferings and hardships that they had to endure.

10 In his *Natural History*, Book V, Pliny describes the Essene movement as follows:

> *On the west* (of the Dead Sea) *the Essenes keep away from the shore as far as it has harmful effects, a solitary race and astonishing above all others in the world, without womenfolk, without sexual intercourse, without money, the companions of palm trees. As time goes by, the assembled throng is reborn in equal numbers by the accession of numerous men weary of life, whom the waves of fortune bring to this manner of life. Thus through the course of thousands of centuries (incredible though it seems) the race is eternal although in it no one is born—so prolific for them is other men's repentance for their past lives.*

Jesus and the Law

1 Jesus and the New Testament writers took issue with the false notions about the content and purpose of the Old Testament writings that arose during the period of Judaism. Paul could say of the Law, "So the law is holy, and the commandment is holy and just and good," Romans 7:12.

2 Paul fought the belief that the Law was given so that people could earn salvation through observing it. He rightly insists that the Law cannot "save" humankind and was never given for that purpose. It was not given to *effect* (bring about) salvation, but to *reflect* salvation.

3 Jesus attacked what the religious experts among the Jews had done, and were doing, with the Law. They had reduced it to a legal code of 613 individual commandments, and insisted that the Law was to be *kept*, not necessarily *understood*. Judaism had turned the Mosaic Law into a multitude of duties and regulations that had to be kept and perpetuated for their own sake. The letter of the Law was all that mattered.

4 The New Testament writers insisted that God gave the Law to serve as a guide for righteous living. They taught that the glory of God and the service of people is what really matters. Jesus attacked the Pharisees for manipulating the Law through their oral traditions to avoid doing the will of God, Mark 7:1–13. Jesus declared His own authority as surpassing oral tradition with, "You have that it was said... but I say unto you," Matthew 5:21–48.

5 The Jews knew that the great commandment of the Law was to love God, Deuteronomy 6:4,5. They knew that Leviticus 19:18 commanded that the neighbor be loved also. However, they interpreted the term *neighbor* to refer to those of their own nation. Furthermore, they set what they considered to be sensible limits to how far one could be expected to go in loving that Jewish neighbor, Matthew 18:21,22.

6 Jesus swept all those notions away and fused together the love of God and the love of neighbor. A person is to live to serve only God (Matthew 4:10), and if the only way to serve that invisible God is by serving the visible neighbor, then the whole of life is to be directed toward the service of God through the service of the neighbor—who is defined simply as any other person on the planet.

7 In the final analysis, the Christian's pattern for living is the life of Jesus. Jesus is the final Torah, the Word become flesh. In summoning the disciples, Jesus said to them, "Follow Me," Mark 1:16–20. In Galatians 3:24,25, Paul speaks of the revelation given at Sinai, including its law-codes, as a *paidagogos* (or "nanny") that was to guide the people of God until Jesus came. Now that Jesus has come, His followers are to live in fellowship with Him as He continues among them in and through the Holy Spirit. The work of the Risen Jesus and the work of the Holy Spirit are one and inseparable in that the Holy Spirit takes the things of Jesus and declares them to Jesus' followers, John 14:26, 16:14. In the final analysis, Christians do not live under a program of laws, but in fellowship with a Person. Their mission as disciples is to make known and visible the invisible but ever-present Jesus.

The Talmuds

The sages who explained and interpreted the *Mishnah* in Palestine and Babylon between A.D. 200 and 500 were known as *Amoraim*. Their discussions are recorded in the *Palestinian* and *Babylonian Talmuds*. The sages ordained by the Sanhedrin in Palestine were given the title of *Rabbi*, while those ordained in Babylon were given the title of *Rav*.

The word *Talmud* is derived from the Hebrew word *lamad*, "to learn." The *Palestinian Talmud* was completed in Palestine about A.D. 450; the *Babylonian Talmud* was completed in Babylon about A.D. 550. The *Babylon Talmud* is about four times larger that the *Palestinian Talmud*, and was recognized as the supreme authority in relation to Jewish teaching by the 11th century A.D. The entire text—written in Aramaic—consists of approximately two-and-a-half million words. It is the major subject of study in Jewish academies (*yeshivot*) and its study is regarded as an important religious duty for Jewish men.

What follows is a brief summary of some of the thoughts and insights that were eventually incorporated into the *Talmuds* concerning what God's people are to believe and how they are to live.

1 God created seven things before He created the world:

a. The Torah
b. Repentance
c. The Garden of Eden (Paradise)
d. Gehinnom (the realm of the dead)
e. The Throne of Glory
f. The Temple
g. The Name of the Messiah

2 The Messiah and the Messianic Age:

a. The Messiah entered the mind of God even before the world was created.
b. Messianic hopes increased in fervor during times of political oppression.
c. Intolerable conditions would prevail prior to the Messiah's coming.
d Travails would accompany the coming of the Messiah.
e. Israel's behavior could influence the Messiah's coming.
f. The Messiah would be human
g. Efforts were made to calculate when the end-time would come.
h. Tremendous fertility would prevail when the Messianic Age broke in.

3 Ten things would be renewed in the Hereafter:

a. God would illumine all with His presence.
b. Running water would flow forth from Jerusalem to heal all ailments.
c. Trees would produce fruit every month, and all ailments would be healed.
d. All cities would be rebuilt, including Sodom and Gomorrah. There would be no ruins.
e. God would rebuild Jerusalem with sapphires. Nations would come to look at it.
f. The animal world would live in peace and harmony.
g. God would make a covenant between Israel and the animal world.
h. There would be no more weeping, wailing, sighing, groaning, anguish.

i. Death would cease.
j. All would be happy.

4 Prior to the Messianic Age, Jerusalem would be rebuilt—never to be destroyed again:

a. The Temple would be rebuilt.
b. The sacrificial system would not be needed. The only offering would be thanksgiving.
c. All tribes would be reunited.
d. The righteous dead would be raised to participate.
e. Only one language would be used in the world to come: Hebrew.
f. Some taught that the Messianic Age would only be a transitory period between this world and the World to Come.
g. No Gentile would be permitted to join Israel during the Messianic Age.

5 Life after death:

a. The Sadducees and the Samaritans did not believe in the resurrection of the body.
b. Some within Judaism spoke of a universal resurrection.
c. Some said that only the righteous would rise—those who deserved it.
d. Others said that only those who took the Torah seriously would rise again.
e. Some said that the resurrection would take place only in the Holy Land.
f. Some said that the bodies of the righteous dead would have to be transported back to Israel before they could come to life again.
g. Some taught that God would dig a tunnel from Babylon to the Holy Land to enable the bodies of the dead to roll back to the Holy Land so that they might be reunited with their souls and rise from the dead.
h. The dead would rise with any handicaps they had during their previous life.
i. Elijah would bring about the resurrection.
j. Martyrs would have an eminence beyond all others.
k. Those who entered The World to Come would enjoy rest from this world's present routines and sit on thrones of glory.

6 Who would participate in the life to come, and who would not?

a. All Israel would participate.
b. Rabbis debated whether or not Gentiles would participate in the world to come.
c. The Gentiles would be judged for their cruel treatment of Israel.
d. The deeds of all people would be written in a book.
e. Rabbi Shammai (First century B.C.) taught there were would be three classes of dead:
   - The perfectly righteous who would be guaranteed eternal life.
   - The completely wicked who were sealed for Gehinnom.
   - The average person who would spend only a short time in Gehinnom to be purified.
f. Some taught that the wicked in Israel, and all Gentiles, would spend 12 months in Gehinnom, and then be annihilated.
g. Some said that the *very* wicked would suffer in Gehinnom forever.

7 How to avoid going to Gehinnom:

a. The best safeguard was to study the Torah.

b. Gehinnom would be cooled for those who pronounce the Great Shema (Deuteronomy 6:4,5) clearly and distinctly.

c. Those who said certain prayers would escape Gehinnom.

d. No circumcised Israelite would go to Gehinnom, unless he had been very wicked.

e. Abraham would sit at the gate to Gehinnom and would not allow circumcised Israelites to descend into it.

f. Heretics and sinners in Israel would descend into Gehinnom because God would extend their foreskin so that they appeared to be uncircumcised.

g. Abraham would help gain the release of Jewish men condemned to Gehinnom short-term, except those who had intercourse with a Gentile woman, or disguised their circumcision to conceal their identity (as some did during the Hellenistic period to be permitted to participate naked in athletic competitions).

8 What would it be like in Gehinnom?

a. The sun is red in the morning because it passes over the roses in the Garden of Eden, and red in the evening because it passes over the fires of Gehinnom. (The name "Gehinnom" was derived from the burning garbage dump in the Hinnom Valley just to the south of Jerusalem.)

b. There are seven storeys, or levels, in Gehinnom (from highest to lowest):

- Sheol
- Abaddon
- Shadow of death
- Nether world
- The Land of Forgetfulness
- Gehinnom
- Silence

c. The fires in Gehinnom would be 60 times hotter than any earthly fire. Although some taught that the fires in Gehinnom would never cease, Rabbi Hillel taught that they would do so.

d. In Gehinnom there would be total darkness—derived from the plagues of Egypt.

e. Some taught that those suffering in Gehinnom would have relief every Sabbath.

9 Gan Eden (The Garden of Eden):

a. Gan Eden (Paradise) has seven levels to accommodate seven levels of righteousness. From the top to the bottom level, these are:

- Presence
- Courts
- House
- Tabernacle
- Holy Hill
- Hill of the Lord
- Holy Place

b. Every righteous person would be assigned a place according to the honor due to him.
c. The happiness in store for the righteous was symbolized by a wonderful banquet.
d. Those who studied the Torah would be given a special welcome. They would recline on large banqueting couches with beautiful covers.
e. Life in Gan Eden would be lavish. The greatest joy would be to live in God's presence.

The Good Inclination (*Yetzer ha-tov*) and the Evil Inclination (*Yetzer ha-rah*):

a. An early reference to the *Yetzer ha-rah* is found in (the apocryphal book) Sirach 37:3.
b. References to the concept of the evil inclination are found also in 4 Ezra 3:20–22 and 4:30–32. Asher 1:6 contains the first reference to the *Yetzer ha-tov*: "Therefore if the soul takes pleasure in the good impulse, all its actions are in righteousness." (4 Ezra and Asher are Pseudepigraphical writings).
c. Some said the *Yetzer ha-tov* was located on the right side, the *Yetzer ha-rah* on the left.
d. Some said the Yetzers were located in the kidneys, but most said "in the heart." (The heart stands for the volitional, intellectual elements in man.)
e. The *Yetzer ha-rah* urges/inclines people to all kinds of sin—particularly to unchastity and idolatry.
f. Although God also created the *Yetzer ha-rah* ("and it was good," Genesis 1), it is not evil in itself. It is the urge to self-preservation and propagation that can be mastered and put to good use. If it were not for the evil impulse, man would not marry, build a house, have children, or engage in a trade. The evil impulse is to be directed and controlled.
g. The chief means of protection against the *Yetzer ha-rah* was the study of Torah. If man yielded to the evil impulse, there was still a cure: *Repentance!*
h. In the Age to Come, the evil impulse to unchastity and idolatry would be no more!

SUMMARY

41A Beyond the period of the Babylonian exile, the Davidic dynasty was no more. The priests serving at the Jerusalem Temple played a central role in directing the nation. The question of which sacred writings were to be included in the Hebrew scriptures was addressed. Much attention was devoted to the study of the law-codes in Exodus–Deuteronomy, and also those referred to as the "oral traditions." The rabbis taught that obedience to the Torah (Law) would hasten the coming of the Messianic Age—the focus of which would be the role of Jerusalem. Positive and negative attitudes toward the Gentiles prevailed. Little attention was paid to Isaiah's Servant Songs.

41B Worship life centered around rituals within the Temple—the symbol of God's presence among His people.

41C The Jews believed that there was only one God, that they alone belonged to Him, and that the link between God and His people was the Torah, i.e., Genesis–Deuteronomy.

41D Herod the Great, an Idumean (a descendant of Esau), ruled Judea 37–4 B.C. Bitter struggles over who would succeed Herod took place before his death. After his death, his kingdom was divided among three of his sons: Archelaeus, Herod Antipas, and Philip.

41E After Herod's son, Archelaus, was removed from office as ruler of Judea and Samaria, the region was ruled by Roman prefects and procurators from Caesarea—not Jerusalem. Eventually, Herod's grandson, Herod Agrippa 1, ruled the Jewish realm. He was later succeeded by his son, Herod Agrippa II. Both ruled under the watchful eye of procurators who cared little for Jewish whims but much for the will of the emperor enthroned in Rome.

41F Although the Greek mind sought to know and understand "the divine" through reason, the Jewish people believed that God reveals His Person, presence, and will through the Hebrew scriptures. God brought the Jewish people into existence as a nation, and a special relationship existed between God and themselves. Although many Jewish rabbis viewed the Gentiles in negative terms, others showed concern for them and sought to persuade them to embrace the faith and practices of Judaism.

41G The "impure" were progressively excluded from the Temple's innermost shrine, the Holy of Holies. The main observances each year were Passover, Pentecost, Tabernacles, Dedication, Purim, the New Year Festival, and the Day of Atonement. The first five were linked to important historical events.

41H The main Jewish movements in Judea were those of the Pharisees, Sadducees, Galileans, Zealots, Scribes, and Essenes.

41I Jesus radically reinterpreted the will of His Father for both the Jewish people and humanity-at-large—and He lived what He taught: the life of a Servant-without-limit.

41J By the time that Jesus appeared on the scene, the Hebrew scriptures consisted of the Pentateuch (Genesis–Deuteronomy) and the Prophets (Joshua–2 Kings, and Isaiah–Malachi). The Writings were added to the Jewish canon late in the first century A.D. To understand Jesus' ministry and teaching, it is important to know something about the Hebrew scriptures, the "oral traditions," the Mishnah, and the Jerusalem and Babylonian Talmuds.

5 SECTION

UNITS 41–50

The Gospels and Acts

UNIT 42

Mark (I)

The Messianic Kingdom: The Claim

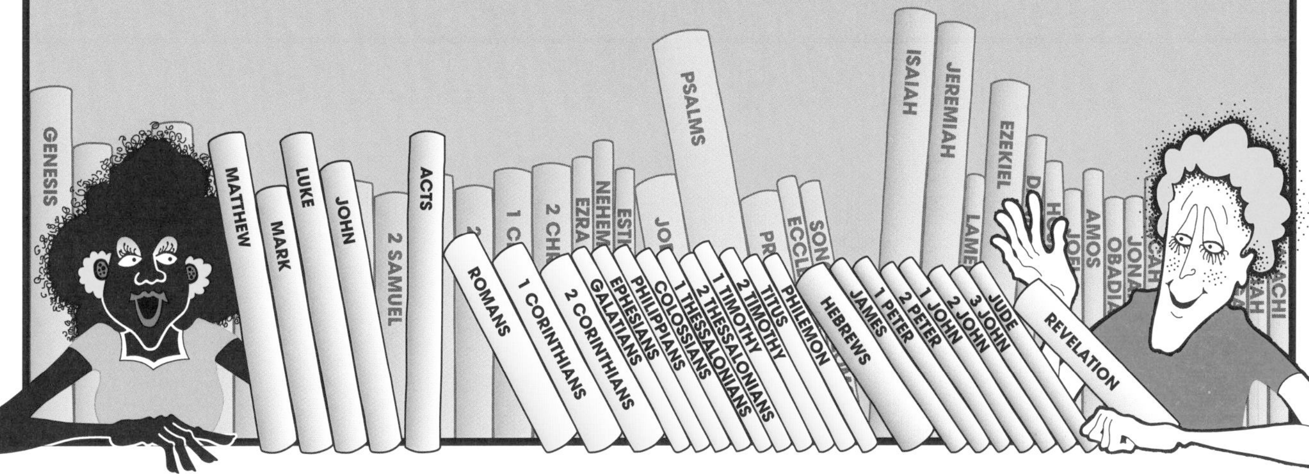

42A
Sidon
Damascus
PHOENICIA
Mt. Hermon
Tyre
Caesarea Philippi
MEDITERRANEAN SEA
GALILEE
Capernaum
GAULANITIS
Ptolemais
Chorazin
Gennesaret
Bethsaida
Magdala
Cana
Gergesa
Mt. Carmel
Tiberias
SEA OF GALILEE
Nazareth
Nain
Gadara
DECAPOLIS
Caesarea
Aenon
Salim
Sebaste (Samaria)
Sychar
Gerasa
PEREA
Mt. Gerizim
SAMARIA
Jordan River
Joppa
Arimathea
Ephraim
Ramah
Jericho
Emmaus
Bethphage
Bethany beyond Jordan
Jerusalem
Bethlehem
Bethany
DEAD SEA
JUDEA
Machaerus
Gaza
Hebron
Masada
PALESTINE DURING THE MINISTRY OF JESUS
Herod Antipas
Philip
Pontius Pilate
Gentile Territory
IDUMEA

Geographical Palestine in Jesus' Day 42A

ILLUSTRATION 42A depicts regions and locations referred to in the four Gospels.

1 Herod the Great came to power in 37 B.C. In the second decade of his reign, he expanded his kingdom to northern Palestine and large parts of northern Transjordan. Herod enlarged the city of ***Samaria*** (called ***Sebaste***, Greek for "Augustus") and built a temple to Caesar Augustus within its walls. He erected a palace on the western side of Mt. Zion, surrounded by gardens and courts, and flanked by three huge towers. This complex served as Herod's seat of government, and later was used by the Roman procurators. (It is possible that the *praetorium* in which Pilate tried Jesus was located in this complex.) Herod also built lavish winter palaces at ***Jericho*** and ***Masada***; these, and other palaces that he built for himself, were marvels of architecture. He built the city of ***Caesarea*** (formerly Strato's Tower) on the Mediterranean coast, complete with an artificial harbor with huge breakwaters surmounted by towers. According to Josephus, John the Baptist was imprisoned and beheaded in the fortress Herod rebuilt at ***Machaerus*** east of the ***DEAD SEA***.

2 After Herod the Great died in 4 B.C., his realm was divided among his three sons: Archelaeus, Herod Antipas, and Philip.

a. Archelaeus ruled ***JUDEA*** and ***SAMARIA*** until A.D. 6 when he was disgraced, deposed, and deported by the Romans. Roman procurators now ruled these regions.

b. ***Herod Antipas*** ruled ***GALILEE*** and ***PEREA***.

c. ***Philip*** ruled the region of ***GAULANITIS***, to the east and north of the ***SEA OF GALILEE***.

3 The **DECAPOLIS** (Greek for "Ten Towns") consisted of a number of independent and predominantly Gentile cities. It did not come under Jewish control, although many Jewish people lived within the region. ***Gadara*** is possibly referred to in Matthew 8:28. ***Gerasa***, an important city in the DECAPOLIS, is mentioned only with reference to the country of the Gerasenes, Mark 5:1; Luke 8:26.

4 According to John's Gospel, John the Baptist carried out his ministry at ***Bethany beyond Jordan*** (1:28) and at ***Aenon*** near ***Salim***, 3:23.

5 ***Mt. Gerizim*** played an important role in the Old Testament narrative. It is located near what was formerly Shechem, but in **ILLUSTRATION 42A** is called ***Sychar*** (today *Nablus*, derived from its Roman name *Neapolis*). The events outlined in John 4 took place in this vicinity. Because the Samaritans said that the only legitimate place of worship was their temple on Mt. Gerizim, the Jews despised them and their temple.

6 Although ***Gaza***, ***Joppa***, and ***Ptolemais*** are not referred to in the Gospels, they are referred to in Acts (8:26, 9:32–43, 21:7).

7 Herod Antipas founded ***Tiberias*** about A.D. 20, named it after the Emperor Tiberius, and made it his capital. Because it was located on ground that had served as a graveyard, Tiberias was seen to be unclean in Jewish eyes. No reference is made to Jesus visiting it. However, after the Romans destroyed Jerusalem in A.D. 70, Tiberias became the chief city of Jewish learning, and both the *Mishnah* and *Palestinian Talmud* were compiled there in the 3rd and 5th centuries respectively. Today, little remains of ***Magdala***, ***Capernaum***, and ***Bethsaida***, located on the shores of the ***SEA OF GALILEE*** and mentioned in the New Testament.

8 The Romans moved their capital from ***Jerusalem*** to Caesarea in A.D. 6—after deposing Archelaeus and appointing a procurator to rule Judea. Nevertheless for most Jews, Jerusalem was "the center of their affections and the navel of the earth," Jubilees 8:19; Josephus, *The Jewish War 52*. After Jerusalem fell to the Romans in A.D. 70 at the end of the First Jewish War, emperor Titus gave orders that it be leveled to the ground. After the Second Jewish War in A.D. 135, emperor Hadrian rebuilt the city as Aelia Capitolina, erected a temple to Jupiter within its walls, and forbad any circumcised person to enter the city.

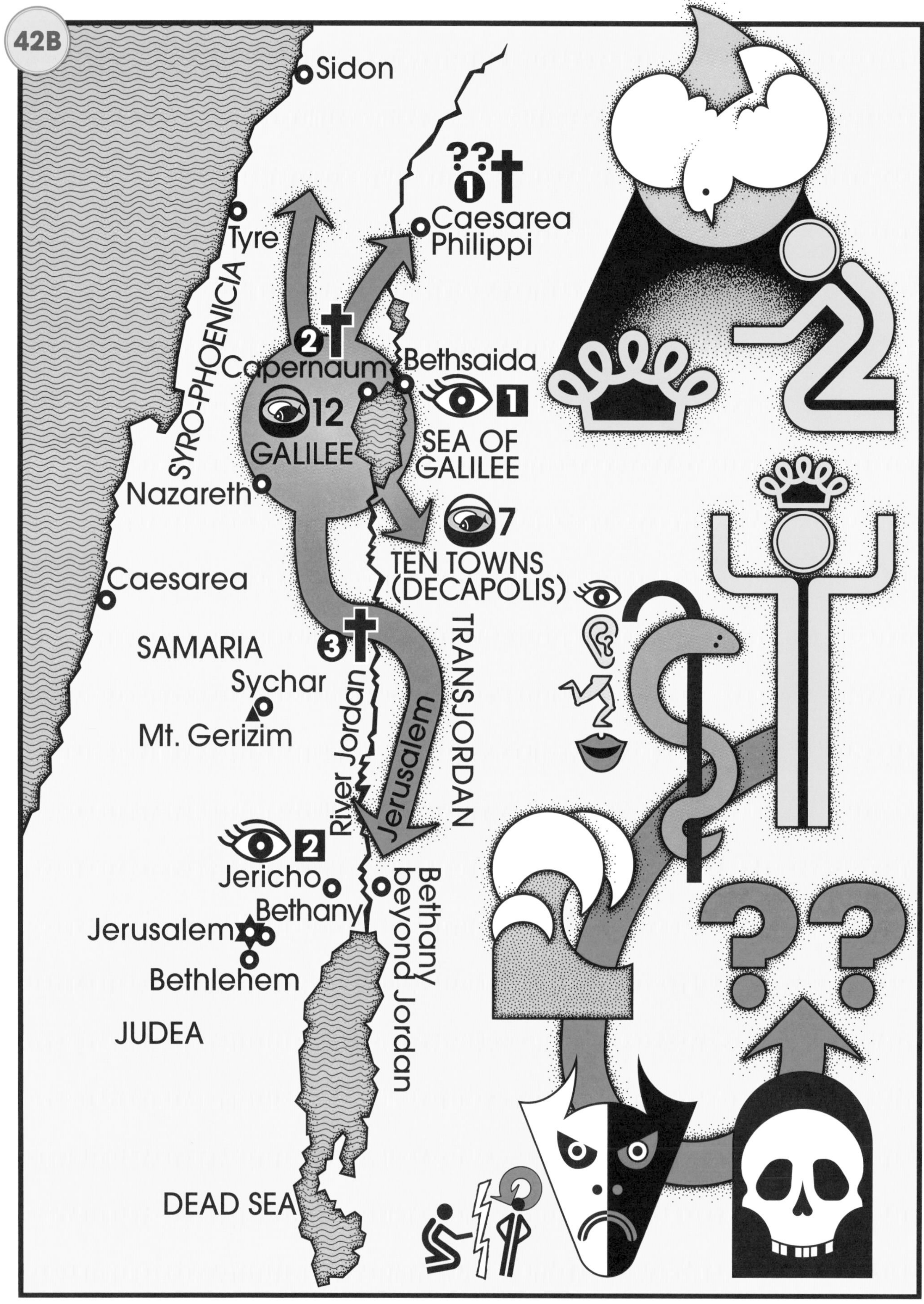
42B
Sidon
Tyre
SYRO-PHOENICIA
Caesarea
Philippi
Capernaum
Bethsaida
12
GALILEE
1
SEA OF
GALILEE
Nazareth
7
TEN TOWNS
(DECAPOLIS)
Caesarea
SAMARIA
3
Sychar
Mt. Gerizim
River Jordan
Jerusalem
TRANSJORDAN
2
Jericho
Bethany
Bethany
beyond Jordan
Jerusalem
Bethlehem
JUDEA
DEAD SEA

Where, What, When?

Units 42 and 43 describe the breaking in of the Messianic Age as outlined in the Gospel according to St. Mark. In what follows, all quotes are from Mark's Gospel, unless otherwise stated.

WHERE?

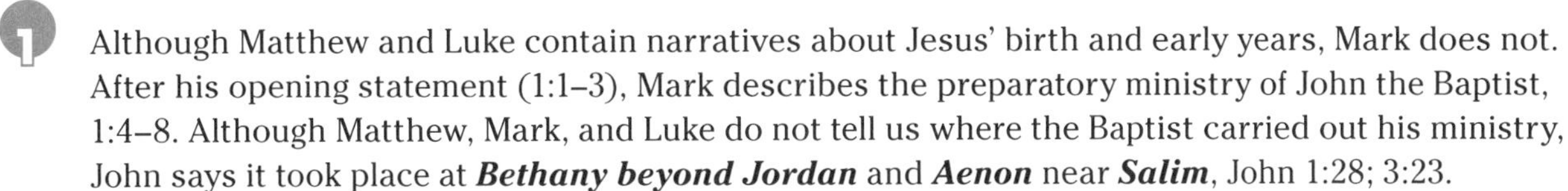

1 Although Matthew and Luke contain narratives about Jesus' birth and early years, Mark does not. After his opening statement (1:1–3), Mark describes the preparatory ministry of John the Baptist, 1:4–8. Although Matthew, Mark, and Luke do not tell us where the Baptist carried out his ministry, John says it took place at ***Bethany beyond Jordan*** and ***Aenon*** near ***Salim***, John 1:28; 3:23.

2 Jesus goes south from ***Nazareth*** in ***GALILEE*** to John to be baptized, 1:9–11. The ***dove*** and ***drop of water*** (*top right*) symbolize events associated with Jesus' baptism. The ***crown*** and ***servant figure*** point to titles ascribed to Jesus on that occasion (*King* and *Servant*; see 42D Frame 4).

3 After being baptized, Jesus goes into the wilderness (according to tradition, to the west of the ***River Jordan***) to confront Satan, 1:12,13.

4 Jesus then returns to Galilee where He carries out a lengthy ministry, 1:14–7:23 (with a visit to the Gentile ***DECAPOLIS*** region in 5:1–20). He then goes north into ***SYRO-PHOENICIA*** to the region of ***Tyre*** and ***Sidon*** (7:24–30), southeast to the Decapolis (7:31–8:10), north to ***Caesarea Philippi*** (8:27), and finally back to Galilee and ***Capernaum***, 9:30,33.

5 Eventually, Jesus leaves Galilee and heads south for ***Jerusalem***, traveling part of the time via the ***TRANSJORDAN***, 10:1. The only place mentioned along the way is ***Jericho***, 10:46 (about 800 feet [.25 kilometers] *below* sea level). After Jesus arrives in the vicinity of Jerusalem (11:1; about 3,000 feet [1 kilometer] *above* sea level), He enters the city on Palm Sunday, attacks the Temple system on Monday, and is crucified the following Friday. After rising from the dead on Sunday morning, He returns to Galilee, 16:7.

6 Although Jesus does not spend time in Jerusalem prior to Palm Sunday, Jerusalem plays a role throughout the narrative. Those who seek to destroy Jesus (3:22; 7:1ff.) come from this *city of opposition*. When Jesus finally sets His face to go to Jerusalem, He knows full well that He is going to a dangerous city—a city where His opponents live and where plans are being made to put Him to death, 8:31; 9:31; 10:32–34. When, for the first time in Mark's Gospel, Jesus confronts the disciples with the question of His identity, He does so in the vicinity of Caesarea Philippi—about as far away from Jerusalem as He ever traveled during His ministry. Furthermore, prior to His death He told His disciples that He would meet them again after His resurrection, not in Jerusalem, but in Galilee, 14:28; see also 16:1–8.

WHAT?

1 Had Jesus, during His early ministry, declared Himself to be the long-awaited Messiah openly and publicly in *words*, He would have had to deal with fierce opposition from the Jewish religious leaders, and the threat of death at the hands of the Roman occupying powers. He chose to reveal His identity through the following *signs* and *actions*.

- ***Serpent around staff*** (symbol of healing, Numbers 21:4–9)***:*** Isaiah 35:5,6 stated that when the messianic age broke in, the blind would see, the deaf would hear, the lame would be healed, and the dumb would be empowered to speak (eye, ear, legs, mouth).
- ***White-capped waves:*** In stilling the storm at sea (4:35–41) and walking on the water (6:45–52), Jesus showed Himself to possess the same power over the forces of nature as did His Father, the Creator of the universe, Psalm 65:7, 89:9, 107:23–32.

- ***Demonic face:*** Jesus revealed the true nature of the Satanic realm, and conquered it. Mark makes frequent reference to Jesus exorcising demons from people, e.g., 1:21–28, 32–34, 39; 3:19–27.
- ***Tombstone with skull:*** Jesus raised the dead, 5:21–23, 35–43; see Isaiah 26:19, Daniel 12:1–3.

2 Jesus ministered to *Gentiles* as well as to *Jews.*

- He traveled to the Gentile region of the ***DECAPOLIS*** where He healed a man possessed by a host of demons, 5:1–12.
- He went to the Gentile region of ***SYRO-PHOENICIA*** where He entered a house (most likely a *Gentile* house), and exorcised a demon from a girl, 7:24–30.
- He then returned to the Decapolis where He healed a deaf-mute and fed 4,000 Gentiles with bread and fish, 7:31–8:11.

3 Mark's Gospel contains two accounts of Jesus feeding the multitudes: 5,000 Jewish people in the Jewish territory of ***GALILEE*** (***basket containing bread and fish, 12*** baskets of leftovers; 6:30–44) and 4,000 Gentile people in the ***DECAPOLIS*** region (***basket containing bread and fish, 7*** baskets of leftovers; 8:1–10).

4 After feeding the 4,000 Gentiles, Jesus traveled north toward ***Caesarea Philippi***. Along the way, He healed a blind man in two stages at ***Bethsaida***, 8:22–26 (***eye, 1***). He also predicted His approaching passion for the *first* time, 8:27–38 (***❶, cross, two question marks***).

5 Jesus then headed south and predicted His passion for a *second* time (***❷, cross***) in the region to the west of ***Capernaum***, 9:30–35.

6 Jesus then left Galilee (10:1) and headed south for Jerusalem. Along the way, He predicted His passion for a *third* time (***❸, cross***), 10:32–45. Along the way, He passed through ***Jericho***.

7 Immediately after leaving Jericho, Jesus met and healed blind Bartimaeus (***eye, 2,*** 10:46–52). Remarkably, in Mark's narrative, *blind* Bartimaeus is the first person to address Jesus as "Son of David"—a title suggesting that Jesus is the Messiah. Although Bartimaeus is *blind*, he can *see*. Then, five days before His death, Jesus entered Jerusalem for the first time during the course of His public ministry, 11:1.

WHEN?

1 Mark's comments about issues of time in Jesus' ministry are often vague—"In those days," 1:9; "after some days," 2:1; "One sabbath," 2:23; "Six days later," 9:2 (six days after what?), etc. It is traditional to think of Jesus' ministry lasting three years, a conclusion arrived at by counting the number of Passover observances referred to in John's Gospel, 2:13,23; 6:4; 11:55. Mark refers to only one Passover (14:1,12,14,16) and gives the impression that Jesus' ministry lasted for one tumultuous year. The narratives in Matthew and Luke are based on Mark's time-frame.

2 Matthew (Units 44,45) follows Mark's geographical outline closely, although he includes an initial nativity narrative, as does Luke. In Luke (Units 46,47), Jesus does not travel to Syro-Phoenicia, the Decapolis, or to Caesarea Philippi. He conducts His ministry in Galilee and along the way from Galilee to Jerusalem. Furthermore, although Jesus does not minister to the Gentiles in Luke's Gospel, He does minister to the Gentiles (through the apostles) in Luke's second writing, the Acts of the Apostles.

3 Jesus' geographical movements in John's Gospel (Units 48,49) are different. John does not focus on the sequence of Jesus' geographical movements, but on what Jesus' ministry implied for the validity and continuing relevance of the beliefs and practices of Judaism.

One Story—Four Lenses

1 How are we to study the Gospels? Should we study Matthew first because it is placed first among the Gospels? If we dig deeply into Matthew, do we need to dig deeply into the other three Gospels? Why not study all four Gospels at the same time and use scissors and glue to fit their respective narratives into one harmonious whole?

2 It is not as simple as that. Any attempt to mix all four Gospels into a single account gains nothing and loses much. When, in about A.D. 150, Tatian tried to combine the Gospels into a single writing, the early church realized that the insights each Gospel offers were lost in the process. To mix the Gospels together is to blur the final, total picture that emerges when each is studied in its own right.

3 Although there is but one "Jesus story," each Gospel writer ("photographer") looks at that one story through his own lens and focuses on details that highlight his major emphases. To put it another way: Jesus' person and ministry are like a beautiful diamond with countless facets. Each Gospel writer concentrates on particular facets of the one diamond.

4 When each evangelist wrote his respective Gospel, his goal was not to present his readers with a complete account of events in Jesus' life. He describes the life, ministry, and mission of Jesus only in broad outline. What details he selects are chosen for a purpose—that his readers may "believe" and "have life," John 20:30,31.

5 It is generally agreed that Mark was written first, and that Mark served as a basis for the writing of both Matthew and Luke. Mark contains 661 verses. Matthew reproduces 606 of these and Luke 320. Only 31 of Mark's 661 verses do not appear in either Matthew or Luke. Matthew occasionally varies Mark's order of events within his Gospel. Luke does the same. However, Matthew and Luke *together* never vary the order; one of them always agrees with Mark's order of events, and most often both do. A knowledge of Mark enables us to read Matthew and Luke more intelligently.

6 During the latter part of the second century A.D., Papias served as the bishop of Hierapolis in South Phrygia—today's northwestern Turkey. Papias took a great interest in collecting information about the Gospels. On one occasion, he wrote that Mark contains the material that Peter used in his preaching. He stated that Mark was Peter's interpreter, and that he wrote down the things Peter taught about Jesus. If Papias' statement is correct, the implication is that in Mark we have virtually an eye-witness account of Jesus' life. If this is so, one can understand why Mark quotes an occasional word of Jesus in Aramaic: "Talitha cum," 5:41; "Ephphatha," 7:34; "Abba," 14:36. We can also understand why Mark often uses a tense referred to as an "historic present," such as, "She says to me, and I say back to her." Mark uses the historic present 151 times in his original Greek. Because translators usually strive to "improve" Mark's grammar and style in order to produce a more polished literary product, these "historic presents" are usually not found in English translations.

7 Other features of Mark's style are worthy of note. Mark makes frequent use of that little word "and." Often when telling a story, he joins its details together by adding "and... and... and... and." In the original Greek version of chapter three, 29 of 35 verses begin with "and." Mark is also fond of the word "immediately." He uses it 41 times in his Gospel—10 times in the first chapter alone. His use of the word creates a sense of urgency: "There is no time to waste. Listen now! Believe now! Follow now!" Mark's story does not just march along. It gallops along with such speed that imaginative readers have little time to catch their breath.

42D
1
2
3
4
5
6
7
8
9
10
11
1 2 3 4 5 6 7 1 2 3 4 5 6 7

MARK 1–8 (Part 1)

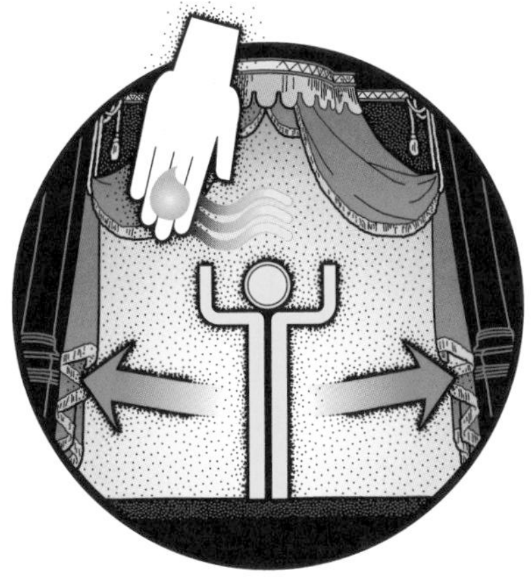

Frame 1

Stage with open curtains; standing Jesus; hand anointing Him with oil: Mark begins his Gospel with, "The beginning of the good news of Jesus Christ, the Son of God," 1:1. This statement might be better translated, "The beginning of the good news of *Jesus the Messiah*, the Son of God." The "good news" is brought by Jesus and is about Jesus. He, the Christ, the Messiah, the *Anointed One*, is ushering in that New Age the Jewish people have been expecting for centuries. The "good news" is that they need wait no longer. *The Messianic Age has arrived! The stage is set. The curtains have been drawn apart. The Messianic drama is about to begin.* Mark's narrative focuses on the question, "What was the nature of the Messianic Age that broke in with Jesus? What does Jesus' Messianic mission imply for those who claim Him as their Savior and Lord?"

Traditionally, the term "Son of God" (1:1) is interpreted to mean that Jesus is true God. He was and is that. In Him, the fullness of Deity took into Himself the fullness of a human nature, so that in one Person, Jesus the Messiah, a union of two natures takes place. That which is fully God has united itself with that which is fully human. However, in 1:1 the term says more than that. In the Old Testament, the nation of Israel is called "the son of God," Exodus 4:21–23; Hosea 11:1. Therefore, to call Jesus "the Son of God" is to declare that the traditional "son of God" (Israel) has been superseded by a new "Son of God." The remnant of the true people of God now numbers one: Jesus the Messiah. This new Son of God is not some upstart or usurper. He is a descendant of such Jewish "greats" as Abraham and David. Through Him, God is not merely continuing the history of His people. God is making a *new beginning* to His people. The term "Son of God" would also have been a challenge to any first century audience steeped in the propaganda of the Roman Empire which declared that the emperor was the Son of God.

Frame 2

Person walking along a highway, with hills either side, and with the ground plan of the Jerusalem Temple on the horizon: The prophet Malachi proclaimed (3:1a) that God would send His messenger to prepare the way before Him. In quoting this verse, Mark expects his readers to be aware of the second half of the verse (a Jewish practice referred to as *remez*), "and the Lord whom you seek will suddenly come to His Temple." So, in and through Jesus, God will eventually visit the Jerusalem Temple, observe what is taking place within its walls, and express His opinion concerning what He sees.

Mark 1:3 reflects the contents of Isaiah 40:3–5. Isaiah addressed these words to the exiles in Babylon. He assured them that God was about to come to Babylon to rescue His people from captivity and lead them back to their homeland. A great highway would appear—on which God would travel to Babylon, and along which He would lead the exiles back to Jerusalem. The height of the mountains would diminish, the valleys would be filled in, and rough and uneven ground would be made smooth. The return journey would indeed be a comfortable one! In the four Gospels, the message is:

> *God is about to carry out the great and final rescue of His people. They are captive, not to Egypt, Assyria, Babylon, Persian, Greece, or Rome but to the power of sin, Satan, and death. They are also captive to their own traditions and rituals, and to their obsession with their descent from Abraham and family genealogies. Jesus is coming to free them from these bonds, and to lead them into the liberty of true children of God.*

Frame 3

John the Baptist; drop of water; large Star of David over the Holy Land; small Star of David over location of Jerusalem; small circle to the east of the River Jordan; arrow pointing from west to east of the Jordan River: John the Baptist (dressed like Elijah, 2 Kings 1:8) is the one sent by God to prepare the people for the coming of God's Messiah. He carries out his mission in the wilderness (see John 1:28), the place of expectations and new beginnings, the place where God said He would take His people to renew them and draw them closer to Himself, Hosea 2:14,15. "People from the whole Judean countryside and all the people of Jerusalem" go out to John and are baptized by him in the River Jordan, confessing their sins in the process.

That Jews submitted to John's baptism is remarkable, for traditionally only Gentiles were baptized when they converted to Judaism. Furthermore, it would seem that John baptized people in the vicinity where the Israelites first entered the land under Joshua—suggesting that John's baptism constituted a new beginning, a new entry into the Promised Land, for the people of God.

John does not baptize to draw attention to himself. He does so to prepare the way for the One who will follow after him—One who will be much greater than he is. John says that he does not deserve even to be the Messiah's slave, to perform the most menial task for Him—to untie the thongs of His sandals (a task that only a Gentile slave would perform). John can baptize with water, true! But the One to whom he points will baptize with the Holy Spirit. Imagine! He will bestow the Holy Spirit, not just on a few select ones in the Jewish nation such as judges, kings, and prophets, but on all who come to Him to receive what He has to give; see Joel 2:28,29. And eventually, the Holy Spirit will come on the Gentiles, Acts 10:44–48.

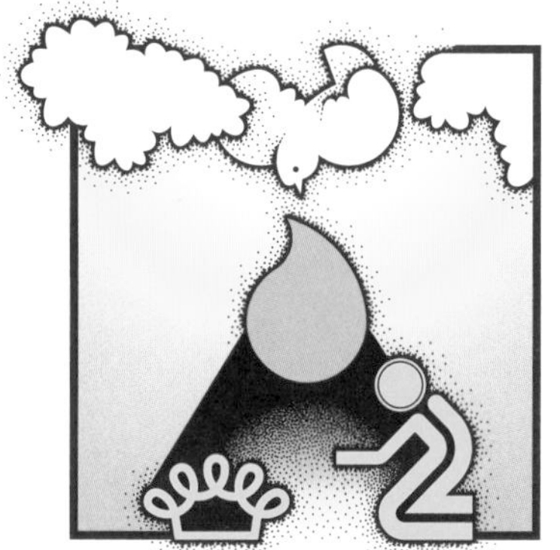

Frame 4

Dove between clouds; drop of water; crown; Jesus in servant posture: Jesus, who is living in the northern region of Galilee when John begins his work, heads south so that John might baptize Him also. Jesus does not need baptism for the forgiveness of any sins. He seeks baptism by John to identify Himself with the New Age that His Father is about to begin in and through Him. After all, He is the new Son of God. As the old son of God, Israel, passed through the waters of the Red Sea and the River Jordan, so the new Son of God must pass through water—the water of John's baptism. Jesus will lead His people into the inheritance of an eternal relationship with the Father.

When Jesus comes out of the water after His baptism, He sees the heavens torn apart and the Spirit descending like a dove on Him, 1:10. Centuries before, the prophet had cried out, "O that you would tear open the heavens and come down," Isaiah 64:1. At Jesus' baptism, the heavens are indeed torn open, and the Spirit comes down in a form that resembles a dove and hovers over the head of Jesus. The rabbis (teachers) spoke of the dove as a symbol of the nation of Israel; see also Hosea 7:11, 9:11, and 11:11. At Jesus' baptism, the Spirit in the form of a dove hovers over the head of the new Son of God, the true Israel. Jesus will lead a life directed entirely by the Holy Spirit.

At His baptism Jesus is anointed into the office defined by the voice from heaven: "You are My Son, the Beloved; with you I am well pleased," 1:11. This statement reflects Psalm 2:7—a Psalm used in ancient Israel at the coronation of a king from the line of David. Its use at Jesus' baptism declares that God has kept His promise; the line of David will not die out. Jesus is, indeed, the long-awaited descendant of David, the long-expected Messianic King, who has come to rule God's people and empower them to carry out God's mission to the world.

The direction the life of this Messianic King will take will be different from what many are expecting. "With you I am well pleased" is a quotation from the first of Isaiah's Servant Songs, 42:1–4; note v. 1. As Messianic King, Jesus will be *The Servant.* He will be despised, rejected, and His people will do their very worst to Him. They will finally crucify Him! However, through His death He will lavish on them the offer of a complete, perfect, and eternal pardon, and draw them into a relationship with Himself in which they will find true life, now and forever.

Frame 5

After Jesus is anointed into office as the long-awaited King and the nature of His Kingship is defined, the Spirit leads Him into the wilderness for *forty days.* After passing through water, Old Israel was taken into a wilderness for *forty years* to be tested and tried—but did little else but sin. Israel's behavior in the wilderness left everything to be desired. The people murmured, grumbled, and sinned constantly. Although Israel's behavior in the wilderness brought forth death and alienation, Jesus' sustained obedience brings forth the new Israel of God.

Servant-King; satanic face; symbol for sin: The new Israel, the new Son of God, is led by the Spirit into the wilderness to be tested and tried by Satan. Mark's temptation narrative consists of only three words, "tempted by Satan," 1:12. In their respective narratives, Matthew (4:1–11) and Luke (4:1–13) list three confrontations between Jesus and Satan. Although both Matthew and Luke conclude their temptation narratives with a reference to Satan *departing* from Jesus, Mark makes no such statement. Most likely, Mark's point is that throughout His ministry, Jesus (the King who walked the way of a servant-without-limit) engages in a non-stop battle with Satan—and finally conquers him when He gives away His life at Calvary. In confronting Jesus, the Servant-King, Satan does not meet his match; he meets his Conqueror!

The first miracle Jesus performs in Mark after His temptation involves a struggle with a demoniac, 1:21–28. And while preaching in synagogues throughout Galilee, He throws out numerous demons, 1:39. Until Jesus takes control of a land and the hearts of its inhabitants, they are under the control of demonic powers.

Angel; lion and serpent: Mark 1:13b states, "Jesus was with the wild beasts; and the angels waited on him." According to the rabbis of Jesus' day, the first fall into sin took place when some of the angels refused to honor Adam and Eve. But now the angels are serving and honoring the New Adam, the true Son of God.

Furthermore, Isaiah (11:6–9; 65:25) stated that when the Messianic Age finally broke in, the members of the animal world would live together in peace, and would not harm one another or humanity; see Hosea 2:18.

Frame 

Servant-Jesus; ringing alarm clock; symbol for sin cancelled out; symbol for serving God and others with approval sign: After John is arrested, Jesus returns to Galilee to launch His public ministry. He begins it by proclaiming a message that causes many Jewish hearts to beat wildly with excitement: "The time is fulfilled, and the kingdom of God has come; repent, and believe in the good news," Mark 1:15. We might summarize Jesus' message as follows:

The age that you and your ancestors have longed for has finally arrived—in Me. Your dreams are about to be fulfilled. The kingdom of God has broken into history! Change your whole way of thinking and living. Rejoice! Embrace the good news of the Messianic Age in all that you believe, think, say, and do.

Some Jewish expectations about the dawning of the Messianic Age were extravagant. However, the setting for Jesus' opening statement is anything but spectacular. There is no display of cosmic fireworks when Jesus speaks. Jesus' audience sees no halo around His head, no regal clothing, no retinue of servants or royal guards, no pomp, and no splendor. Indeed, the setting and Jesus' appearance are anticlimactic to the Jews. To the best of their knowledge, Jesus is the son of Joseph the carpenter and his wife Mary. Even so, the claims the New Testament makes about who Jesus is, and the implications of His opening statement, are profound.

When Jesus declared that the kingdom of God broke into history with Him, He was doing something that was politically dangerous. To announce any kingdom was to challenge the power of the Herods—and behind the Herods were the Roman authorities and emperor.

Frame 7

Crowned Jesus with arms extended calls the first disciples—fishermen—to follow Him: On the coastline of the Sea of Galilee, Jesus begins to gather about Himself a new people 1:16–20. He confronts Peter and Andrew, James and John, and says, "Follow Me!" 1:17. They follow. Jesus conducts no test to ascertain whether they are worthy of being in His company. He makes no study of their family background to check out their pedigree; see 2:13–17. He issues only an urgent summons, 2:13,14. A little later, the Twelve are set aside as the nucleus of the New Israel that is being formed, 3:13–18. The Messianic ministry is getting under way, and the Messianic community is being formed.

Frame 8

Synagogue; Star of David; arrow from male figure to demonic face: Next, Jesus and the first four disciples enter a synagogue in Capernaum on a Sabbath day, 1:21–34. Those present are astonished by Jesus' teaching. His teaching *with authority*, making an absolute claim on His hearers, is in the best tradition of the ancient prophets—not the rabbis and scribes of His day.

A man possessed with an "unclean spirit" comes before Jesus—"unclean" because of the spirit's resistance to the holiness of God. The demonic presence knows who Jesus is and why He has come, and fears Jesus' power to destroy his influence. It addresses Jesus as "Jesus of Nazareth—the Holy One of God"—an action reflecting the belief that the use of the precise name of an opposing spirit guarantees mastery over him. Jesus forbids the demons to speak! After Jesus casts the demon out of the man, the crowd is even more astonished and Jesus' fame begins to spread throughout Galilee.

Immediately after Jesus and the four disciples leave the synagogue, they go to the home of Simon Peter and Andrew—whose mother-in-law is sick with a fever, 1:29–31. Despite the fact that *it is still Sabbath* (when healing of the sick—deemed as work—should not take place), Jesus heals her.

That evening, *after the Sabbath is over*, crowds from Capernaum come to the home where Jesus is, bringing to Him many who are sick, 1:32–34. Jesus heals many of the sick, and casts out many demons.

Very early the next morning, Jesus goes out of the house to pray in a lonely place, 1:35–39. The disciples search for Jesus, find Him, and tell Him that everyone is searching for Him. Jesus then summons them to go with Him to surrounding towns where He will proclaim His divine message. In the course of doing this, Jesus preaches in synagogues and casts out demons.

Eventually, a leper comes to Jesus and begs for healing, 1:40–45; see also Numbers 12:10–15, 2 Kings 5:1–14. Jesus touches the leper *before healing him*. According to the rabbis at this time, Jesus makes Himself unclean by touching an unclean person—a tradition that Jesus ignores and sets aside. In curing the leper, Jesus assumes that the priests will reinstate the cured man into the religious community.

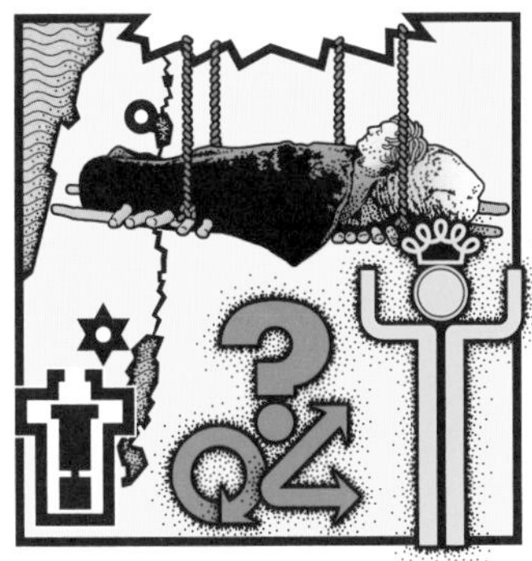

Frame 9

Man on a stretcher being lowered from an opening in a roof; symbols denoting locations of Capernaum and Jerusalem; Temple ground-plan; question mark above symbols for sin (*at left*) ***and God's will for humanity*** (*at right*)***; crowned Jesus:*** Jesus then returns to Capernaum and enters a house—which is soon crowded with people, 2:1–12. Some men bring a paralyzed man to the house, carry him to the roof, make an opening in the roof, and lower the into the room below. (The house would have had a flat roof, with an outside stair case leading up to it.) Although those present expect Jesus to heal the man, He does not do that. He says to the man, "Son, your sins are forgiven." The scribes who are present are furious with Jesus. Their position is that only God can forgive sins. If the paralyzed wants to be forgiven he should go to the Jerusalem Temple and observe the appropriate rituals. Who is Jesus to offer to offer forgiveness—outside of the Temple and free of charge?

To deal with His adversaries, and validate His divine authority to forgive, Jesus then heals the man. If Jesus' second statement has authority and power, His first word must also have authority and power. The "sin management system" is now out of the Temple. It resides in Jesus! He is the forgiving Presence of God! When speaking to His opponents, Jesus refers to Himself as "the Son of Man," a term with links to Daniel 7:13 where the term "Son of Man" refers to the true, eternal, authoritative people of God (which Jesus is!).

Immediately after declaring the paralytic forgiven and healing him, Jesus calls a tax collector, Levi (possibly the Hebrew name for Matthew), to follow Him, 2:13,14. Levi immediately rises from his seat in the tax booth and follows Jesus. Tax collectors were regarded as sinners, outcasts of society, and collaborators with Rome. They and their families were looked upon with scorn and disgrace.

Frame 10

Roman helmet and coins; food and drink; new patch on an old piece of cloth; wine flowing from hole in a wineskin: Jesus then goes to Levi's house and dines with him and other tax collectors and "sinners," 2:15–22. When some scribes of the Pharisees see what Jesus is doing, they protest to Jesus' disciples. After all, the Jewish elite look on Levi and his friends as despised collaborators with the Romans! Jesus responds by telling them that He has come to serve those who are aware of their need of spiritual healing. Those who see no need for spiritual healing cut themselves off from what they desperately need—something that only Jesus can give.

Jesus then says that His message and ministry is so radical that it is impossible to harmonize it with previous beliefs and practices—even as it is impossible to attach a piece of new cloth to an old, worn, tattered garment, or to pour new wine into old wineskins. The new cloth will tear away from the old, and the new wine will break open the old wineskins.

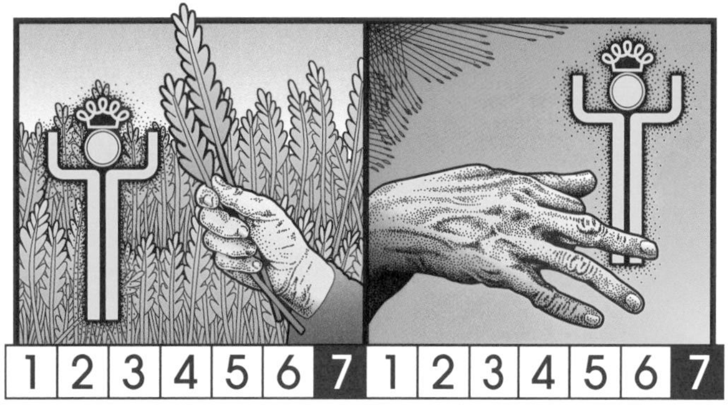

Frame 11

Frame 11 contains two sections. A ***crowned Jesus*** is seen in both of them. A symbol denoting the ***seventh day of the week (Sabbath)*** is placed beneath each.

Grain crop; hand holding plucked grain-stalks: When Jesus permits the disciples to pluck heads of grain on a ***Sabbath***, some Pharisees protest that their action is unlawful and sinful, 2:23–28. Jesus responds by referring to an event in David's life (1 Samuel 21:1–16), and then states that the Sabbath is intended to serve people—and is not merely a ritual that people are to serve. Furthermore, Jesus declares Himself (the Son of Man) to have authority over the Sabbath—an authority that, according to the Pharisees, only God has; see also Matthew 12:1–8.

Withered hand: When Jesus again enters a synagogue on a ***Sabbath***, a man with a withered hand is brought to him. And Jesus heals the man—despite the fact that it is again a Sabbath day, 3:1–6.

In Jesus' day, some religious leaders taught that if all Jews were to *observe* two consecutive Sabbaths strictly, the Messiah would appear. Jesus, however, *breaks* two consecutive Sabbaths—with the result that the Pharisees conspire with some Herodians to determine how best to destroy Jesus! The Pharisees need the help of the Herodians, supporters of Herod Antipas (Tetrarch of Galilee and Perea), if they are to take action against Jesus.

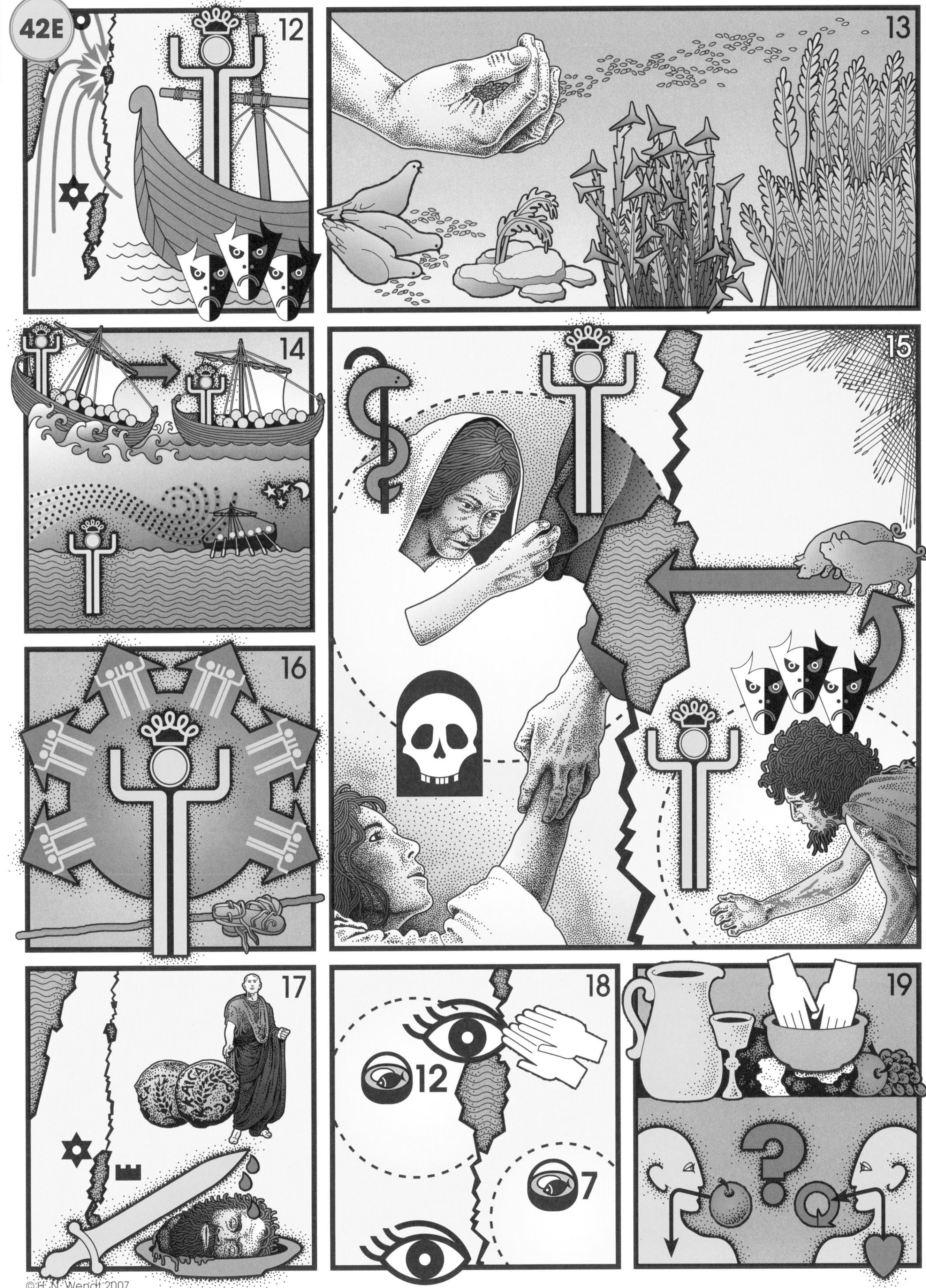

42E
12
13
14
15
16
17
18
12
7
19

Frame 12

Crowned Jesus standing in a boat; arrows from a variety of locations pointing to the Sea of Galilee; demonic faces: When Jesus and His disciples go to the Sea of Galilee, crowds flock to Him from Judea, Jerusalem, Idumea, Beyond the Jordan, and Tyre and Sidon in Syro-Phoenicia. Jesus tells the disciples to provide Him with a boat so that He might cope with the crowds, and not be crushed by those who hope to touch Him so that they might be healed. And once again, the demons recognize who Jesus is, fall down before Him, and shout, "You are the Son of God!" (3:7–35)

Jesus then takes the disciples up a mountain, and commissions them to proclaim His message and to cast out demons, 3:13–19a. Here and elsewhere, the mountain is associated with solemn moments in the acts and mission of self-revelation of Jesus, 6:46; 9:2–8; 13:3.

Next, when Jesus returns to His home, the crowds flock around Him. Some say that Jesus has lost His mind. Scribes who come from Jerusalem insist that Jesus is doing all things with the help of Satan and the demonic realm, 3:19b–22. Jesus responds by telling the scribes that if He is working hand in hand with the Satanic realm, then there must be chaos in that realm because Jesus is *fighting* the powers of the demonic! The truth is that Jesus has come to bind and destroy the powers of the demonic, 3:23–27.

Mark 3:28–30 puzzles many. Its message is best understood as follows: Jesus states that He can understand why people might reject and blaspheme Him during the course of His earthly ministry. However, after that ministry has been vindicated by Jesus' resurrection, those who reject the message that the Holy Spirit seeks to make known about the risen Jesus cut themselves off from God's forgiving grace and mercy.

In the closing section of ch. 3 (vv. 31–35), Jesus points out that His "family circle" is much wider than His genetic mother and siblings. His family consists of all who know and do the will of God that Jesus teaches and demonstrates.

Frame 13

Hand scattering grain; birds eating some of the grain; grain sprouting amid rocks; grain stalks and weeds intertwined; healthy and abundant grain crop: While seated in a boat, Jesus shares many parables with His audience, 4:1–34. In the parable of the sower (4:1–20), Jesus teaches His hearers that His message will meet with a mixed reception.

- In some cases, it will be destroyed before it even takes root (it will not make any inroads into the human heart).
- In other cases, although it may sprout, it will soon wither away (it will make only a superficial, short-term impact).
- While some might initially sprout in an encouraging manner, it will be throttled by weeds that grow up with it (the message will be destroyed by the seductions and temptations of the world order).
- But—praise God—some will produce an abundant harvest: they will dedicate life to knowing, following, and sharing Jesus! The narrative indicates that Jesus presents the message of His Kingdom to the disbelieving crowd in one manner (4:1–8), and to His disciples in another, 4:9ff.

Frame 14

Jesus' power over the storms and the sea: Jesus tells the disciples to take Him by boat across the Sea of Galilee—from the west bank to the east bank, 4:35–41. Along the way, Jesus falls asleep and a storm erupts. The frightened disciples wake Jesus and ask Him to do something about their dangerous situation. Jesus rebukes the wind and commands the sea to be still. A dead calm follows! The disciples are overawed by what they see, and ask one another, "Who then is this, that even the wind and sea obey Him?" The answer is found in Psalm 65:7, 89:9, and 107:23–32; Jesus is God!

The illustration also contains a depiction of Jesus walking on the water—an incident referred to in 6:45–52. Here again Jesus demonstrates power over the created order; *He is the Creator!*

Frame 15

Frame 15 depicts the three events outlined in ch. 5. When Jesus asks the disciples to take Him to the region to the southeast of the Sea of Galilee, they are deeply disturbed. That region is not Jewish territory. Gentiles live there—and they have pigs! After the group arrives at their destination, we are told that only Jesus gets out of the boat, 5:1,2.

Lower right
Crowned Jesus; man with scars on his body; demonic faces; arrow from man to pigs to the Sea of Galilee: When Jesus disembarks, He is recognized from a distance by a man, possessed by a "legion" of demons, who lives among the (ritually unclean) tombs and is an outcast from society, 5:1–20. No one can restrain him—not even with chains and shackles. The man constantly howls and bruises himself with stones. When he comes into Jesus' presence, he bows before Him and shouts out that he knows that Jesus is the Son of the Most High God. Jesus commands the demons within the man to leave him. When the demons plead with Jesus not to send them out of the region in which they live, Jesus commands them to enter a nearby herd of 2,000 pigs—which they do. (*Only Gentiles kept pigs.*) The pigs then rush into the Sea of Galilee and are drowned—taking the demons with them. There are parallels between this incident and the Exodus from Egypt under Moses. Although in the Exodus event, the enemies who drown are Egyptian soldiers, in this healing miracle the enemies who drown are demons—the real opponents of Jesus' Messianic Kingdom!

The people who live in the region are disturbed! They have lost their pigs—their source of income. They beg Jesus to leave their neighborhood—and He does. The man whom Jesus has healed wants to go with Him—but Jesus says "No!" and tells him to remain in the region and tell his family and others about Jesus—which he does. A little later (8:1–10), Jesus feeds 4,000 Gentiles in this same region—Gentiles who gather around Jesus. Did they come as a result of the witness of the man Jesus healed?

Upper left
Crowned Jesus; distressed woman reaching out to touch Jesus' outer robe; symbol of healing—serpent around a staff: When Jesus returns to the west side of the Sea of Galilee, He is met by Jairus,

a leader of a local synagogue, who begs Jesus to come to his home as quickly as possible, 5:24b–34. His 12 year-old daughter is dying! At this point, there is a break in the Jairus narrative. A woman creeps up to Jesus, and secretly (so she hopes) touches His cloak. The woman has been suffering from a menstrual disorder for twelve years—a condition that makes her an unclean outcast in her family and community. Her hope is that if she can but touch Jesus' cloak, she will be healed. She touches Jesus' cloak—and is immediately healed! Jesus, sensing what has taken place, asks, "Who touched My garments?" The woman is forced to "confess"—which she does with fear and trembling, expecting Jesus to rebuke her in no uncertain terms. Jesus does not rebuke her. He addresses her as "Daughter," commends her for her faith, and bids her to go in peace! In relating to the woman in this manner, Jesus once again does away with concern for laws having to do with ritual purity.

Lower left
Tombstone with skull—symbol for death; Jesus takes hold of the hand of Jairus' daughter: After Jesus heals the woman with the menstrual disorder, He is told that Jairus' daughter has died.

However, Jesus goes to Jairus' house, taking with Him Peter, James, and John. After arriving at the house, He goes into the room where the dead girl lies—taking with Him the three disciples, and Jairus and his wife. He then takes the (ritually unclean!) dead girl by the hand, and commands her to return to life. Those who witness her restoration to life are amazed! Jesus then commands them not to tell others what He has done—and asks them to give the girl some food.

It is intriguing to note that the woman had been hemorrhaging for *twelve* years, and that Jairus' daughter was *twelve* years of age. Jesus' actions in Mark 5 become more profound and radical when we understand that, according to the Jewish religious elite, the two worst things a person could do were to touch a dead body, or to touch a menstruating woman. Those who touched such people were required to wash both their body and clothes—and resume normal life only next day. Jesus dispenses with such rituals, and His touch, rather than making Him unclean, brings healing and wholeness to those He touches.

Jesus then returns to Nazareth where He preaches in the town synagogue (6:1–6a), and encounters problems! His opponents refer to Him as "the carpenter, the son of Mary." No other Gospel refers to Jesus as "the carpenter," but as the carpenter's son, Matthew 13:55. Furthermore, Jewish practice was to refer to a male as the son of his father. Perhaps Mark's desire is to express his conviction that God is the Father of Jesus. Jesus responds to His opponents by telling them that the opposition He is experiencing is but a foretaste of things to come.

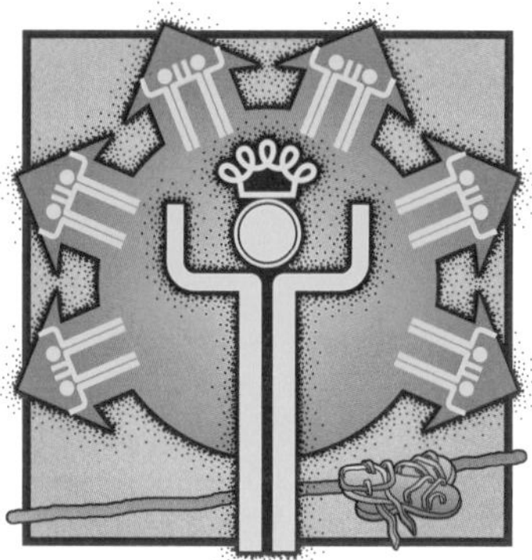

Frame 16

Crowned Jesus, staff and sandals; six protruding arrows with two persons in each: When Jesus and His disciples returns to Nazareth, Jesus' hometown, He teaches in the local synagogue on the Sabbath—but encounters ridicule and mockery, 6:1–6a. He then travels throughout nearby villages and teaches. Eventually there comes the day when He sends out the twelve disciples, two by two—and gives them authority to deal with the unclean spirits, 6:6b–13. The disciples are to "travel light." They are to take with them no bread, no bag, and no money—only a staff and a pair of sandals. Furthermore, they are to wear only one tunic—not two, as was the custom. He also gives them instructions on how to deal with whatever reception they receive as they enter a new place. (Mark, unlike Matthew, makes no mention of any prohibition to visit pagan territory or to enter Samaritan towns.) The disciples then go out, call their hearers to repent, cast out many demons, and cure many who are sick.

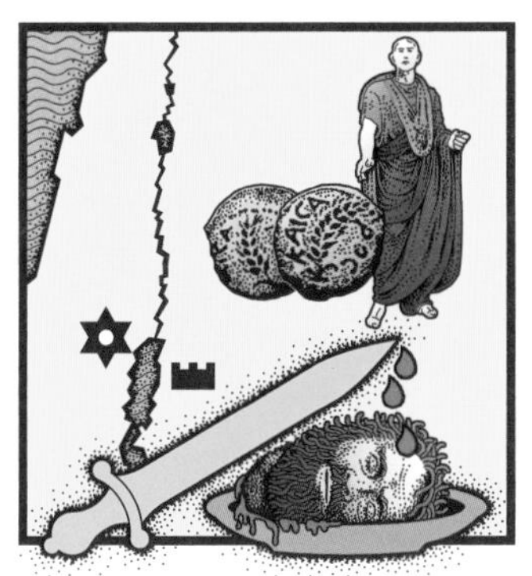

Frame 17

Herod Antipas in royal garb; coins used in Herod's realm; fortress denoting the location of Machaerus; sword; the head of John the Baptist on a platter: When Herod Antipas, ruler of Galilee (to the west of the Sea of Galilee), and Perea (to the east of the Jordan river), hears about Jesus' ministry, he is perplexed. Some within his court suggest that John the Baptist has come to life. Others link Jesus to the long-awaited Elijah, Malachi 4:5,6. Herod expresses the opinion that John the Baptist (whom he had beheaded) has returned to life, 6:14–16.

Mark 6:17–29 describes the events associated with the beheading of John the Baptist. After Herod married Herodias, his brother's wife, John rebuked him—and was imprisoned. (Herodias had divorced her previous husband, Herod Philip. At that time, for a woman to divorce her husband was unthinkable and unheard of. Herodias also insisted that Herod divorce his first wife—a Nabatean princess—in order to marry her.) Herodias wanted John killed—and eventually managed to force Herod to have him beheaded when her husband made a rash promise after watching Herodias' daughter (according to tradition, Salome) perform a dance to entertain him and his guests. The hatred of Herodias toward John reflects that of Jewish leaders toward Jesus.

Although the Pharaoh's birthday was celebrated with a banquet (Genesis 40:20), Herod Antipas' birthday was celebrated with a beheading, Mark 6:21, 26–28.

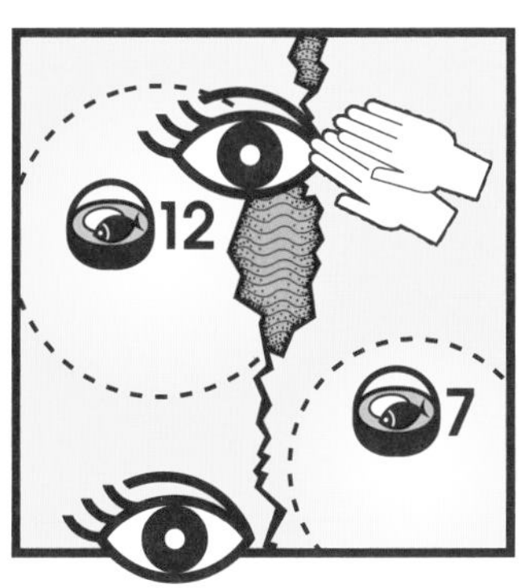

Frame 18

Frame 18 depicts two feeding events, and two incidents involving the healing of the blind.

Basket containing bread and fish, 12: When Jesus feeds 5,000 Jewish men in Galilee with bread and fish, there are twelve baskets of leftovers, 6:32–44.

Basket containing bread and fish, 7: When, in the Decapolis, Jesus feeds 4,000 Gentiles with bread and fish, there are seven baskets of leftovers, 8:1–10. In the verses that follow (8:11–21), the Pharisees ask Jesus to give them some kind of a sign to prove His identity; Jesus refuses to do so and takes His leave of them, 8:11–13. In the conversation that follows (8:14–21), Jesus challenges His disciples to think through the significance of the *twelve* and *seven* baskets of leftovers, 8:14–21.

The message is this: When Jesus feeds the 5,000, the number *twelve* signifies that the nation of Israel originally consisted of *twelve tribes*. Furthermore, Jesus called *twelve disciples* to follow Him and make Him known. When Jesus fed the 4,000 Gentiles, the number *seven* has links to the fact that the ancient Israelites referred to the seven nations living on their borders in derogatory terms, Deuteronomy 7:1,2; Joshua 3:10; Ezekiel 25–32. Although the Jewish priestly and political leaders despise the Gentiles, Jesus has compassion on them. When Jesus feeds the 5,000 in Galilee, the people take their place in rows of hundreds and fifties—reminiscent of the groupings of Israelites encamped in the desert, Exodus 18:21–25. Furthermore, a hope embraced by many Jews in Jesus' day was that when the Messianic Age arrived, the manna would fall from the sky once again, 2 Baruch 29:8. The implications of these two feeding events are enormous!

Eye, with two hands nearby: After feeding the 4,000 in the Decapolis, Jesus eventually heads north toward Caesarea Philippi, 8:27. Along the way, He meets a blind man at Bethsaida—on the northeast corner of the Sea of Galilee, 8:22–26.

Eye to the west of the River Jordan: After Jesus leaves Jericho, He meets another blind man, Bartimaeus, and restores his sight, 10:46–52.

When healing the man in the vicinity of Bethsaida, why did Jesus touch him twice? The message is that although the disciples will soon "see" and confess Jesus to be the Messiah, their vision remains blurred. They do not understand the nature of His Messianic ministry. They need a second touch so that they might see the true nature of Jesus' ministry, and what it will mean for their lives as His disciples and apostles.

The message in relation to the healing of blind Bartimaeus is more obvious. Jesus is surrounded by people who can see with their eyes but are blind in their *hearts*. However, although Bartimaeus cannot see with his *eyes*, he can see within his *heart* and addresses Jesus as "Son of David"—and is the first person in Mark's Gospel to do so.

It is significant that these two incidents involving giving sight to the blind bracket the three accounts of Jesus finally revealing the nature of His Messianic ministry to the disciples, 8:27–30; 9:30–32; 10:32–34. The disciples do not seem to understand what Jesus is saying to them. They will "see" the truth about Jesus' Person and ministry (and its implications for them!) only after Jesus' resurrection when He finally meets with them in Galilee, 16:1–8; note vs. 7.

Frame 19

Food, drink containers; person washing hands: When some Pharisees confront Jesus about the fact that His disciples do not practice ritual washing prior to eating, Jesus responds that although the Pharisees pay much attention to external, ritual purity, they pay little or no attention to inner spiritual purity, 7:1–13.

Question mark; symbol of food entering the body via the mouth; symbol for sin leaving the heart via the mouth: Jesus points out that what enters a person is of no great consequence; it enters the stomach and passes through the body, 7:14–23. What matters is what comes out of the heart via the mouth. Jesus then lists the thoughts and actions that flow from the heart and mouth and truly defile. In setting aside ritual requirements with regard to clean and unclean food, Jesus opens the way for unity between Jew and Gentile.

In the three narratives that follow, *Jesus shows mercy toward Gentiles living in Gentile territory.* (Had Jesus gone to the Gentiles first, the Jewish people would have equated Him with the devil!)

- *First*, He heals the demon-possessed daughter of a woman living in Syro-Phoenicia, 7:24–30. Many find Jesus' statement in 7:27 puzzling. The following insights help. Prior to meeting with the Syro-Phoenician woman, Jesus has been working with and among Jewish people—none of whom have truly understood His identity, message, or mission. However, the Gentile woman falls at Jesus' feet and addresses Him as "Lord." Jesus then helps the woman by healing her daughter. He shows compassion to a Gentile whom the Jews and His disciples would have referred to in abusive terms as a "dog." (They also believed that when the Messiah came, the Jews would participate in the Messianic Banquet—and that dogs would share scraps placed under the table.) Jesus wants the woman to understand that He is more than ready to help one whom the Jewish people despised.
- *Second*, Jesus travels to the Decapolis—again, Gentile territory—where He gives hearing, the ability to speak, and a language to a deaf-mute, 7:31–37. (Because the man had been deaf, he would not previously have heard words and would not have known any language.)

- *Third*, Jesus feeds 4,000 Gentile men living in the Decapolis, and there were seven baskets of leftoversv, 8:1–10. (See Frame 18 above.)

When Jesus refuses to give the Pharisees a "sign" (8:11–13), His response shows that a sign in response to human demand will not be provided. Jesus then warns the disciples to be on their guard concerning the leaven (the influence) of the Pharisees, and challenges them to unravel the significance of His two feeding miracles, 8:14–21. He then heals a blind man in the vicinity of Bethsaida—touching him twice in the process, 8:22–26.

Then, on the way to Caesarea, Jesus asks the disciples who the crowds and they themselves think Jesus really is. Although the crowds don't "get it," the disciples do. Peter declares Jesus to be the Messiah! When Jesus then—for the first time in Mark's narrative—explains what fate awaits Him in Jerusalem, Peter protests! Jesus tells Peter that anyone who wishes to stop Him from completing His mission in Jerusalem is on the side of the devil—and explains that, in Jesus' upside-down, back-to-front Kingdom, people find life by giving it away, 8:27–38.

When predicting His coming passion in Jerusalem, Jesus states that His death will take place as a result of His rejection by the elders, chief priests, and scribes, 8:31. The supreme council in Jerusalem, called the Sanhedrin, was made up of 71 members of these three groups and presided over by the High Priest. It exercised jurisdiction over the Jewish people in religious matters.

The cycle of *prediction—confusion—clarification* surfaces two more times in the narrative that follows. The relevant passages, Mark 9:30–50, 10:32–45, will be dealt with in Unit 43. In all three passion predictions, Jesus refers to Himself as "the Son of Man"—a term found in Daniel 7; see 7:13. Jewish leaders in Jesus' day treasured the book of Daniel; its seventh chapter gave them the hope that they ("the son of man," "the saints of the Most High") would eventually rule the nations of the world forever. Jesus radically reinterpreted that hope and called them to *serve* the nations of the world. Jesus' reinterpretation cost Him His life!

SUMMARY

42A After the death of Herod the Great in 4 B.C., Herod's three sons ruled Judea-Idumea-Samaria (Archelaus), Galilee-Perea (Herod Antipas), and Gaulanitis (Herod Philip). Although Jews lived also in the Decapolis (Ten Cities), they did not rule the region.

42B Mark's Gospel contains no infancy narrative. It begins by telling us how Jesus went from Nazareth in Galilee to where John was working to be baptized. At His baptism, Jesus was anointed into His Messianic office, His titles were announced (King and Servant), and the nature of His mission was defined. After His baptism, Jesus returned to Galilee.

Jesus' ministry took place in and around Galilee. He left Galilee to minister in the Decapolis, and in the region of Tyre and Sidon. After revealing His identity to the disciples in the region of Caesarea Philippi, Jesus headed south for His first and final visit to Jerusalem. He revealed His identity on two more occasions while traveling from Caesarea Philippi to Jerusalem—first in the vicinity of Capernaum and again after leaving Galilee.

Although Jesus taught extensively during His ministry, Mark reports only a limited amount of what Jesus actually said. He concentrates more on Jesus' actions, in particular, His miracles. These can be classified as (1) the Isaianic signs, (2) miracles over nature, (3) miracles over the realm of the demonic, and (4) miracles over death. Jesus fed 5,000 Jewish men in Galilee and 4,000 Gentile men in the Decapolis, and healed blind men near Bethsaida and after leaving Jericho on His way to Jerusalem.

It is difficult to determine precisely how long Jesus' ministry lasted. Mark gives the impression that it was short; he mentions Jesus' attendance at only one Passover observance (as do also Matthew and Luke). Although John makes reference to Jesus being in Jerusalem for two Passover observances, his focus is not so much chronology but how Jesus radically reinterprets the beliefs and practices of Judaism.

42C To study the four Gospels is to look at Jesus' life and ministry through four different lenses. Although what they teach about Jesus' Person and Messianic ministry is similar, each tells the story its own way.

42D The Old Testament narrative reveals the origins of the Jewish people, their rescue from bondage in Egypt, God making a covenant with them at Sinai, their gaining possession of the "Promised Land" and establishing Jerusalem and the Temple system. Mark's narrative focuses on Jesus preparing to visit the Temple to deal with its religious system—its "salvation marketing system." Prior to dealing with the Temple system, Jesus reveals His Father's love and will for people of all nations and lands. He invites people to leave the "kingdoms of the world" and to enter into the "Kingdom of God"—and to believe and do what membership in that Kingdom implies. Throughout the first half of Mark's account, Jesus discourages people and evil spirits alike from declaring who He is. Although He wanted people to come to faith in Him as God's Messiah, He wanted them to see clearly what kind of a Messiah He had come to be. He consistently refused to use His power to benefit Himself in any way. The people, the authorities, and His disciples found it difficult to relate His lifestyle to traditional expectations about what the Messiah would be like and what He would accomplish. Although they were waiting for the coming of their Messiah, they got Jesus of Nazareth instead.

CROSSWAYS®
5
SECTION
UNITS 41-50
The Gospels and Acts
UNIT 43
Mark (II)
The Messianic Kingdom: The Verdict
GENESIS
MATTHEW
MARK
LUKE
JOHN
2 SAMUEL
ACTS
PSALMS
ISAIAH
JEREMIAH
EZEKIEL
ROMANS
1 CORINTHIANS
2 CORINTHIANS
GALATIANS
EPHESIANS
PHILIPPIANS
COLOSSIANS
1 THESSALONIANS
2 THESSALONIANS
1 TIMOTHY
2 TIMOTHY
TITUS
PHILEMON
HEBREWS
JAMES
1 PETER
2 PETER
1 JOHN
2 JOHN
3 JOHN
JUDE
REVELATION
AMOS

ILLUSTRATION

43A

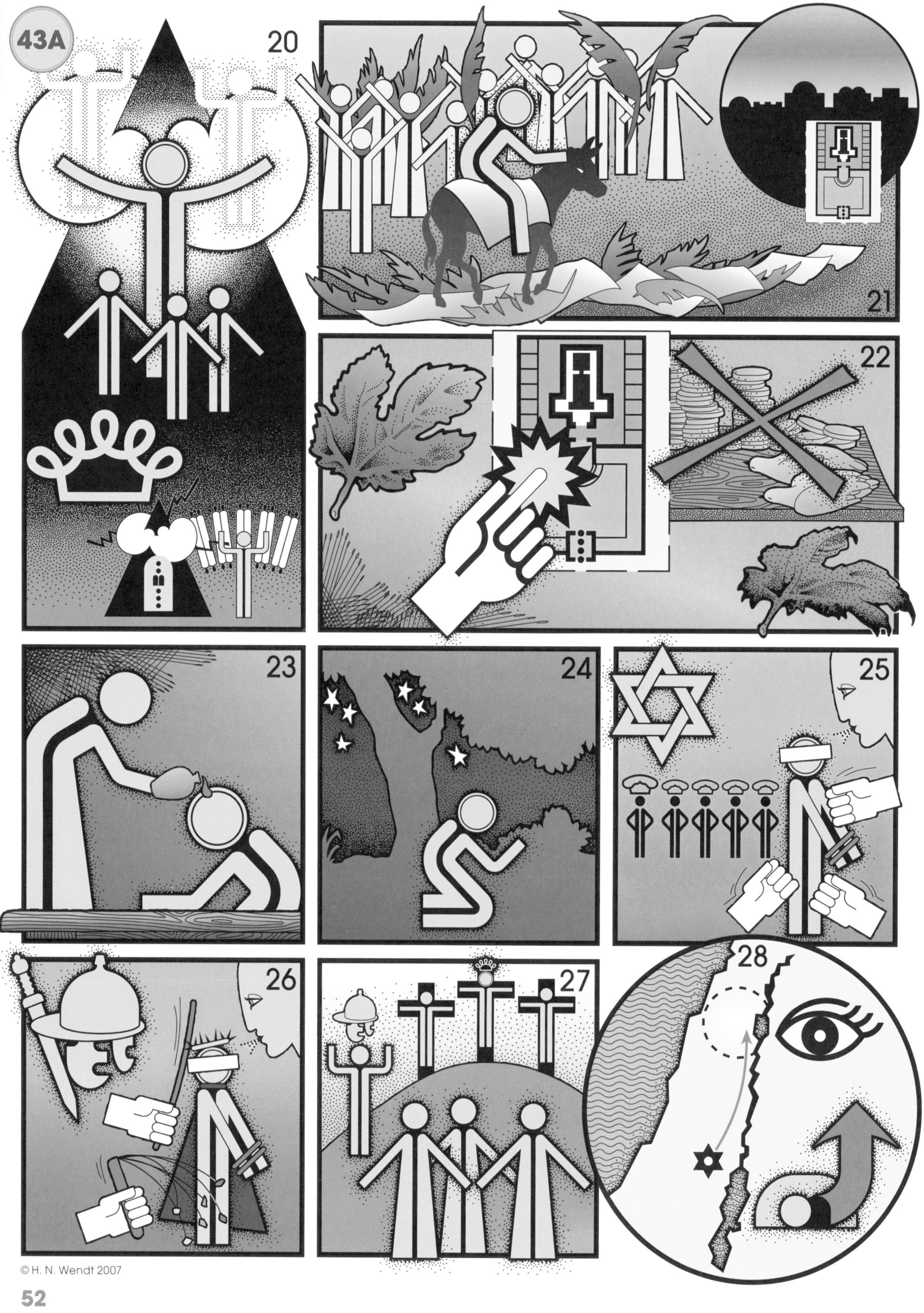

20

21

22

23

24

25

26

27

28

Frame 20

There comes the day when ***Jesus*** leads ***Peter***, ***James***, and ***John*** up a ***high mountain***, 9:2–13. When they reach its summit, Jesus is transfigured before them and His clothes become dazzling white. ***Moses*** and ***Elijah*** appear and engage in conversation with Jesus. Peter offers to build a dwelling for Jesus, Moses, and Elijah. A ***cloud*** then overshadows the group and a voice declares, "This is My Son, the Beloved; listen to Him." The experience and vision then come to an end—and the disciples see only Jesus. What is the message of the voice from the cloud?

Crown: The statement, "This is My Son, the Beloved" reflects Psalm 2:7—a coronation Psalm used when a descendant of David was anointed into office as king. (The very name "David" means "beloved.") Its message in the transfiguration event is: "You are getting your kings back. The Davidic line is being restored" (but in a very different way from what they were expecting!). ***Mt. Sinai; cloud; covenant symbol; five scrolls (Torah); Moses:*** The words "Listen to Him!" reflect Deuteronomy 18:15—a verse that states that God will eventually provide His people with a prophet to whom they must listen. Jesus is that new prophet—but He will share with His people guidelines for a way of life radically different from that which they have been observing.

The *disciples* did not understand the message of the voice from the cloud until after Jesus' resurrection. However, the *Roman centurion* who stood at the foot of Jesus' cross declared, "Truly this man was God's Son!", 15:39.

Frame 21

S	M	T	W	T	F	S	S

Jesus finally enters Jerusalem (***skyline***), ***seated on a donkey*** (see Zechariah 9:9) on which the disciples place some ***cloaks***, 11:1–11. Some of the pilgrims place their ***cloaks*** and ***leafy branches*** on the road along which Jesus is traveling. The crowds join in shouting words from Psalm 118:26. Jesus eventually enters the ***Jerusalem Temple***, observes what is taking place within it walls, and then—together with the disciples—returns to Bethany.

After Elisha anointed Jehu as king of Israel, those who eventually welcomed Jehu into the royal headquarters spread garments before him, 2 Kings 9:1–13. When the Jewish people welcomed Judas Maccabeus and his follower into Jerusalem in 164 B.C., they waved fronds of palms when doing so, 2 Maccabees 10:1–9. They welcomed Simon, Judas' brother, in a similar manner in 142 B.C., 1 Maccabees 13:51.

Frame 22

S	M	T	W	T	F	S	S

The next day (Monday), Jesus returns to the ***Temple*** and attacks (***pointing hand***) what is taking place within its walls, 11:12–20. He drives out those who are selling and buying, and overturns the tables of the ***money-changers*** and those who are selling ***doves***—marketing practices that took place within the Court of the Gentiles.

Within the Temple, Jesus teaches that although the Temple was intended to be *a house of prayer for all nations* (Isaiah 56:7), the religious leaders have turned the Court of the Gentiles into a marketplace where corrupt business ventures are practiced, Jeremiah 7:11.

Two fig tree leaves:

- While traveling from Bethany to the Temple, Jesus sees a fig tree, and goes to it in the hope of finding some fruit under its leaves (***leaf***, *upper left*). However, after finding no figs on the tree, He curses it.
- When Jesus and the disciples return to Jerusalem the next day (Tuesday), the fig tree is withered away to its roots (***withered leaf***, *lower right*).

Jesus' seemingly unreasonable action conveys a powerful message—a message that reflects Micah 7:1–6 and Jeremiah 8:13, passages that refer to God's people as a useless fig tree that bears no fruit. Jesus is stating that the Temple's "salvation marketing system," its "sin management system" has the worth of a dead fig tree, and will soon be uprooted and destroyed. (The Romans eventually demolished the Temple structure in A.D. 70.)

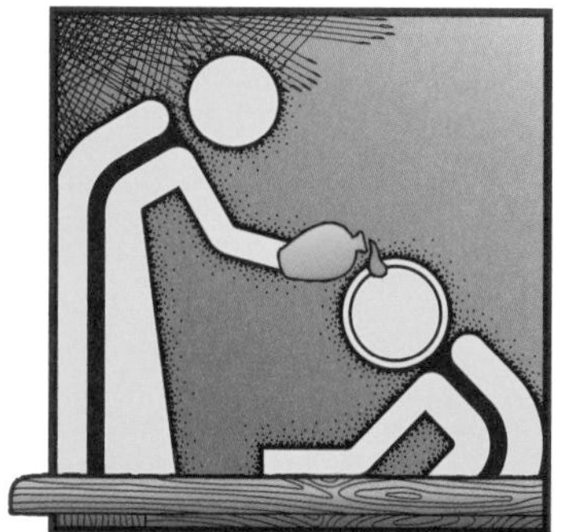

On the Wednesday of Holy Week, Jesus dines in the home of Simon the leper in Bethany. While ***Jesus is seated at a table***, a ***woman comes with a jar of costly ointment that she uses to anoint Jesus' head***. Some of those present are angry, say that this is an expensive waste, and scold the woman. Jesus rebukes the woman's accusers and commends her generous pre-burial anointing of His body, 14:1–9.

After celebrating the Passover in an Upper Room, ***Jesus*** goes with His disciples to the ***Garden of Gethsemane*** ("oil press") where He ***prays to His Father*** for strength to cope with the painful death that He must soon suffer, 14:12–42. While Jesus prays, the disciples sleep! Jesus prayed for help *three times*; the disciples fell asleep *three times*. As Adam and Eve became aware of their nakedness in the Garden of Eden (Genesis 3), so too a young follower of Jesus fled naked from Jesus' presence in the Garden of Gethsemane, 14:51. Eventually, Peter denied Jesus *three times*, 14:66–72.

Frame 25

While Jesus is in the Garden of Gethsemane, He is captured by a crowd (led by Judas, one of His disciples) who lead Him away to a gathering of Jewish chief priests, scribes, and elders (***Star of David, High Priest, Chief Priests***). After trying Jesus, they sentence Him to death, ***blindfold*** Him, ***bind*** Him, ***strike*** Him, and ***spit*** on Him, 14:43–72.

Frame 26

The Jewish leaders eventually take Jesus to Pilate, the Roman procurator (***Roman helmet and sword***), and manipulate him into having Jesus crucified. Prior to crucifying Jesus, Pilate has Jesus flogged (***scourge***). Roman soldiers then dress Jesus in a ***purple robe*** (signifying "royalty"—but in mockery), place a ***crown of thorns*** on His head, ***spit*** on Him, and ***beat Him with a reed***, 15:1–20.

Frame 27

S	M	T	W	T	F	S	S

Jesus is then crucified between two bandits (most likely, two Zealot rebels). Although the disciples desert Jesus and run for their lives, ***three women*** remain at the foot of Jesus' cross. A Roman centurion (***Roman helmet above male figure with raised hands***) observes what is taking place and proclaims, "Truly this man was God's Son!" (15:21–27)

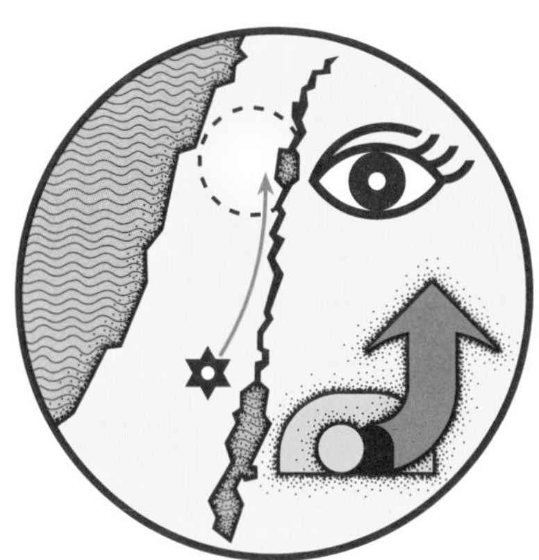

Frame 28

S	M	T	W	T	F	S	S

On Easter Sunday morning, Mary Magdalene, Mary the mother of James and Joses, and Salome go to the tomb in which Jesus has been buried, and find it open and empty. (These three women played a supportive role in Jesus' Galilean ministry, and in Mark's burial and resurrection narratives; 15:40,41,47; 16:1–8.) After entering the tomb, the three women are told by a young man clothed in a white robe that Jesus has been restored to life (***open tomb, rising arrow***), 16:1–8.

The women are to tell the disciples (and Peter, who had denied Jesus three times!) to go to Galilee (***arrow leaving Jerusalem***) where they will *see* Jesus (***eye***). Indeed, Jesus' own disciples are the ones who, like the blind man at Bethsaida (8:22–26), need the "second touch." They will get that second touch when they meet the risen Jesus. Their eyes will finally be open to see who Jesus really is, what He has come to achieve, and what is involved in being His disciples—and apostles!

43B
TRANSFIGURATION
TO JERUSALEM
1
2
3

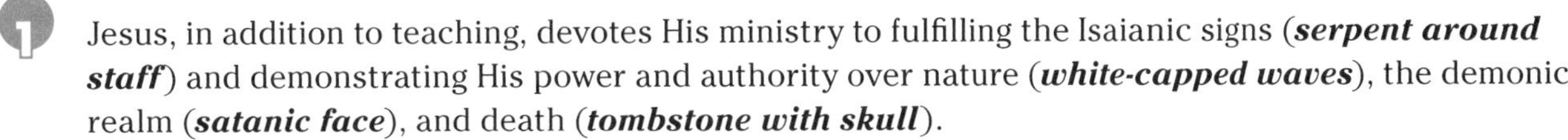

"Seeing" the Big Message

Some of the symbols used in **ILLUSTRATION 42B** appear again in **ILLUSTRATION 43B**.

Upper section

1. Jesus, in addition to teaching, devotes His ministry to fulfilling the Isaianic signs (***serpent around staff***) and demonstrating His power and authority over nature (***white-capped waves***), the demonic realm (***satanic face***), and death (***tombstone with skull***).

2. Eventually Jesus asks the disciples ***two questions***: Who do the *people* think that He is? Who do they, the *disciples*, think that He is? Although the disciples have concluded that Jesus is the Messiah, they do not understand the nature of His Messiahship, 8:27–38.

3. ***Three arrows pointing to three crosses:*** Jesus predicts His approaching passion three times, 8:31; 9:30–32; 10:32–34. The *first* takes place toward the close of Jesus' ministry in Galilee, the *second* after the transfiguration event, the *third* on the way from Galilee to Jerusalem. Each time Jesus predicts His coming passion, three elements are woven into the narrative:
   - **Prediction:** Jesus speaks of His coming crucifixion.
   - **Confusion:** The disciples just do not understand what Jesus is talking about.
   - **Clarification:** Jesus clarifies what believing in Him as the Messiah implies for how life is to be used.

4. ***Eye, 1 and eye, 2 —to the left and right of the three crosses:*** Jesus' three passion predictions are bracketed by incidents in which He gives sight to the blind, Mark 8:22–26, 10:46–52.

5. ***Cross, person in posture of praise to right of cross:*** When Jesus is finally crucified, the only person who seems to be aware of His true identity is a Roman centurion, 15:39.

Center section

The illustration depicts four confrontations that take place after Jesus finally enters Jerusalem on Palm Sunday.

1. ***Coin, question mark:*** Some Pharisees and Herodians try to trap Jesus with a question concerning whether or not Jews are under any obligation to pay taxes to their Roman overlords, 12:13–17.

2. ***Divided door, with portion of a skull to left, and slats to right, question mark:*** The Sadducees deny belief in the resurrection of the body. Their view of death is grim (***skull***). Jesus declares that life does not end with death; the body will indeed rise. Jesus' followers, already in this life, can know and see what lies beyond death (***door with slats***), 12:18–27.

3. ***Law-code, with single arrow pointing to God and neighbor, question mark:*** The Pharisees question Jesus about "the great commandment in the Law." They think of loving God and others as two separate commandments. However, Jesus insists that they are not two, but form a unity, 12:28–34.

4. ***Crown, question mark:*** Although the Jews are waiting for David's "lord" to come, the One who has come is David's "LORD" (i.e., David's God), 12:35–37. In a very real sense, the Messiah, God in flesh, wears a crown much bigger than they expected!

Lower section

1. ***Crowned Jesus*** (*left*)***:*** When Jesus begins His ministry, He is *Israel reduced to one*.

2 ***Four question marks:*** Although Jesus never openly declares Himself to be the Messiah, He does things that indicate Him to be the Messiah. (The question marks relate to the four groups of miracles depicted in the left of the *upper section.*)

3 ***Expanding lines to the right of Jesus:*** As Jesus' ministry progresses, the crowds gather and His community grows.

However, when the people hear Jesus talk about the nature of self-sacrificial servant discipleship in His Kingdom (***Servant-King***), they desert Him (***lines converging***).

4 ***Crowned Jesus on cross:*** Finally, Jesus goes to the *cross—alone.*

5 ***Open tomb, rising arrow, cloud, eye, dove:*** However, beyond the cross come the resurrection *(**open tomb**)* and eventually the ascension (***arrow rising into cloud***). The disciples eyes (***eye,*** **3**) are finally opened when they meet with the Risen Jesus in Galilee. When Jesus ascends, He does not *withdraw* His presence; He *transforms* it. Jesus remains among His people invisibly. We, His brothers and sisters, wait for His "final appearing." While we wait, the Holy Spirit (***dove***) uses God's "written Word" to help us know, believe in, trust in, and follow God's Living Word, Jesus the Messiah.

Confrontations in Jerusalem

Jesus' ministry confronts humanity with a gift and a demand. In Jesus, God comes to die for humanity, to remove the burden of guilt, to cleanse the lepers, to heal the sick, to find the lost, to assure humanity that the door to God's house stands open, and to summon beggars to the heavenly banquet. Yet, the gift of such limitless grace comes with a call—a call that summons people who have been gathered in grace into the Kingdom of God to give away life in limitless, loving service of God and of others in their every need. The comments that follow outline the confrontations that take place between Jesus and the Jewish authorities after His entry into Jerusalem.

1 A few days prior to His death, Jesus stands on the Mount of Olives and looks across the Kidron Valley to Jerusalem. The manner in which He chooses to enter Jerusalem is no accident. Long before, Zechariah pointed out that when Zion's king eventually came to her, he would come in humility on an ass, Zechariah 9:9. A king rode on a horse when going to war; he rode on an ass when on a mission of peace. Jesus wants His mode of entry to say to the crowds that He has not come to stir up a revolt against Rome. He has come to give God's forgiveness and peace to sinners and to teach humanity to walk in the ways of forgiveness and peace with one another. Jesus' audience misses the point—and no wonder. They want a Messiah who will be a carbon-copy of David of old—a king who will restore to them their ancient borders, freedom from foreign control, and the national prestige that they once enjoyed. *They are blind to the truths associated with Jesus' real ministry.*

2 After Jesus enters Jerusalem, He goes to the Temple. What He sees angers Him. The next day He returns to the Temple and creates holy havoc among the money changers and animal sellers. He sends their wares flying and forbids anyone to carry anything through the Temple (the *Mishnah* forbade the irreverent use of the Temple platform as a short cut, 11:16). His audience is not left without explanation: "Is it not written, 'My House shall be called a house of prayer for all peoples' (Isaiah 56:7)? But you have made it a den of robbers (Jeremiah 7:11)."

3 A little background knowledge helps us understand Jesus' actions. A dividing wall separated the inner courts of the Jerusalem Temple from the outer court. The Chief Priest, High Priest, priests, and Jewish men and women were permitted to enter the various inner courts assigned to them. However, the Gentiles could not go beyond the dividing wall. Fastened to it were bilingual inscriptions (in Latin and Greek) warning Gentiles not to enter the inner Temple area. About a hundred years ago, one of these inscriptions was found during excavations near the Temple site. It states: "Any non-Jew who passes beyond this balustrade will have only himself to blame for the death that will follow as a consequence." Non-Jews, then, were permitted access only to the Court of the Gentiles.

4 The tables of the money-changers and animal-sellers were located within the Court of the Gentiles. These stalls were for the convenience of pilgrims who had to buy animals for sacrifice, and who had to change their Greek and Roman money into coinage acceptable for use within the Temple precincts—including the payment of Temple dues. The priestly class controlled these stalls, and ran rackets in changing foreign currencies and in selling animals for sacrifice. This meant that when Gentiles came to Jerusalem hoping to have contact with the God of the Jews, their impressions were colored by what they saw in the part of the Temple to which they were restricted. The Temple was anything but a house for all the nations. The Jewish religious and political leaders had turned it into their private club. Furthermore, they used it as a place of refuge, a den, after committing crimes in the community, Jeremiah 7:11. However, in Jesus, the Lord has come to His Temple, Malachi 3:1. His coming causes sudden shock!

5 It is significant that the two sections of the cursing of the fig tree event "book-end" the cleansing of the Temple, 11:12–14, 20,21. This incident is to be understood in the light of Micah 7:1–6 and Jeremiah 8:13. Although God created Israel to produce much spiritual fruit, Israel is fruit-less and therefore rejected!

When Jesus cleanses the Temple, He passes the point of no return. His actions stir His opponents to strive more zealously to get rid of Him, 11:18. The authorities confront Him with that thought in mind.

a. In the first open clash with the authorities, a deputation from the chief priests, scribes, and elders demands that Jesus tell them on what authority He bases His actions. Jesus answers with a counter-question about John the Baptist that leaves the deputation hanging on the horns of a dilemma, 11:27–33.

b. Jesus then tells a parable to illustrate that the Kingdom is about to be taken away from the Jews and given to the Gentiles. This statement does not win Him friends and influence among the Jews. Their reaction is to be expected. They seek to arrest Jesus, 12:1–12.

c. Next come representatives of the Pharisees and Herodians. They pose a question designed to trap Jesus. The issue is taxation. The Jews are required to pay a tax to the Roman Emperor's treasury. The requirement to do this is like salt in an open wound, because it signifies subjection to a foreign power. The delegation's opening statement makes use of flattery, but Jesus springs their trap. He knows that if He answers their question with "No!" His foes will embroil Him with the Romans. He also knows that if He answers "Yes!" He will incur the wrath of every patriotic Jew. He responds by insisting that the issue is not one of "either-or," but of "both-and," 12:13–17.

   But there is more! In Jesus' day, two types of coins were used. Coins used by Torah-observant Jews had no human or animal images on them. But Roman coins had images—the head of the emperor on one side (and the words, *Augustus Tiberius, son of Divine Augustus*), and the words *High Priest* on the other side; the emperor was, after all, thought to be the head of a divine cult. Many Jews would never look at a Roman coin, or touch or use it. But Jesus' interrogators had at least one (and possibly many more) in their possession—exposing their willingness to embrace the politics of collaboration with the ruling foreign power.

d. It is the Sadducees' turn next. The Sadducees consist of the priestly aristocracy and are theologically conservative. They reject any belief in the resurrection of the body, angels, and spirits. Accordingly, they confront Jesus with a question designed to reduce the doctrine of the resurrection to the level of absurdity. Jesus reminds them that the promise of the resurrection does not depend on any natural power within human control or understanding, but on the power and promise of God, 12:18–27.

e. The next incident indicates that not all are opposed to Jesus, 12:28–34. A scribe's question to Jesus is one frequently discussed. There is no doubt among the Jews concerning which is the greatest commandment, for the faithful within the nation repeat "the Great Shema" (Deuteronomy 6:4,5) several times daily. However, in answering, Jesus does something distinctive. *He joins the love of God to the love of neighbor.* Even some Jewish scholars today assert that Jesus was the first rabbi to meld these two commandments into one. True, Leviticus 19:18 spoke of love for one's neighbor, and Rabbi Akiba called this the greatest principle of the Torah. Furthermore, Rabbi Hillel summed up the Law in the *negative* form of the Golden Rule. But Jesus expresses the Golden Rule positively and links it inseparably to the love of God.

f. The issue in 12:35–37 is as follows: The Jewish leaders believed that the Messiah would come from the house of David, but Jesus points out that in Psalm 110 the Messiah is spoken of as David's LORD. Jesus is indeed David's descendant (*lord*, lower case), but He is much more than that. He is David's *LORD* (upper case, therefore GOD)! Their understanding of Jesus' Person is far too limited.

Mark 12 closes with a warning against the scribes and their hypocrisy, and the account of the widow's mite, 12:38–40, and 41–44. Mark 13 contains two predictive threads of thought. One speaks of the coming destruction of Jerusalem by the Romans in A.D. 70. The other outlines what the disciples and Jesus' community will experience in the period between Jesus' Ascension and His Final Appearing. In the closing section of the chapter, Jesus exhorts His hearers to be ready at all times for the Final Day of history.

Mark's Passion Narrative

JESUS' LAST HOURS

1 The passion history is outlined in chs. 14 and 15. Mark 14:1–11 outlines what transpired on the Wednesday of that final, climactic week; the remainder of these chapters describes the events of Good Friday. Why devote so much space to the events of one day? Jesus' life culminated very differently from traditional expectations. It was necessary to demonstrate that what appeared to be *tragedy* was really *triumph*.

2 On the Wednesday morning of Holy Week, the chief priests and scribes discuss how to get rid of Jesus, 14:1,2. That same morning a woman anoints His head with ointment. The value of the ointment is approximately a year's wages, for a denarius is the usual amount paid for a day's work. Jesus accepts the gesture as a loving preparation for His coming burial, 14:8. Others express more mercenary concerns, 14:4,5.

3 Events follow in quick succession. Judas makes arrangements with the Chief Priests for Jesus' betrayal. Mark does not mention Judas asking the Chief Priests for money, although they promise to give him some, 14:10,11. Preparations are then made for the celebration of the Passover. Jesus tells His disciples they will have no trouble finding a room for observing the Passover, for a man carrying a jar of water will lead them to it, 14:13. (Usually only women carried water jars; men carried water containers made of skins.) During the Passover celebration, Jesus tells the disciples that one of them will betray Him, but mentions no name; see Matthew 26:14–16, 20–25; Luke 22:3–6,14,21–23; John 13:21–30.

4 The Passover observance involved the observance of rituals and the eating of specified foods to remind the Jews of their miraculous deliverance from Egypt. It also pointed forward to the time when the Messiah would accomplish a second mighty deliverance for His people. That night in the upper room the disciples share table with the expected Deliverer. However, He has come to deliver them, not from the Romans, but from Satan, sin, death, judgement, damnation, and themselves. With Jesus' coming, the Passover observance has completed its time of useful service. Jesus replaces it with another observance—one in which He gives His new community His own body and blood together with the bread and wine that He passes around. This observance is an assurance that what Jesus has come to accomplish is *for them*. It is also an assurance that Jesus will remain among them throughout life.

Furthermore, it is (as Paul reminded them, 1 Corinthians 11:26) to encourage them to look two ways: *backward* and *forward*. They are to look *backward* to that event in which Jesus has delivered them from the powers of sin and death. They are to look *forward* to the time when He will come again to lead them across that "final Jordan" of death into the Heavenly Canaan. Finally, in sharing the Lord's cup they are declaring their willingness to embrace and perpetuate their Lord's mission and to use their lives as He used His—in the service of the Heavenly Father and others. The continuing observance of the Lord's supper is to celebrate that Jesus' brothers and sisters are eternal servant/subjects of their eternal forgiving Savior and Servant Lord; see Mark 14:22–25.

5 During the Passover meal, Jesus tells the disciples that they will all desert Him. Yes, even Peter will do that. However, after His death and resurrection they will meet Him again in Galilee.

6 After the Passover observance, Jesus goes with His disciples to the garden of Gethsemane. There, the realization of what is to happen within a few hours crushes Him. The disciples find it difficult to keep Him company in His prayer vigil; they fall asleep. Eventually, Judas arrives with an armed group

intent on taking Jesus into custody. (Perhaps Judas' initial offer to the authorities was to lead them to Jesus at a time and place where there would be no opportunity for the crowds to protest. Judas' use of a kiss was not unusual; a kiss was the customary greeting that a disciple offered to his teacher.) Jesus' capture frightens the disciples. They flee. Peter follows at a distance but, when pressured, he denies Jesus, 14:66–72.

In relation to Judas' betrayal, it is rather unlikely that Judas expected that his actions would lead to Jesus' crucifixion. Most likely, his hope was to force Jesus to declare Himself to be the Messiah whose goal was to mobilize a Zealot uprising and drive out the hated Romans. After all, if Judas expected Jesus to be crucified, why did he despair and hang himself? Would he not instead have congratulated himself on the success of his move? Furthermore, the last thing that Satan wanted was that Jesus walk the way of a servant all the way to death on the cross. Satan's desire was to divert Jesus from doing that. However, Jesus did go to His cross—an event in which Jesus got crucified and Satan got nailed!

7 Jesus' first trial takes place at night, a factor that makes the proceedings illegal. The members of the Sanhedrin (High Priest, priests, elders, and scribes) have assembled with the express purpose of doing away with Jesus as quickly as possible. However, the assembly has trouble with its witnesses. They are unable to agree about what Jesus actually said. Finally, the High Priest confronts Jesus with a question, 14:61. He asks Jesus if He is indeed the Messiah, "the Son of the Blessed." ("The Blessed" is a Jewish term for God.) Jesus answers with, "I AM" (see Exodus 3:14), and continues with a statement based on Daniel 7 in which He declares that He is the Son of Man, the "representative Israel," the true People of God to whom the Kingdom of God has been given and in whom it exists. The High Priest responds by ritually tearing his clothes and accusing Jesus of blasphemy. His colleagues concur and demand the death penalty. Jesus is then subjected to vile treatment, 14:53–65.

8 The next morning the Sanhedrin meets, no doubt to ratify the previous meeting's decision, and then sends Jesus to Pilate, the Roman governor. Although the Jewish leaders have judged Jesus to be deserving of the death penalty, they are not permitted to put anyone to death because they are a people subject to a foreign power. Only their Roman overlords can execute a criminal. The question Pilate discusses with Jesus is enlightening. He asks Him: "Are You the King of the Jews?" 15:2. Perhaps the Sanhedrin charged Jesus with claiming to be the king of the Jews to create in Pilate's mind the idea that Jesus is stirring up disloyalty to Rome. This charge is in sharp contrast to Jesus' ministry, which was clearly non-political and non-threatening to the Roman authorities.

9 In the incident that follows, Pilate gives the people the opportunity to choose between Jesus and Barabbas. (Barabbas had been involved in an insurrection and had killed in the process. In the minds of many Jews, his ambitions were more messianic than were those of Jesus.) Pilate remains puzzled and perplexed. He has difficulty relating what the Jews *say* about Jesus to what he *sees* in Jesus. However, he hands Jesus over to his soldiers for scourging and crucifixion. Before they put Jesus to death, the soldiers sarcastically dress Jesus as a king and pay Him mock homage. The soldiers then lead Jesus out for crucifixion. Simon of Cyrene is pressed into service to carry Jesus' cross, 15:21. Before the soldiers nail Jesus to the cross, they offer Him a drink designed to dull the senses and deaden the pain, but Jesus refuses it, 15:23. They also divide His garments among themselves. (These were considered legitimate perquisites for executioners.) Finally, at about 9 a.m., Jesus is crucified, 15:25.

10 When Jesus begins His ministry, "the true Israel" numbers one person, Himself. As He carries out His ministry, the numbers grow: Peter, Andrew, James, John, the other disciples, and the crowds. As the implications of Jesus' message become clear, the group diminishes in size. The Jerusalem authorities,

who remain hostile toward Him, stir up the crowds against Him. Judas betrays Him. The disciples fall asleep in the Garden of Gethsemane and flee when His captors arrive. Peter denies Him. The crowds beneath the cross mock Him. The thieves, who are his companions in death, revile Him, 15:32. Furthermore, Mark reports only one word from the cross, "My God, My God, why have you forsaken Me?" 15:34; see Psalm 22:1. It seems that even His Father has forsaken Him!

Jesus' last words in Mark and Matthew are traditionally referred to as a cry of dereliction. However, they constitute the first verse of a psalm containing 31 verses. Psalm 22, in the Jewish mind, belonged to a group of three psalms—Psalms 22, 23, and 24—that contain many verses expressing hope and assurance. When a rabbi quoted a verse from one of these Psalms, he expected his hearers to know the contents of the entire psalm and of the other two psalms—a practice that was referred to as *remez*. It follows that Jesus, in praying Psalm 22:1, is expressing the sure hope that, despite His present agony, His Father will rescue and vindicate Him.

11 Then comes death. Jesus seems to be so very alone. Or is He? A Roman centurion stands beneath His cross and confesses the truth expressed in the opening verse of the Gospel ("the Son of God," 1:1), "Truly this man was God's Son!" 15:39. He confesses the very truth the Sanhedrin has denied. Joseph of Arimathea, *a member of the Sanhedrin*, assumes responsibility for Jesus' burial, 15:42–47. (In doing this, Joseph of Arimathea treats Jesus as a member of his family—but makes himself ritually unclean, unfit to observe Passover, and open to suspicion and possible charges.) Some of the women who have been with Jesus take note of Joseph's activities, and observe the location of the tomb in which Jesus' body is placed.

JESUS' RESURRECTION AND VINDICATION

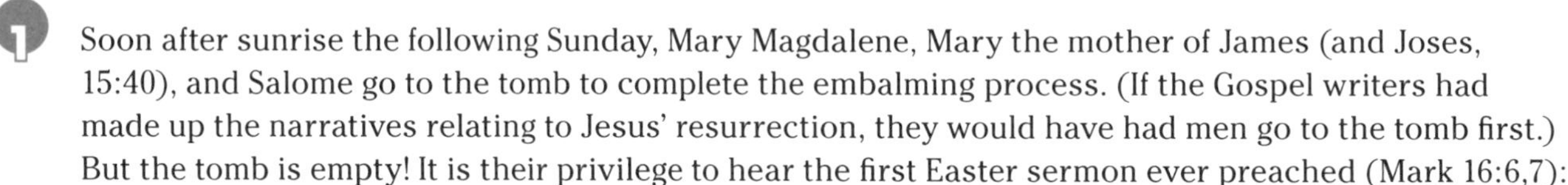

1 Soon after sunrise the following Sunday, Mary Magdalene, Mary the mother of James (and Joses, 15:40), and Salome go to the tomb to complete the embalming process. (If the Gospel writers had made up the narratives relating to Jesus' resurrection, they would have had men go to the tomb first.) But the tomb is empty! It is their privilege to hear the first Easter sermon ever preached (Mark 16:6,7):

> *Do not be alarmed; you are looking for Jesus of Nazareth, who was crucified. He has been raised; He is not here. Look, there is the place where they laid Him. But go, tell His disciples and Peter that he is going ahead of you to Galilee; there you will see him, just as he told you.*

2 Jesus is alive! His followers will *see* Him again—and soon! In Galilee! The reference to Peter picks up Jesus' prediction in 14:28. Mark makes no mention of the risen Jesus being seen in Jerusalem. He will be seen in Galilee.

MARK'S LONGER ENDING

1 A problem arises regarding Mark 16:9–20. It is not found in the oldest manuscripts. Although some argue that Mark intended to end his work at 16:8, others find it hard to accept that it was intended to conclude so abruptly. Several suggestions have been made:

a. Mark's original manuscript was mutilated soon after it was written.

b. Mark died before he could complete the work.

c. He wrote more after 16:8, but, for some unknown reason, it was suppressed.

2 If the conclusion was lost, it was lost at an early date. The longer ending can be outlined as follows:

a. The appearance to Mary Magdalene, 16:9–11; see also John 20:11–18.

b. The appearance to the two travelers, 16:12–13; see also Luke 24:13–35.

c. The appearance to the eleven, 16:14–18; see also Matthew 28:16–20; Luke 24:36–49; John 20:19–23.

d. The ascension, and the commencement of the apostolic mission, 16:19–20; see also Luke 24:50–53.

3 It seems likely that the Gospel actually closes at 16:8. It presupposes the resurrection of our Lord. The message of 16:1–8 culminates in the reaction of the women (v. 8), and challenges God's people to face the Gospel's claims about Jesus' Person and Messianic ministry. In raising His Son from the Dead, God the Father gives His Son the best possible endorsement! The verses beyond 16:8 are likely later additions derived from other sources used in the Early Church to describe Jesus' ministry.

The Central Issue in the Gospels

1 Some believe that the central issue in the Gospels and in the whole of the New Testament is that, in Jesus, the long-expected Savior finally came, died for the sins of the world, rose from the grave, and ascended to prepare a place for those who believe in Him and look to Him for forgiveness. Although these truths are central to the teachings of the New Testament, they tend to focus largely on personal salvation in the life to come. More is at stake.

2 The central issue in the Gospels is the nature of Jesus' Messiahship. Although the Jewish people were waiting for the coming of a Messiah, they were not expecting that Messiah to take the form of a Servant-Messiah. As George McDonald, the president of Harvard University, once wrote:

They were all waiting for a king
To slay their foes and raise them high;
Thou cam'st a little baby thing
that made a woman cry.

To which might be added two lines:

Thou cam'st to do Thy servant thing,
On cruel cross to die.

3 The point is: The Jewish people were waiting for a Messiah who would restore the long-defunct Davidic dynasty, reestablish the Davidic kingdom, gain freedom from Roman control and establish political independence. Instead, they got a King who walked the way of a servant-without-limit, sought the company of those considered nobodies and outcasts, and washed the disciples' feet (an act in which He did what no Jew would ever do; only Gentile slaves washed feet).

4 **ILLUSTRATION 43D** shows the nature of the kingdom that Jesus came to establish. Although it reflects Jesus washing the disciples' feet in the Upper Room as described in John 13:1–17, it describes the foundational issue at stake in each Gospel. At *lower right*, ***Jesus washes Peter's feet***. Peter appears *awkward* and *embarrassed*, for surely Messiahs do not perform tasks traditionally allocated to Gentile slaves! Jesus is then shown at *center* as *King* (***crown***) and ***Servant***. At *right* are symbols of the ***crucified Jesus*** and the ***empty tomb***; when Jesus' Father raised His Son from the dead, He endorsed the nature of Jesus' Messiahship. Shown in stylized form around Jesus are the ***members of Jesus' new community***. Naturally they are called to do more than hold hands; they are called to serve Jesus by serving each other and the world around them. The Risen Jesus continues among His brothers and sisters today in and through His *Holy Spirit* (***dove***). The entire New Testament points beyond itself to God's Word-in-Flesh, a strange King who *does feet* and summons the members of His community to do the same.

43F

SUN
MON
TUES
WED
THURS
FRI
SAT
SUN
1 MARK
PASSOVER
2 MATTHEW
PASSOVER
3 LUKE
PASSOVER
4 JOHN
PASSOVER
1 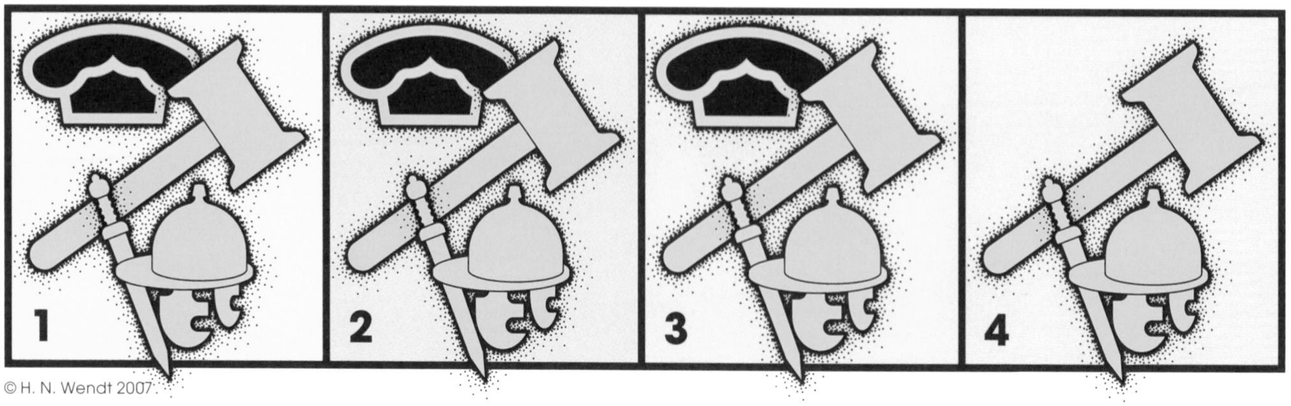
2
3
4

Passion Narratives to Come 43F

ILLUSTRATION 43E depicts in simple form the Holy Week narratives in the four Gospels. Because Mark's narrative is surveyed in Unit 43, his narrative is listed first.

MARK—Holy Week Narrative

1. Jesus enters Jerusalem on a ***donkey*** on Palm Sunday. Although He notes what is taking place within the Temple, He does not yet attack the Temple system, 11:1–11.
2. When Jesus returns to the Temple on the following day, Monday, He does attack the ***Temple*** system. On the way into Jerusalem, He curses a ***fig tree***. When He returns to Jerusalem *the next day* (Tuesday), the ***fig tree*** is dead, 11:12–24.
3. Jesus celebrates the Passover with His disciples on Thursday evening and shares His ***Holy Supper*** with them, 14:12–25.
4. Jesus is crucified at ***9 a.m.*** on Friday morning, 15:25. Darkness (***vertical dark lines***) covers the region from ***midday until 3 p.m.***, 15:33. Jesus gives up His life at about ***3 p.m.*** (15:34) and returns to life (***open tomb, rising arrow***) on Sunday morning, 16:1–8.

MATTHEW—Holy Week Narrative

1. Matthew makes reference to a ***donkey and a colt*** being brought to Jesus. Jesus enters Jerusalem on Palm Sunday morning and attacks the ***Temple*** that same day, 21:1–17.
2. Jesus curses a ***fig tree*** on Monday, and it dies immediately, 21:18,19.
3. Jesus celebrates the Passover with the disciples on Thursday evening, and shares His ***Holy Supper*** with them, 26:17–29.
4. Jesus is *presumably* (***question mark***) crucified at ***9 a.m.*** on Friday morning. Darkness covers the region from ***midday until 3 p.m.***, 27:45. Jesus gives up His life at about ***3 p.m.*** (27:46), and returns to life (***open tomb, rising arrow***) on Sunday morning, 28:1–10.

LUKE—Holy Week Narrative

1. Jesus enters Jerusalem on a ***donkey*** on Palm Sunday, and attacks the ***Temple*** that same day, 19:29–46.
2. Jesus celebrates the Passover with the disciples on Thursday evening, and celebrates his ***Holy Supper*** with the disciples, 22:7–38.
3. Jesus is *presumably* (***question mark***) crucified at ***9 a.m.*** on Friday morning. Darkness covers the region from ***midday until 3 p.m.***, 23:44. Jesus gives up His life at about ***3 p.m.*** (23:44–46) and returns to life (***open tomb, rising arrow***) on Sunday morning, 24:1–12.
4. Luke refers to Jesus' ascension (***glorified Jesus***) as taking place on the same day as His resurrection, 24:50–52.

JOHN—Holy Week Narrative

1. Jesus enters Jerusalem on a ***donkey*** on Palm Sunday, 12:12–15. (His attack on the Temple is reported in John 2:13–25, but is not linked to Palm Sunday.)
2. On the Thursday evening, ***Jesus washes the disciples' feet*** (13:1–17), and then shares a ***meal*** with them, 13:18, 21–30. (The meal referred to cannot be a Passover observance, for in John's Gospel

Passover begins at sunset on Friday evening, 18:14.) John makes no reference to the institution of the Lord's Supper.

3 John tells us that *Pilate hands Jesus over for crucifixion* on Friday at ***midday*** (19:14)—at the hour when those preparing to celebrate the Passover (which in John takes place from sunset on Friday to sunset on Saturday) begin to bring their lambs to the priests for ritual slaughter. We are not told how much later He is lifted on to His cross (***question mark***). John makes no mention of darkness covering the region at midday. Although John does not state that Jesus gave up his life at about ***3 p.m.***, we might *presume* (***question mark***) that He did so at about that time—in light of the narratives in Mark, Matthew, and Luke, and because Joseph of Arimathea and Nicodemus would have needed time to attend to Jesus' burial prior to the commencement of the Sabbath at sunset.

4 Jesus returns to life (***open tomb, rising arrow***) on Sunday morning, and that evening breathes on the disciples and gives them the ***Holy Spirit***, 20:1–23.

Who tries Jesus?

1 2 3 In Matthew, Mark, and Luke, Jesus is tried (***gavel***) by the Jewish religious and political leaders (***priest's hat***), and also by the Romans (***Roman helmet and sword***).

4 In John's Holy Week narrative, virtually nothing is said about Jesus being tried by the Jewish religious and political leaders. They try Jesus (*in absentia*) and condemn Him to death immediately after He raises Lazarus from the dead, 11:14–53. In the passion narrative itself, John refers to the High Priest Annas asking Jesus questions about His disciples and teaching, (18:19), and then sending Jesus to Caiaphas (18:24) who sends Him to Pilate, 18:28. No information is offered about what Caiaphas and the Sanhedrin might have asked Jesus or done to Him. John's Good Friday narrative focuses on Jesus being tried (***gavel***) by Pilate, the Roman procurator (***Roman helmet and sword***), 18:28–19:16.

Additional Insights

1 Mark reports that Jesus stilled a storm (4:35–41) and walked on the water, 6:45–52. There is more to these miracles than the wonder of the event. The Jews were afraid of the oceans and the deep. They never became a seafaring people and let other peoples (such as the Phoenicians) provide their needs in relation to sea transportation. One senses a sigh of relief in Revelation 21:1 where John speaks of the coming of "a new heaven and a new earth," and adds, "The sea was no more." However, Jews took comfort in the fact that God could control the seas, the oceans, and the storms. Psalm 65:7 praises God with, "You silence the roaring of the seas, the roaring of their waves." Psalm 89:9 is similar in tone, "You rule the raging of the sea; when its waves rise, you still them." When Jesus stilled the storms on the Sea of Galilee and walked on the water, He demonstrated that He Himself possessed the powers that Jews had always assigned to God, Psalm 107:23–32.

2 During the latter part of the intertestamental period, much attention was focused on the demonic realm. In Jesus' day, many believed that the world was subject to the rule of Satan and his demonic hosts. Infirmities, generally, were attributed to the power of Satan and his co-workers. Jesus declares that One stronger than Satan has come and is despoiling his goods. Jesus' ministry marks the beginning of an onslaught on the powers of evil that will end in Satan's complete overthrow—at the cross. The reign of God is putting an end to the reign of Satan (3:27), who wants people to walk through life as anything but servants of others.

3 Mark contains one account of Jesus raising the dead, 5:22–43; see also Matthew 9:18,19,23–25. Luke reports Jesus raising the widow's son at Nain, 7:11–17; his account reflects his interest in Jesus as the New Elijah-Elisha who re-enacts in the Shunem locality the great deeds of these saints of old, each of whom restored a dead son to a widowed mother, 1 Kings 17:17–24; 2 Kings 4:18–37. John reports the raising of Lazarus, ch. 11. Jesus' actions in raising the dead fulfill the hope expressed in Isaiah 25:8, where the prophet describes the joys the people of God will experience when the Messianic Age arrives. Isaiah wrote: "He will swallow up death forever. Then the Lord God will wipe away the tears from all faces"; see also Isaiah 26:19. Jesus' miracles of raising the dead are also anticipations of His own resurrection and the resurrection of all believers. Jesus is Lord over death itself—in Himself and in others.

4 Jesus consistently refused to use His divine power to perform a miracle to serve His own personal needs. Even when He was hungry, He chose to remain hungry rather than change stones into bread, Matthew 4:1–4. Jesus was always "the Servant"; He sought only to place Himself and His powers at the service of humanity.

5 As Jesus moved among people, He demonstrated a remarkable compassion. For example, before healing a leper, He reached out and touched him, 1:40–45. The Pharisees on occasion threw rocks at lepers and said that their suffering was the result of some sin they had committed. Furthermore, Jesus sought the company of "sinners, tax collectors," and the like, 2:15–17. His actions upset the scribes and Pharisees for they felt that, if He really was the Messiah, He would seek out the "righteous" (namely, themselves). Jesus' concern for the Gentiles would also have been repugnant to many in Israel who believed that, when the Messianic Age finally came, the Gentiles would be destroyed, or at best made slaves of the Jews; see 7:24–30.

6 In Mark's narrative, Jesus performs His miracles "up north"—in Galilee, Syro-phoenicia, and the Decapolis. Jesus performs only one miracle after leaving Galilee; He heals blind Bartimaeus after leaving Jericho, 10:46–52. Remarkably, *blind* Bartimaeus can "see" who Jesus is prior to having his

sight restored (10:47,48) and is the first to address Jesus as "Son of David." Jesus performs no miracles in or near Jerusalem, the "city of opposition."

Jesus declared that He possessed authority to reveal the secrets of the Kingdom of God, 4:10,11,34. The Jewish teachers believed that they knew what the Kingdom would be like, and that *they were able to influence its coming.* The Kingdom that broke in with Jesus took the Jewish leaders by surprise. It came despite their opinions and actions.

The following paragraph does not summarize the contents of this Unit, but describes the challenge that Jesus' Person and ministry pose. It was written by H.G. Wells. Its implications are timeless.

> *Jesus was too great for His disciples. And in view of what He plainly said, is it any wonder that all who were rich and prosperous felt a horror of strange things, a swimming of their world at His teaching? Perhaps the priests and rulers and rich men understood Him better than His followers. He was dragging out all the little private reservations they had made from social service into the light of a universal religious life. He was like a terrible moral huntsman, digging mankind out of the snug burrows in which they had lived hitherto. In the white blaze of His kingdom there was to be no property, no privilege, no pride and no precedence, no motive and reward but love. Is it any wonder that men were dazzled and blinded, and cried out against Him? Even His disciples cried out when He would not spare them that light. Is it any wonder that the priests realized that between this Man and themselves there was no choice, but that He or their priestcraft should perish? Is it any wonder that the Roman soldiers, confronted and amazed by something soaring over their comprehension and threatening all their disciplines, should take refuge in wild laughter, and crown Him with thorns and robe Him in purple and make a mock Caesar of Him? For to take Him seriously was to enter into a strange and alarming life, to abandon habits, to control instincts and impulses, to embrace an incredible happiness. Is it any wonder that to this day this Galilean is too much for our small hearts?*
>
> *The Outline of History*, Vol. 1, pp. 425–426

SUMMARY

43A After Jesus predicts His coming passion for the first time, He takes Peter, James, and John up a mountain, is transfigured before them, and a voice declares Him to be the long-awaited King and the "new Moses." After entering Jerusalem on Palm Sunday, Jesus notes what is taking place in the Temple, and the next day attacks its "sin management system." While dining with Simon the leper, an unnamed woman anoints His head with oil—a preliminary anointing of His soon-to-be-dead body.

After eating a Passover Meal with the disciples on the Thursday evening, Jesus prays in the Garden of Gethsemane, is captured, tried, sentenced to death, and abused by Jewish and Roman leaders. Although the disciples desert Jesus after His capture, three woman remain near His cross, and a Roman centurion declares Him to be the "Son of God."

Jesus returns to life on Easter Sunday morning. A young man clad in white meets the same three women in the empty tomb, tells them that Jesus is alive, and instructs them to inform the disciples that they are to return to Galilee where they will meet and "see" Jesus. The disciples gain full spiritual sight concerning Jesus' identity and mission only after He returns to life.

43B During the course of His ministry, Jesus' actions point to His identity and mission. Although He predicts His crucifixion three times, His disciples remain spiritually blind. Jesus is referred to as "Son of God" in the first verse of Mark's Gospel, and, at the cross, is declared to be God's Son by a Roman centurion. After Jesus attacks the Temple system, He deals with confrontations by Pharisees, Herodians, and Sadducees. Although initially crowds flock to Jesus, when they begin to understand the implications of His Messianic ministry, they desert Him. They "see clearly" only after His resurrection.

43C Jesus' actions in the Temple are not a "cleansing of the Temple," but an "attack on the system." Things such as the prestige of priestly rank, the superiority of men over women, the desire to keep Gentiles at a distance, and the Temple's corrupt "salvation marketing system" anger Jesus. His cursing of a fig tree on His way into the Temple points to what will soon overtake the Temple system; it will soon be torn up and discarded like a useless fig tree. When the Pharisees show Jesus a coin bearing the image of the Emperor, they reveal that they have what they are not supposed to have—a foreign coin with a human image on it. To them, money matters!

43D When celebrating the Passover on the night before His crucifixion, Jesus not only shares table fellowship with the disciples, but links their eating and drinking to celebrating the new and final rescue event that lies at the very center of Jesus' ministry. When, next morning, Pontius Pilate gives the Jewish people the choice of freeing either Jesus or Barabbas ("son of the father"), they choose Barabbas—a Zealot whose desire is to free them from Roman domination by force.

43E The Jewish people see no need for a Savior from sin! Little wonder, then, that they reject Jesus and chose Barabbas. However, they will have to do a lot of thinking after Jesus returns to life. They have to give thought to the fact that the One to whom they had looked to free them from Roman control calls them to walk the way of a servant-without-limit—even to the point of washing each other's feet—an act of humility that only Gentile slaves would be expected to do.

43F Although there are similarities in the passion narratives, there are also differences. The goal of each is to highlight aspects of Jesus' actions in conquering the powers of Satan, sin, and death.

43G Jesus' actions in relation to touching outcasts and the ritually unclean would have caused many of His observers to question the nature of His ministry. Jesus was "too great" for His disciples—and remains "too much" for many small human hearts still today!

UNITS 41–50

The Gospels and Acts

UNIT 44

Matthew (I)

From Bethlehem to Egypt—to Galilee—to Jerusalem

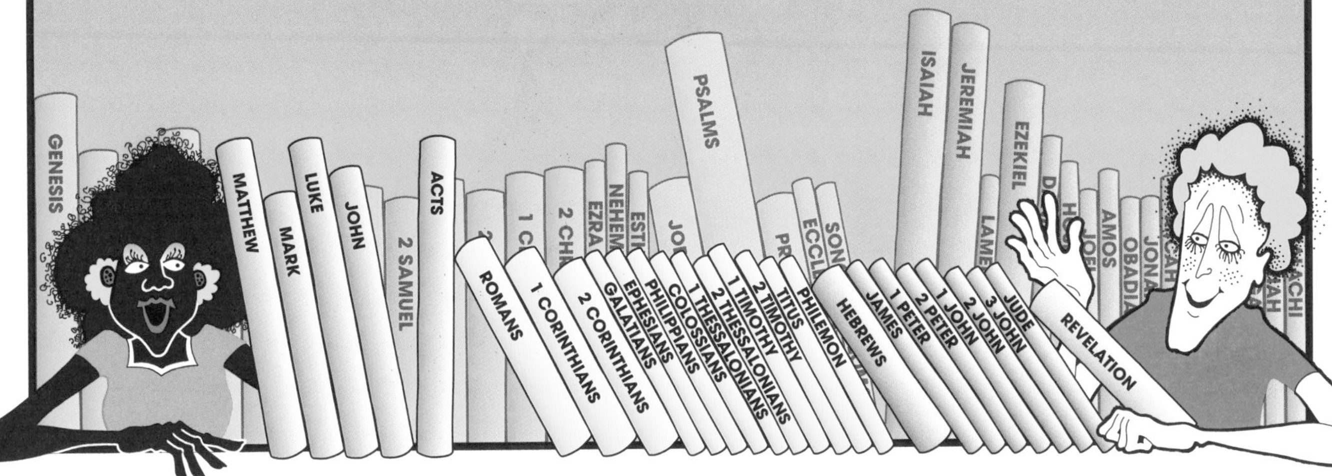

44A

Jesus Reenacts Israel's History

Already during the second century A.D., Irenaeus, one of the early church fathers, noted that many events in Jesus' ministry reflect events in the history of ancient Israel. **ILLUSTRATION 44A** depicts the major parallels—all of which are found in Matthew's Gospel. All biblical passages quoted are from Matthew, unless otherwise indicated.

1. ***Manger in the vicinity of Bethlehem:*** King David was born in Bethlehem, 1 Samuel 16:1; Jesus is born in Bethlehem, Matthew 2:1. The Egyptian pharaoh tried to kill the Old Testament "son of God," Exodus 1:15–22; Herod the Great tries to destroy the new Son of God, Matthew ch. 2. (In both cases, there was a slaughter of male infants.) The kings of the earth came to Solomon to hear his wisdom and brought him gifts of gold, silver, and spices, 1 Kings 10:23–25; wise men bring gifts of gold, frankincense, and myrrh to Jesus, 2:7–12. "One greater than Solomon is here," 12:42.

2. ***Broken line from manger to Egypt:*** Old Testament Israel went from Canaan to Egypt, Genesis 37–50; Jesus' parents take Him to Egypt, 2:13–15.

3. ***Line leaving Egypt:*** God called Old Testament Israel out of Egypt, Hosea 11:1; God calls Jesus out of Egypt, 2:14,15,19–21.

The parallels that follow are now theological rather than geographical.

4. ***Drop of water, with dove*** (symbol for the Holy Spirit) ***superimposed:*** God opened up the waters to free the Israelites from Egypt (Exodus 14:21–29), and again to enable them to enter the Promised Land, Joshua 3:14–17. In His baptism, Jesus passes through the waters of the Jordan into the Promised Land to free God's people from their sins, 3:13–17.

5. ***Satanic face cancelled out:*** Old Testament Israel was tested and tried in the wilderness during the *forty* years of wanderings—and failed by its continuous sinning. Jesus is tested in the wilderness by Satan for *forty* days—but does not yield to Satan's temptations, 4:1–11.

6. ***Symbols for Sinai and community:*** God took the Old Testament community of Israel to Sinai. Jesus takes His disciples to a mountain and forms a new community out of them.

7. ***Symbol for serving God and neighbor:*** At Sinai, God gave Old Testament Israel 613 commandments based on loving God and others; see Deuteronomy 6:4,5 and Leviticus 19:18. Jesus welds the love of God to the love of neighbor, 22:34–40. He makes the two key Old Testament commandments one and inseparable.

8. ***Servant-King Jesus:*** God took up residence among the Israelites in the Tabernacle and guided them during their time in the wilderness, Exodus 40:34–38. Jesus dwells among His people through the Holy Spirit, and promises to remain among them and guide and empower them to the close of the age, Matthew 28:16–20.

9. ***Bread and cup:*** God provided His people with water, manna, and quails to sustain them during their time in the wilderness. The Risen Lord shares a Holy Meal with His brothers and sisters to sustain them during their earthly pilgrimage.

10. ***Line passing through Jordan; Jesus on cross; open tomb:*** God opened up the waters to enable the Israelites to enter the Promised Land, Joshua 3. By going to the cross and conquering the powers of death, Jesus opens up a way through death to enable His disciples to enter the eternal Promised Land, 25:34,46.

11. ***The risen, glorified Jesus in the midst of His community:*** God dwelt among the Israelites as "Immanuel," Isaiah 7:14; 1 Kings 9:3. The risen Jesus lives among His people forever, Matthew 28:20.

ILLUSTRATION 44B

JESUS' GENEALOGY

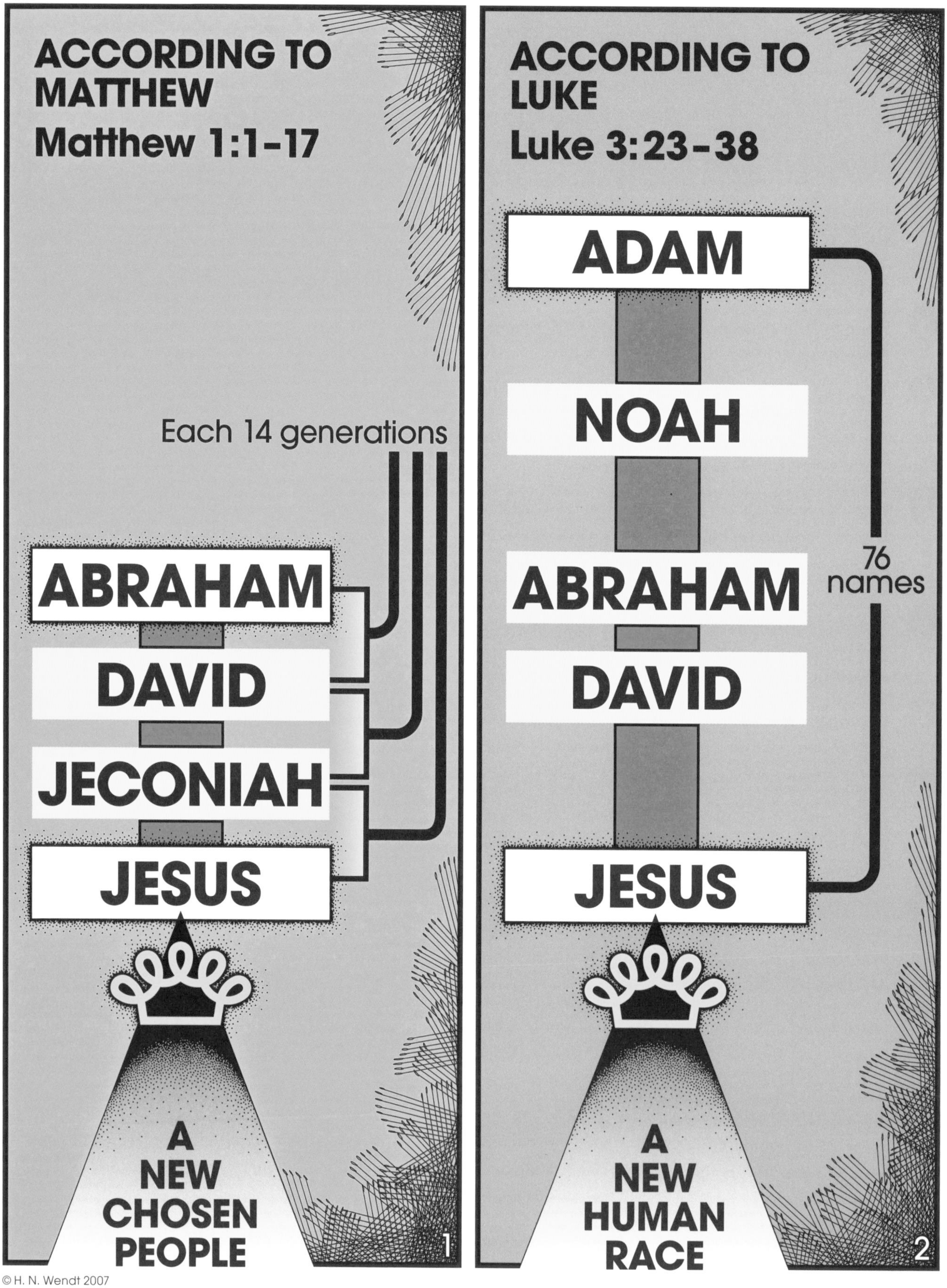
ACCORDING TO MATTHEW
Matthew 1:1-17
Each 14 generations
ABRAHAM
DAVID
JECONIAH
JESUS
A NEW CHOSEN PEOPLE
1
ACCORDING TO LUKE
Luke 3:23-38
ADAM
NOAH
ABRAHAM
DAVID
JESUS
76 names
A NEW HUMAN RACE
2

Genealogy and Theology

ILLUSTRATION 44B outlines the genealogies that Matthew and Luke present in their respective Gospels. These genealogies make significant theological statements.

MATTHEW

1. The opening verse of Matthew's Gospel reads, "An account of the genealogy of Jesus the Messiah, the son of ***DAVID***, the son of ***ABRAHAM***." Although Abraham came before David, Matthew mentions David's name first. In Matthew, Jesus is called "Son of David" more often than in all the other Gospels put together, 1:1; 9:27; 12:23; 15:22; 20:30,31; 21:9,15. (Mark uses the title only in 10:47,48; Luke in 18:35–39, and John not at all.)

2. The list of names in Matthew 1:1–17 consists of three sections of fourteen names each. Matthew 1:17 points out the historical significance of each section: from Abraham to David; from David to the Babylonian exile; and from the Babylonian exile to the birth of Jesus. The third section contains mostly unknown names. In Hebrew, David's name (D-V-D—no vowels) has the mathematical value of fourteen: D = 4, V = 6, D = 4.

3. Matthew's genealogical table omits the names of kings Ahaziah, Joash, Amaziah and queen Athaliah, 1:8. He also refers to Josiah's descendants as Jechoniah and his brothers, 1:11. (Note that according to 2 Kings 22–25, ***JECHONIAH*** [or Jehoiachin, Coniah] was a son of Jehoiakim and a grandson of Josiah. Josiah was succeeded by three sons and a grandson: his son Jehoahaz, his son Jehoiakim, his grandson Jehoachin, and his son Zedekiah.) Some suggest that Matthew edits his lists to ensure they ***each*** contain ***14 generations***.

4. The table contains the names of several women: Tamar, Rahab, Ruth, Bathsheba ("the wife of Uriah," 1:6), and Mary. Women were not always held in high esteem in the ancient world, but they were and are precious to God. Some of the women listed were anything but saints. However, none of the patriarchs or kings was a saint either.

5. Although the exiles hoped that King Jehoiachin would live through the exile and return to Jerusalem to reestablish the Davidic dynasty, he died in Babylon, 2 Kings 25:27–30. Later hopes in relation to Jehoiachin's grandson, Zerubbabel (Haggai 2:20–23; Zechariah 4:6–10), were frustrated when apparently he was removed from the scene by the Persians. Matthew's message is: God has kept His promise to David; the Davidic dynasty is finally being restored.

6. In tracing Jesus' genealogy back to Abraham, Matthew shows that the new chosen people were not an upstart group. It grew directly out of the old people of God, for Jesus was a descendant of Abraham. Jesus is, therefore, the first of ***A NEW CHOSEN PEOPLE***, and the King of that people. The mention of Abraham may be due also to Matthew's interest in the universal scope of Jesus' mission; see Genesis 22:18, "...in your descendants all the nations of the earth shall find blessing" (NAB).

LUKE

7. In Luke's genealogy, most of the persons from ***DAVID*** to ***JESUS*** are unknown, 3:23–31. David's place in the list does not receive the emphasis that it does in Matthew's genealogy.

8. Luke traces Jesus' origins back through ***DAVID***, ***ABRAHAM***, and ***NOAH*** all the way back to ***ADAM***. Luke's point is: Jesus is not merely the first of a new chosen people; He is the first of ***A NEW HUMAN RACE***. In Jesus, there takes place a new beginning to creation and history. Jesus is God's anointed Lord over creation, humanity, and history.

Matthew's Outline

1 Although Matthew's two opening chapters contain details about Jesus' birth and early childhood that are not reported in Mark, beyond that point his *geographical* outline is similar to Mark's.

2 As in Mark, Jesus goes from Nazareth to John the Baptist to be baptized (3:13), and then returns to Nazareth, 4:12,13. He works in and around Galilee, in Syro-Phoenicia (15:21–28), in the Decapolis (15:29–39), crosses back and forth over the Sea of Galilee (15:29–39, 16:5), travels north to the region of Caesarea Philippi (16:13), and finally leaves Galilee to head south to Jerusalem, 19:1. He enters Jerusalem on Palm Sunday (21:1–11), is put to death five days later on Good Friday, and rises from the dead the following Sunday. After His resurrection, He is seen near Jerusalem by women (28:1–10, not reported in Mark) and establishes contact with His disciples again in Galilee, 28:16–20.

3 Mark contains sixteen chapters, Matthew twenty-eight. Although Mark frequently says that Jesus taught, he reports only a limited amount of what Jesus *said* and focuses instead on Jesus' *actions*. On the other hand, Matthew devotes whole chapters and groups of chapters to Jesus' sayings.

4 At the close of each of his five blocks of Jesus' sayings, Matthew says something like, "And when Jesus had finished these sayings," 7:28, 11:1, 13:53, 19:1, 26:1. Scholars believe that Matthew has structured his Gospel along the lines of a new five-book Torah, a new five-book Pentateuch. The outline below divides Matthew into five sections, with an introductory prologue to span the period from the Old to the New Testament.

	From the Old to the New Testament (1:1–4:16)	
PROLOGUE	1:1–2:23	Infancy Narratives
	3:1–4:16	John the Baptist and Jesus
	The Kingdom of God is at Hand (4:17–9:34)	
1	4:17–7:29	Introduction & DISCOURSE 1
	8:1–9:34	Narrative
	The Lost Sheep of the House of Israel (9:35–12:50)	
2	9:35–10:42	DISCOURSE 2
	11:1–12:50	Narrative
	I Will Build My Church (13:1–17:27)	
3	13:1–58	DISCOURSE 3
	14:1–17:27	Narrative
	The True Israel (18:1–23:29)	
4	18:1–35	DISCOURSE 4
	19:1–23:39	Narrative
	The Final Victory (24:1–28:20)	
5	24:1–25:46	DISCOURSE 5
	26:1–28:20	Narrative

5 In His discourses, Jesus addresses the following audiences:

- The crowds, 5:1–7:29; the Sermon on the Mount.
- The disciples, 10:1–42. Jesus instructs and commissions them.
- A crowd of people, 13:1–58. Ch. 13 contains a number of parables.
- The disciples, 18:1–35.
- The disciples, chs. 24,25.

Jesus—the Disciples—the Crowd

The manner in which each evangelist arranges his materials says much about the message he wishes to convey. A thread that depicts the interplay between Jesus, the disciples, and the crowds runs through Matthew's account of Jesus' unfolding message and ministry. There are five stages in the attitudes displayed by the crowds and the disciples; these coincide with the five "books" listed in Matthew's outline.

a. In **Matthew 4:17–9:34**, Jesus meets the crowds and a few disciples. He calls the disciples to follow Him. They witness what Jesus says and does, but do not carry out a ministry of their own. The crowds are also present during this time and respond enthusiastically.

b. In **Matthew 9:35–12:50**, the atmosphere changes. Jesus meets opposition from the people. At the same time, the disciples begin to share Jesus' ministry and encounter similar opposition.

c. In **Matthew 13:1–17:27**, Jesus speaks to two very distinct groups. On the one hand, there are those who cannot hear or understand what He is saying. On the other hand, there are the disciples whose eyes begin to open and whose ears begin to hear. Although they understand what Jesus says to them, they still need further instruction.

d. In **Matthew 18:1–23:29**, Jesus gathers His disciples around Himself and gives them instructions about life in His community. A wide variety of issues is dealt with. The disciples repeatedly approach Jesus with questions—which He answers. The "old Israel" is now no longer the people of God; it has refused to recognize Jesus as Messiah and the Son of God. Only Jesus has the right to sit on Moses' seat.

e. In **Matthew 24:1–28:20**, Jesus instructs His disciples about the coming destruction of Judah, Jerusalem, and the Temple (ch. 24), and the implications of His eventual reappearance at the close of the age, ch. 25. Chs. 26–28 describe Jesus' trial, crucifixion, and resurrection.

2 What message does this thread convey? Jesus is the Messiah, but not the Messiah of Jewish expectation. Jesus is the humble Son of Man, the lowly Messiah, and the friend of the poor. He renounces wealth and power, and calls on His disciples to do the same. He accomplishes His final victory through His suffering, death, and resurrection.

3 Although the reign of God breaks in with Jesus, it is not the reign of a kingly messiah over a Jewish world empire. Instead, it demonstrates itself in submission to the gracious will of God. The truths about Jesus' Messiahship emerge against a backdrop of Jewish unbelief and hostility. As Jesus' ministry progresses and His meaning becomes increasingly clear, old Israel turns on Him and rejects all that He stands for. However, Jesus gathers some out of old Israel to Himself and molds them into His new people: the true Israel.

4 Entwined in the structure of Matthew's outline is the conviction that Jesus is a new Moses who forms the new and true Israel, rescues it from bondage to Satan, sin, and death, instructs it, bestows on it the new and true Law/Torah/Pentateuch, and leads it into the true inheritance of eternal life. Claim to membership in the people of God does not rest on national ties or rituals rightly performed, but on faith in, and allegiance to the true Son of God, the Savior of the world, and the King of creation.

Opening Narratives

Nativity Narrative, Matthew 1:18–25

1 Joseph features prominently in Matthew's nativity narrative, 1:18–25. God communicates with him through dreams, 1:20; 2:19; see Genesis 37:5–11,19. Matthew 1:22 introduces a formula Matthew uses numerous times, "All this took place to fulfill what had been spoken by the Lord through the prophet." The events associated with Jesus' birth and ministry were predicted and planned. Matthew does not refer to Joseph and Mary traveling to Bethlehem; he merely states that Jesus was born there, 2:1.

2 The name that the angel instructs Joseph to give Mary's Son defines Jesus' mission (Jesus, "God saves"). In Judaism at this time, many Jewish people believed that they were saved because they were descendants of Abraham. Mary's Son will make it clear that membership in the new and true Israel is based on a different principle, 1:21.

3 Mary's Son is no ordinary human being. He has no human father. His conception is caused by the gracious, supernatural intervention of the Holy Spirit. The child is Emmanuel, "God is with us," 1:23. Mark uses the term "Son of God" in his opening verse, and repeats it at Calvary, 15:39 (see also Matthew 27:54). Similarly, Matthew uses the term "Emmanuel" ("God is with you") in 1:23 and again in the closing verse of the Gospel, "I am with you always, to the close of the age," 28:20. Matthew's message is that the incarnate Son of God did not come to pay His people a brief call, but to take up residence among them until the close of the age.

The Visit of the Wise Men, Matthew 2:1–23

1 The identity of the wise men has been the subject of much speculation. The Bible does not say that they were three in number, that they rode camels, that they were kings, or that they were Gentiles. Possibly the message is that the wise of this world come to Jesus to find true wisdom and bring their gifts to Him (just as they did with King Solomon, 1 Kings 4:34, 10:23–25), for in Jesus One greater than Solomon has come, Matthew 12:42. If they were indeed Gentiles, the message is that the Gentiles can see what the Jewish people cannot see. The term "magi" used in relation to the wise men was used to refer to those thought to have more than human knowledge. The reference to their seeing a star rising in the east suggests that the wise men were also astrologers; see also Numbers 24:17 where the term "star" is not linked to an astral phenomenon but to the king himself.

2 Although the wise men bring Jesus gifts fit for a king, those in the power structures (Herod and all in Jerusalem) are perturbed and troubled, 2:3. Jesus' coming threatens their authority, and the manner in which they obtain and exercise it. Herod in particular is determined to deal with the problem. He therefore attempts to destroy the new Son of God just as another ruler, the Pharaoh in Egypt, had sought to destroy the former son of God (Exodus 1). Herod's efforts result in Jesus being taken to Egypt—as a homeless refugee with a price on His head—and the eventual recapitulation of Hosea 11:1, "Out of Egypt I called my son." Egypt was a traditional place of refuge for those fleeing from danger in Palestine, 1 Kings 11:40; Jeremiah 26:21. In their meeting with Herod, the wise men referred to their desire to make contact with "the King of the Jews." Later, Roman soldiers will use the term when mocking Jesus (Matthew 27:29), and the sign placed above Jesus' head will include the term, 27:37

3 After Joseph and Mary return from Egypt, they settle in Nazareth in Galilee—again, an act that is viewed as a fulfillment of prophecy, 2:23. Matthew links the name "Nazareth" to the Hebrew word for "branch" (nezer) in Isaiah 11:1. The name Nazareth is not mentioned in the Old Testament.

John the Baptist, Matthew 3:1–12

1 John carries out his ministry in the Judean wilderness. His dress resembles that of Elijah, 2 Kings 1:8. John bitterly attacks those Jews who look to national origins for spiritual security, summons them to

repentance and faith, and baptizes many who respond. To baptize Jews was a radical practice, for only Gentile proselytes were baptized when they converted to Judaism.

2 John's appeal declares that the yardstick the Jews have been using to determine membership in the people of God is invalid. God is not interested in family trees, but seeks a circumcision of the heart—repentance. The consequences of rejecting God's summons are serious indeed, 3:10. Throughout his ministry, John points beyond himself and his ministry to a Greater One, 3:11,12.

3 Eventually, Jesus comes to John to be baptized. Because this incident is surveyed in Unit 42, further comment will not be made at this point.

4 Unlike Luke (1:36), Matthew says nothing about John's family background and does not refer to him as a relative of Jesus.

Jesus' Temptation, Matthew 4:1-11

1 Jesus recapitulates the history of the former Israel (tested in the wilderness for *forty years*, Deuteronomy 8:2), even to the point of being tested in the wilderness for *forty days*; see also the reference to Moses spending *forty days* at Mt. Sinai, Exodus 24:18. After passing through the waters of baptism into the wilderness of Judea, Jesus faces a series of Satanic "ifs." Had Jesus yielded to the demonic, Satan would have remained the master of the human race.

2 In the *first temptation* (4:1–4), Jesus, despite severe hunger, refuses to use His divine power to obtain food for Himself. Jesus has come to be a Servant of others, and that means using His powers only to that end. Old Israel regularly complained about its wilderness diet and lack of food. Jesus' behavior is the opposite.

3 In the *second temptation* (4:5–7), Jesus refuses to resort to spectacular deeds to attract attention to Himself, and to presume on His Father's supernatural protection. His servanthood and trusting submission to His Father's will bear witness to the true nature of the Messianic Kingdom.

4 In the *third temptation* (4:8–10), Satan takes Jesus to the top of a mountain and tempts Him to change His goals and seek an earthly Kingdom rather than establish and expand a Servant Kingdom. From the mountaintop Jesus looks across a world that His Father made and owns, a world over which He is already King and for which He must die! He rejects all of Satan's temptations with quotes from Deuteronomy (8:3; 6:16; 6:13), a book set in the wilderness period. After Old Israel crossed the Jordan into the Promised Land, the people sinned repeatedly. The new, true Israel crosses the Jordan (in His baptism) and withstands all Satan's temptations.

5 After Jesus hears about John's arrest, He leaves Nazareth and makes Capernaum His base of operations, 4:12,13. The ministry that follows takes place in and around Galilee, the territory of the former Northern Kingdom destroyed by Assyria in 721 B.C. The region that once experienced great darkness now sees a great light, 4:15,16; Isaiah 9:1.

6 The transition from the Old to the New Testament is now complete. The stage is set. The Messiah is at hand. His work gets underway. While John pointed to a kingdom that was coming, Jesus proclaims that *God's Kingdom has come—in Him.* Matthew states (4:17):

> *From that time Jesus began to proclaim, "Repent, for the Kingdom of God is at hand."*

DISCOURSE 1

Matthew 5-7: The Sermon on the Mount

- The Beatitudes, 5:1–12
- Salt and Light, 5:13–16
- The Law, 5:17–20
- Anger, 5:21–26
- Adultery, 5:27–30
- Divorce, 5:31,32
- Oaths, 5:33–37
- Retaliation, 5:38–42
- Love of Enemies, 5:43–48
- Almsgiving, 6:1–4
- Prayer, 6:5–15 (including the Lord's Prayer)
- Fasting, 6:16–18
- Treasure in Heaven, 6:19–21
- The Light of the Body, 6:22,23
- God and Money, 6:24
- Trusting in God, 6:25–34
- Judging others, 7:1–5
- Pearls before Swine, 7:6
- Answers to Prayers, 7:7–11
- The Golden Rule, 7:12
- The Narrow Gate, 7:13,14
- False Prophets, 7:15–20
- The True Disciples, 7:21–23
- Foundations for Life, 7:24–27

In the Beatitudes (5:1–12), Jesus makes frequent use of the word "blessed." However, Jesus never links it to the enjoyment of materials goods, as does Deuteronomy 28:1–14. He links it only to reflecting His servant manner of life.

Prior to Leaving Galilee for Jerusalem

Narratives in Matthew 8:1–9:38

1 This section contains nine miracle stories arranged in blocks of three, with teachings about discipleship after each block. In the first healing miracle, Jesus heals a leper—an outcast—but touches him before He heals him, 8:1–4.

2 Jesus heals the servant of a (Gentile) Roman centurion—from a distance, from "far off," 8:5–13. Although Jewish religious leaders referred to Gentiles as those "far off," Jesus commends the centurion for his remarkable faith. The centurion believed that Jesus could heal his servant from a distance, from "far off."

3 Jesus heals Peter's mother-in-law of a fever, and again touches her before He heals her, 8:14,15. He then heals many who are sick, and casts out demons, 8:16,17.

4 Jesus deals with two men to the east of the Sea of Galilee, 8:18. The *first* says he will follow Jesus wherever He goes, v. 19; Jesus tells him that if he has hopes of eventually enjoying a lavish lifestyle similar to that of the Herods ("foxes"; see Luke 13:31,32) or exercising political power similar to that practiced by the Romans ("birds"; the eagle was the symbol for Rome), he is misguided. The *second* says that he plans to follow Jesus, but only after his father eventually dies—for his father has first and total claim on his son's life while he is alive, 8:21. Jesus reminds the man that His claim on a person overrides all other claims, 8:22.

This section contains Jesus' first reference to Himself as "the Son of Man," 8:20; see Daniel 7:13. In Matthew's Gospel, the term is used seven times to refer to Jesus' general ministry, nine times in relation to Jesus' passion and resurrection, and 13 times in relation to Jesus' glorious reappearing at the end of the age, e.g., 24:30.

5 While at sea, the disciples wake a sleeping Jesus Who stills a storm, 8:23–27—thereby pointing to His deity, Psalm 107:23–32. The disciples are amazed!

6 After disembarking in the region of the Decapolis, Jesus casts demons out of two (Gentile) men, 8:28–34. Remarkably, the men address Jesus as "Son of God," 8:29. Others in the region ask Jesus to leave the region, for the demons Jesus cast out enter their pigs, and the pigs rush into the Sea of Galilee and drown—and these pig farmers lose their means of earning a living. (The notion that evil spirits were allowed by God to afflict human beings until the time of judgment is found in two non-canonical writings, Enoch 16:1 and Jubilees 10:7–10.)

7 After Jesus returns to the west side of the Sea of Galilee, people bring to him a paralyzed man lying on a stretcher-like bier, 9:1–8. Although Jesus' audience expects Jesus to heal the man, Jesus (*first*) declares him forgiven, and then (*second*) heals him. If Jesus' second word comes to pass, so does His first word—signifying that the "sin forgiveness system" now resides in Jesus and not in the rituals of the Jerusalem Temple system.

8 Jesus calls Matthew, a despised tax-collector who collaborates with the Romans, to follow Him, 9:9. When He then dines with tax collectors and those whom the religious leaders classify as "sinners," the Pharisees protest, 9:10–17! Jesus responds by telling the Pharisees that He has come to heal those who know that they are sick—but the Pharisees sense no need of personal, spiritual healing. What Jesus brings to humanity is something radically new and different. It is impossible to fit the new into the old—even as it is futile to sew a piece of new cloth on to old tattered cloth or to pour new wine into old wineskins.

9 Ch. 9:18–26 contains two healing narratives. Jesus restores Jairus' dead daughter to life, and takes hold of her (ritually unclean) hand prior to doing so, 9:18,19,23,25. He also permits a woman who has

been menstruating for twelve years to touch Him—with the result that she is healed. Although the crowds expect Jesus to rebuke this ritually unclean woman for touching Him, Jesus addresses her as "daughter," 9:20–22.

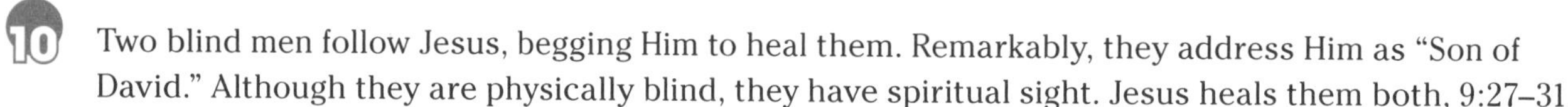

10 Two blind men follow Jesus, begging Him to heal them. Remarkably, they address Him as "Son of David." Although they are physically blind, they have spiritual sight. Jesus heals them both, 9:27–31.

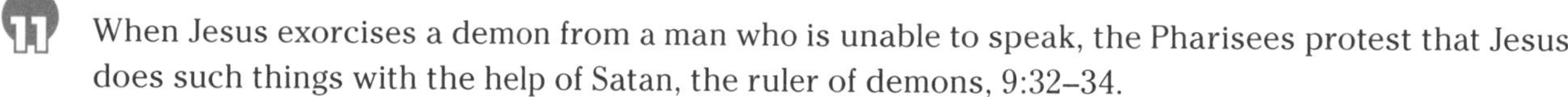

11 When Jesus exorcises a demon from a man who is unable to speak, the Pharisees protest that Jesus does such things with the help of Satan, the ruler of demons, 9:32–34.

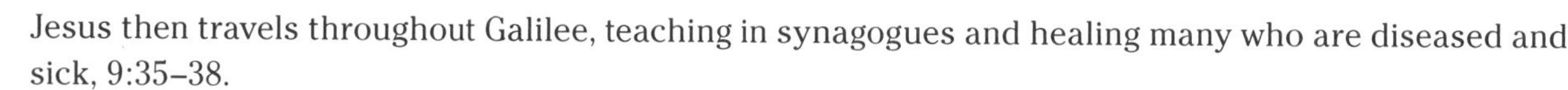

12 Jesus then travels throughout Galilee, teaching in synagogues and healing many who are diseased and sick, 9:35–38.

DISCOURSE 2

Matthew 10

- The Mission of the Twelve, vv. 1–4
- The Commissioning of the Twelve, vv. 5–15
- Persecutions to be expected, vv. 16–25
- Dealing with Persecution, vv.26–33
- Jesus: a Cause for Division, vv. 34–36
- Conditions of Discipleship, vv. 37–39
- Rewards, vv. 40–42

Narratives in Matthew 11:1-12:50

In this section, opposition to Jesus and His ministry increases.

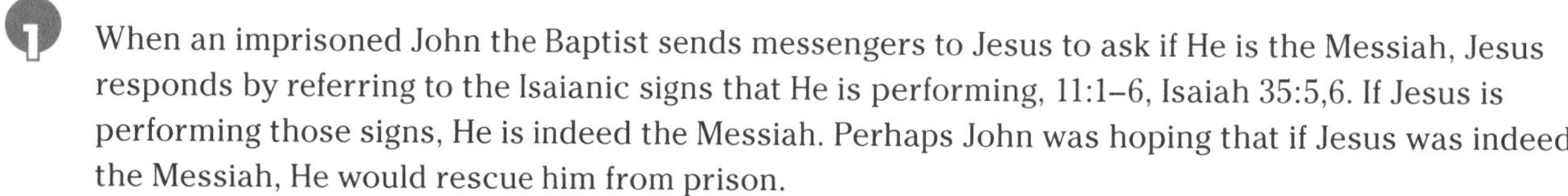

1 When an imprisoned John the Baptist sends messengers to Jesus to ask if He is the Messiah, Jesus responds by referring to the Isaianic signs that He is performing, 11:1–6, Isaiah 35:5,6. If Jesus is performing those signs, He is indeed the Messiah. Perhaps John was hoping that if Jesus was indeed the Messiah, He would rescue him from prison.

2 Jesus then states that if those who went to hear John preach were expecting to see someone reflecting the power and lifestyle of the Herods, they were misguided, 11:7.8. (Herod Antipas put symbols of grain stalks blowing in the wind—symbols of beauty and fertility—on his coins. Those in positions of power wore clothing made of expensive, soft cloth.) Jesus then states that John the Baptist is indeed that prophet referred to in Malachi 3:1. And no matter what lifestyle a prophet pursues—whether it be rigid and controlled (John) or more relaxed (Jesus)—people will find cause to criticize, 11:11–19.

3 Jesus then rebukes the cities (Chorazin, Bethsaida) in which He had carried out His ministry. Although their inhabitants had seen Jesus' deeds of power, they refused to repent. If the people of Sodom had seen what the people of Jesus' day are seeing, they would have repented. He adds that on the Last Day of history, the Gentile Phoenicians (Tyre and Sidon) will receive more mercy than those who claim to be God's people, 11:20–24. In the Old Testament, Tyre and Sidon are denounced as wicked pagan cities, Joel 3:4–7.

4 Jesus then thanks His Father for the honor of being the One called to make Him known, for to know the visible Jesus is to know the invisible Father, 11:25–27. There is perfect reciprocity of knowledge between the Father and Jesus, and Jesus will reveal the knowledge handed over to Him to those whom He wishes. Jesus then invites the weary and the burdened to come to Him to receive the rest that only He can give. They find rest by freeing themselves of the yoke of submission to traditional Jewish law-codes and by taking upon themselves Jesus' yoke—the yoke that calls them to devote life to glorifying God by giving it away in loving service of others, 11:28–30. (The scribes and Pharisees see themselves as those who have taken upon themselves the heavy "yoke" of the Old Testament Torah/Law. Jesus' "yoke" is a radically different one; it is "easy" and His "burden is light."

5 Jesus then breaks two Sabbaths in a row, 12:1–14. He permits His disciples to rub out grain from wheat stalks on a Sabbath (vv.1–8), and then heals a man with a withered hand on a Sabbath 12:9–14. The Pharisees taught that if all God's people would properly observe two Sabbaths in a row, the Messiah would appear. They see Jesus' actions as preventing the coming of the Messiah—and conspire to destroy Jesus. Jesus validates His actions by pointing out that if Temple duties outweigh the demands of the Sabbath law (Leviticus 24:8, Numbers 28:9–10), how much more does the presence of Jesus (something greater than the Temple) justify the conduct of the disciples?

6 Despite the plots of the Pharisees, Jesus continues to heal many—an action that Matthew defines as fulfillment of Isaiah 42:1–4 (Isaiah's first Servant Song), 12:15–21. After Jesus heals a man who is blind and mute, and possessed by a demon, the crowds are amazed and suggest that Jesus might be the long-awaited Son of David. However, the Pharisees insist that Jesus does such things with the help of Satan, 12:22–24.

7 Jesus responds to the Pharisees' charges by pointing out that if He is in league with the devil, then there is a "devil of a mess in hell," for the implication of the Pharisees' charge is that Satan is throwing out demons. Not so! The truth is that a kingdom much more powerful than that of Satan has broken into history—and Jesus, the King of the radically New Kingdom, will finally overthrow Satan's kingdom at the cross. 12:25–31. If those around Jesus see these things being fulfilled during His earthly ministry prior to the cross, they will be forgiven. But after the crucified Jesus has been vindicated by the Father through His resurrection, those who refuse to heed the witness of the Holy Spirit will cut themselves off from God's forgiving grace, 12:31,32. Jesus then defines His opponents as a "brood of vipers, snakes," and reminds them that a day is coming when all will be called to give account to God of how they have used life, 12:33–37.

8 When some scribes and Pharisees ask Jesus to perform a sign to validate His ministry, He responds that those who seek signs belong to an adulterous generation, 12:38,39. However, the sign that humanity will eventually receive will resemble that of Jonah leaving the belly of a fish after spending three days within it: Jesus will return to life after spending three days in a tomb, 12:40. The people of Nineveh, who repented when they heard Jonah's message to them, will rise up in judgment against those who refuse to see in Jesus one greater than Jonah, 12:41. So too will the Queen of Sheba who traveled a great distance to listen to Solomon's wisdom—and in Jesus, one greater than Solomon has come, 12:42. Both the people of Nineveh and the Queen of Sheba (all supposedly "pagans") responded to "lesser opportunities" than those Jesus is offering to the people of Israel!

In Matthew 12, Jesus is referred to as being greater than the Jerusalem *Temple* (v. 6), greater than the *Sabbath* (v. 8), greater than *Jonah* (v. 41), and greater than *Solomon*, v. 42.

9 Jesus goes on to say that while it is important to throw a demon out of a person's life, unless that demon is replaced with God's presence and truth, the demon will return—bringing seven other demons with it, 12:43–45. There is no such thing as a spiritual vacuum within a person; either God rules—or Satan rules!

10 In the closing section of ch. 12 (vv.46–50), Jesus states that His family is bigger than His genetic family. Those who embrace Him as forgiving Savior and Servant Lord are His mother, brothers, and sisters.

DISCOURSE 3

Matthew 13: Jesus teaches in parables

- The Parable of the Sower, vv. 1–9
- The purpose of parables, vv. 10–15
- The privilege of discipleship, vv. 16,17
- The parable explained, vv. 18–23
- The Parable of the Weeds among the Wheat, vv. 24–30
- The Parable of the Mustard Seed, vv. 31,32
- The Parable of the Yeast, v. 33
- The use of parables, vv. 34,35
- The Parable of the Weeds explained, vv. 36–43
- More parables, vv. 44–50
- Treasures Old and New, vv. 51–53

Narratives in Matthew 14:1-17:27

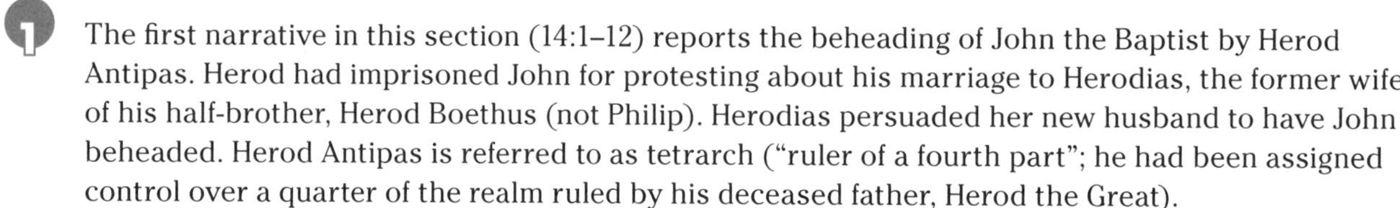
1 The first narrative in this section (14:1–12) reports the beheading of John the Baptist by Herod Antipas. Herod had imprisoned John for protesting about his marriage to Herodias, the former wife of his half-brother, Herod Boethus (not Philip). Herodias persuaded her new husband to have John beheaded. Herod Antipas is referred to as tetrarch ("ruler of a fourth part"; he had been assigned control over a quarter of the realm ruled by his deceased father, Herod the Great).

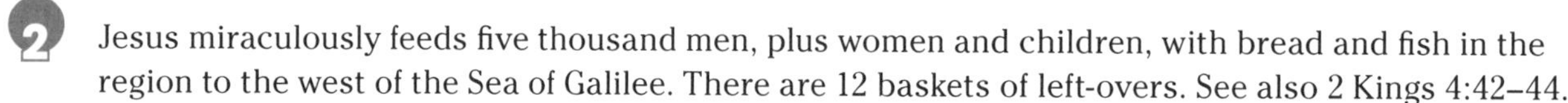
2 Jesus miraculously feeds five thousand men, plus women and children, with bread and fish in the region to the west of the Sea of Galilee. There are 12 baskets of left-overs. See also 2 Kings 4:42–44.

3 After Jesus tells the disciples to travel by boat to the other side of the Sea of Galilee, He goes aside to pray. However, when evening comes the disciples' boat is being tossed about in a storm. Early next morning, the disciples see Jesus walking toward them across the water—and are terrified by what they see. Jesus tells them not to be afraid—He, their Lord and Master, is the one approaching their boat, 14:22–27. When Peter suggests that Jesus enable him to walk toward Him across the surface of the lake, Jesus invites him to do so. But when Peter becomes aware of the presence of a strong wind, he begins to sink into the water and cries to Jesus for help. Jesus takes hold of Peter's hand, and both climb into the boat—and immediately the wind ceases. The disciples respond by worshiping Jesus as the Son of God, 14:28–33.

4 When Jesus and the disciples arrive at Gennesaret (just below Capernaum on the northwest coast of the Sea of Galilee), word of Jesus' presence gets around. Crowds gather around Jesus, bringing with them the sick—whom Jesus touches and heals, 14:34–36.

5 Next, the Pharisees and scribes attack Jesus for not requiring His disciples to practice ritual washing prior to eating. Jesus responds by accusing His opponents of twisting God's law to avoid doing what

it asked them to do. They honor God with their lips but not with their heart. They conform to human whims but not to God's will, 15:1–9.

6 Jesus then points out to His disciples that what people put into their mouth does not defile them. After all, food that enters into the mouth and stomach finishes up in the sewer. What really matters are those vile things that rise within the heart and leave the body via the mouth—and cause pain to others, 15:10–20.

7 Jesus then leaves Galilee and goes to the region of Tyre and Sidon in Phoenicia where He encounters a (Gentile) Canaanite woman who calls out to Him, addressing Him as Lord and Son of David (something that His own people do not do). The woman asks Jesus to help her daughter who is being tormented by a demon. When Jesus tells her that His mission is, above all, to the Jews, she again addresses Him as Lord—twice. Although the disciples urge Jesus to ignore the woman (a Gentile "dog"), He heals her ailing daughter, 15:21–28.

Only Matthew refers to the woman as a "Canaanite"; see Mark 7:24–30. In Old Testament writings, the Canaanites are viewed with scorn, declared to be "cursed" (Genesis 9:24–27), and were to be wiped out in the conquest, Joshua 3:10. In Deuteronomy 7:1,2 they are included in a list of seven nations the Israelites are to hate and destroy. They are to show them no mercy! However, Jesus shows mercy to a Canaanite!

8 Jesus heals many who are lame, maimed, blind, and unable to speak—and the crowds praise Him, 15:29–31. Jesus then feeds 4,000 men, plus women and children, using and multiplying seven loaves and a few small fish in the process. There are seven baskets of left-overs, 15:32–39.

9 The Pharisees and Sadducees again come to Jesus asking for a sign from heaven, 16:1ff. Jesus responds by telling them that although they know how to read signs in the world of nature, they do not know how to read what is happening in relation to divine history. Yes—they will eventually be given a sign—that of Jonah. As Jonah emerged from the belly of a fish after three days, so Jesus will emerge from the tomb of death after three days, 16:1–4. Jesus then warns His disciples (who forgot to bring bread with them) to be on guard against the (corrupt influencing) yeast of the Pharisees and Sadducees, 16:5–12.

10 Jesus takes His disciples to the region of Caesarea Philippi (about 20 miles—or 35 kilometers—north of the Sea of Galilee) where He asks them who the people believe Him to be. They respond that the people are suggesting that He is John the Baptist, Elijah, Jeremiah, or one of the prophets. When Peter, speaking on behalf of the disciples, says that He is the Messiah, the Son of the living God, Jesus declares Peter to be blessed. Jesus then states that He will build His church, His new community, on the truth of Peter's statement. However, Jesus tells the disciples that they are not to tell anyone that He is the Messiah—no doubt because the people-at-large have wrong notions about Jesus' mission, 16:13–20.

11 Next, Jesus predicts His coming suffering, death, and resurrection in Jerusalem. When Peter rebukes Jesus for predicting such a future for Himself (and possibly also for the disciples), He tells Peter that he is on the side of the devil, 16:21–23. And then Jesus tells the disciples that those who claim to belong to Him are to walk the way Jesus walks, to find life by giving it away, 16:24–26. Jesus is indeed the Son of Man, the true people of God (Daniel 7:13), and calls humanity-at-large to accountability with regard to how they use life. During their own lifetime the disciples will witness the breaking in of the true Kingdom of God, the Kingdom of the Son of Man, the Kingdom of the true people of God, 16:27,28.

12 In the event that follows, Jesus takes Peter, James, and John up a high mountain, 17:1–8. Jesus is transfigured before them; His face shines like the sun and His clothes become as white as light; see Exodus 19:16–18; 24:9,10; Daniel 7:9. Moses and Elijah appear on the scene and speak with Jesus.

(Both Moses and Elijah met with God on Mt. Sinai: Moses after the Exodus event; Elijah after fleeing to Mt. Horeb—Deuteronomy's name for Mt. Sinai—after killing the prophets of Baal on Mt. Carmel, 1 Kings 18.) While Peter is suggesting that the disciples construct three tents for Jesus, Moses, and Elijah, a bright cloud envelops them and a voice speaks declaring Jesus to be *King* (Psalm 2:7), *Servant* (Isaiah 42:1,2), and the long-awaited *new Prophet* like Moses, Deuteronomy 18:15. The disciples are overcome with fear when they hear the voice from the cloud. However, Jesus touches them, tells them not to be afraid—and the vision ends.

In the verses that follow, Jesus links John the Baptist to the expected return of Elijah (Malachi 3:1), and refers once again to His coming crucifixion, 17:9–13. He then heals a boy suffering from epilepsy and possessed by a demon, 17:14–21.

Next, Jesus predicts His coming betrayal, crucifixion, and resurrection—a prediction that distresses His disciples, 17:22,23. When the disciples arrive at Capernaum, Jesus provides the necessary coin to pay the required Temple tax in a remarkable way. Peter will find it in the mouth of a fish that he will catch in the Sea of Galilee, 17:24–27. (Before the destruction of the Jerusalem Temple in A.D. 70, every male Jew was obliged to make an annual contribution to fund its upkeep, Exodus 30:11–16, Nehemiah 10:32–39.) In the context of this event, Jesus points out that just as subjects are not bound by laws applying to foreigners, Jesus and His disciples (subjects of the Kingdom of Heaven) are not under legal obligation to pay a tax imposed on them by those who are not members of God's Kingdom.

DISCOURSE 4

Matthew 18: Sayings on humility and forgiveness

- The Greatest in the Kingdom, vv. 1–5
- Temptations to Sin, vv. 6–9
- The Parable of the Lost Sheep, vv. 10–14
- A Brother who Sins, vv. 15–20
- The Parable of the Unforgiving Servant, vv. 21–35

From Galilee to Jerusalem

Matthew 19:1–20:34

1 In 19:1, Jesus leaves Galilee and begins the journey to Jerusalem. When doing so, He travels south along the East Bank of the River Jordan. Large crowds accompany Him, and He heals many. When some Pharisees question Jesus concerning the permissibility of divorce, Jesus takes His questioners back beyond the time of Moses and the giving of the Torah to God's original intention for marriage at the time of creation, 19:1–12.

2 When parents bring their little children to Jesus, He lays His hands on the children, prays, and blesses them. When the disciples protest, Jesus rebukes them, 19:13–15.

3 A man comes to Jesus and asks him what good deed he must do to have eternal life, 19:16–22. When Jesus tells the man that if he wishes to "enter life," he must keep the commandments, the man asks, "Which ones?" Jesus then lists five of the commandments listed in Exodus 20 and Deuteronomy 5, and adds the commandment given in Leviticus 19:18. The man responds that he has kept all these, and asks what else he should do. Jesus tells him to sell his possessions, give the proceeds to the poor—and follow Jesus! The man goes away grieving—for he is a person of wealth, 19:16–22. Jesus follows with a comment that it is indeed hard for the rich to enter the kingdom of heaven; their focus is on what they possess and enjoy now, rather than on what they might experience and enjoy as citizens of God's eternal Kingdom, 19:23–26.

4 The disciples ask Jesus what reward they can expect to receive—for they have given up everything to follow Him. Jesus says that they will eventually receive their reward—even though it will be different from what people hope to receive. After all, Jesus' Kingdom is an upside-down Kingdom in which the first will be last, and the last will be first. In Jesus' Kingdom, greatness is not determined by how much a person acquires for himself, but by how much he gives of himself in the service of others. Jesus assures the disciples that those who leave all to follow Him will eventually benefit richly; they will inherit eternal life, 19:27–30.

5 Next, Jesus tells the parable of the laborers in the vineyard. The message is that those who serve long in God's kingdom cannot expect any greater reward than those who labor for only a short time in that kingdom, 20:1–16.

6 Jesus now predicts His coming passion, crucifixion, and resurrection for the third time, 20:17–19. After He does this, the mother of James and John asks Jesus for a favor. She wants her two sons to occupy the most prominent places in Jesus' coming "coronation ceremony"—little realizing that she is requesting that they be crucified at either side of Jesus, vv. 20–23. When the other ten disciples hear the mother's request, they are angry, 20:24. Jesus responds by telling the disciples that the goal of life in His kingdom is to seek not prominence but opportunities to serve, 20:25–28.

In Mark's Gospel, James and John themselves are the ones who approach Jesus with the request to be granted places of honor in the coming coronation ceremony, 10:35–40. In Matthew's Gospel, their mother makes the request—possibly alluding to Bathsheba seeking the throne on behalf of her son, Solomon, 1 Kings 1:11–31.

7 Jesus then crosses to the West Bank of the Jordan and passes through Jericho. As He takes his leave of that city, two blind men sitting by the roadside twice call out, "Lord, Son of David, have mercy on us!" 20:29–34. Although they are blind in their eyes, they can see in their hearts. Jesus then restores their sight—and they follow Him!

8 *Next stop: Jerusalem!*

SUMMARY

44A In Matthew, Jesus' actions reflect events recorded in the Old Testament, and His teachings reinterpret many traditional emphases. In particular, there are significant parallels between the Old Testament Exodus narrative, and the new rescue event that Jesus carries out: Jesus goes down into Egypt, is called out of Egypt, passes through water, is tempted in the wilderness, and gathers a new people around Himself. And as God gave His Law to old Israel on a mountain, so too Jesus gives His new will to His new people on a mountain.

44B In his opening statement, Matthew declares that God is honoring His promise in relation to the Davidic dynasty. Because Jesus is descended from David (and also a good Jew descended from Abraham), David's dynasty is being restored—but not as expected. Although Matthew presents Jesus as a new beginning to the Davidic dynasty and the Chosen People, Luke presents Jesus as a new Adam—a new beginning to the human race.

44C Although Matthew's geographical and chronological outline resembles Mark's, it reflects a five book structure that declares that Jesus brings a new Torah (Law), a new revelation to His people—and that Torah/revelation is Jesus Himself.

44D As Jesus' ministry unfolds, an increasing division develops between Jesus' followers and the Jewish leaders. Those who remain true to Jesus become the new and true Israel that is to bear witness to Jesus to all nations, and to teach them to believe and do all that Jesus has taught and commanded.

44E Matthew's first four chapters contain narratives that describe Jesus' birth, the visit of the Wise Men, the ministry of John the Baptist, and Jesus' temptation by Satan. These narratives are followed by the first of five discourses that focus on the implications of Jesus' life and teachings for His followers—eventually referred to as His brothers and sisters.

44F While ministering in Galilee, Syro-Phoenicia, and the Decapolis:

- Jesus heals the sick and shows compassion to Gentiles,
- demonstrates His power over the forces of nature, and casts out demons,
- calls a despised tax-collector to follow Him,
- restores the dead to life,
- responds to an inquiry from John the Baptist concerning His identity,
- states that the Gentiles are more ready to believe than are His own people,
- invites His followers to find true rest by taking His yoke upon themselves,
- ignores traditional notions about Sabbath observance,
- states that One greater than the Temple, the Sabbath, Jonah, and Solomon has come,
- feeds 5,000 Jewish men, plus women and children, with bread and fish,
- sets aside the observance of purification rituals,
- feeds 4,000 Gentile men, plus women and children, with bread and fish,
- predicts His coming passion twice, and is transfigured on a mountaintop and
- answers numerous questions from both friend and foe.

44G While traveling from Galilee to Jerusalem:

- Jesus deals with questions from Pharisees, the disciples, and others,
- blesses children and clarifies the nature of true obedience,
- tells several parables and predicts His coming passion a third time, and
- heals two blind men after leaving Jericho for Jerusalem.

UNITS 41–50

The Gospels and Acts

UNIT 45

Matthew (II)

Jesus' Passion, Resurrection, and Final Appearing

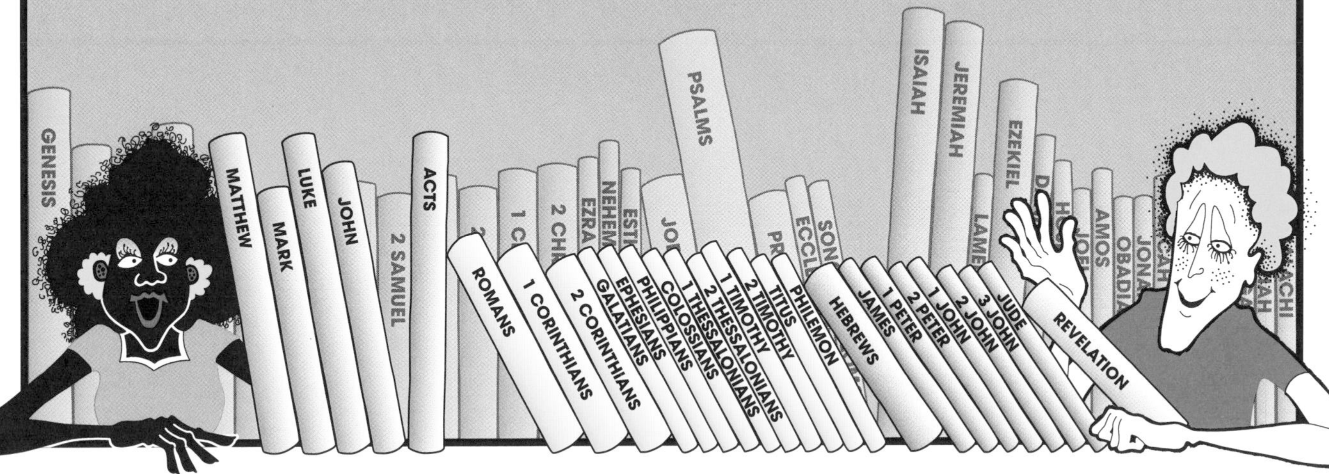

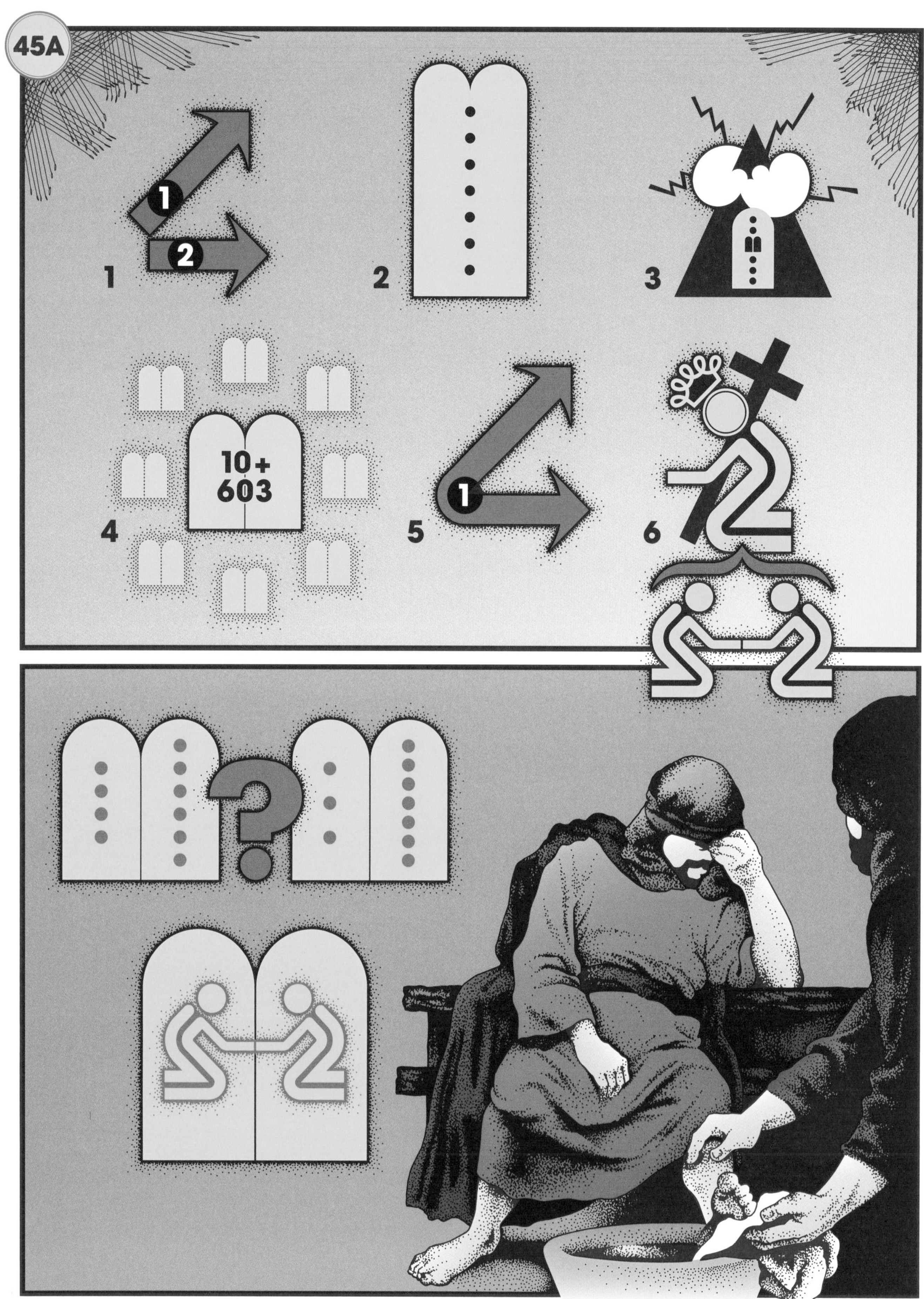
45A
1
2
1
2
3
10+
603
4
1
5
6

God's Will According to Jesus

In Matthew ch. 5, Jesus states a number of times, "You have heard that it was *said* to those of ancient times...," 5:21, 27, 31, 33, 38, 43. The reference is to what was *said* rather than to what was *written*. The things that were *said* had to do with the Jewish *oral traditions*. **ILLUSTRATION 45A** depicts when these oral traditions first surfaced within Judaism, and *what Jesus did with them*,

Upper section

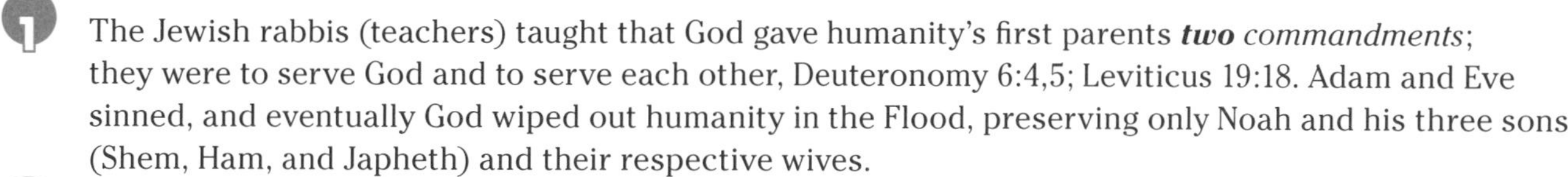

1. The Jewish rabbis (teachers) taught that God gave humanity's first parents ***two*** *commandments*; they were to serve God and to serve each other, Deuteronomy 6:4,5; Leviticus 19:18. Adam and Eve sinned, and eventually God wiped out humanity in the Flood, preserving only Noah and his three sons (Shem, Ham, and Japheth) and their respective wives.

2. According to rabbinic tradition, God gave Noah ***seven*** *commandments*, "The commandments of Noah," which were understood to apply to all humanity. They were the following: (1) The practice of equity. Prohibitions against: (2) Blaspheming the Name of God, (3) Idolatry, (4) Immorality, (5) Bloodshed, (6) Robbery, (7) Eating an uncooked limb torn from an animal.

3. After God rescued the Israelites from Egypt in the Exodus, God made a ***covenant*** with them at ***Mt. Sinai***. The covenant, one that called the Israelites to respond to God's goodness to them, consisted of ***six sections*** with the ***commandments placed at position 3***.

4. The commandments consisted of the ***10*** *Commandments*, plus ***603*** *additional commandments*. The Ten Commandments are given in Exodus 20:1–17, and repeated in Deuteronomy 5:6–21 with minor variations. The 603 additional commandments are given in Exodus, Leviticus, Numbers, and Deuteronomy. Judaism insists, and rightly so, that these 613 commandments were given only to the Israelites and their descendants, the Jewish people.
Smaller law-codes around the 10 + 603: After those taken into exile in Babylon in 597 and 587 B.C. began returning to Judah and Jerusalem in 538 B.C., they began developing the "oral traditions" to supplement, explain, and apply the laws written in the Pentateuch, the first five Old Testament books. Some argued that God had whispered these to Moses, who memorized them and passed them on to Joshua, who passed them on to the elders, who finally passed them on to the members of the postexilic Great Assembly. These oral traditions were finally written down in about A.D. 200 in the *Mishnah*.

5. ***Jesus joined loving God to loving neighbor***, Mark 12:28–34. He welded the *two* into ***one***. Furthermore, Jesus defined "neighbor" as any person from any nation—not just one's own ethnic group, Luke 10:25–37.

6. Jesus lived what He taught. He walked the way of a loving ***Servant-without-limit*** all the way to giving away His life on a cross, and calls ***His brothers and sisters*** to do the same.

Lower section

Top left: Christians continue to debate how the Ten Commandments should be numbered: ***Four to God*** and ***six to neighbor***? Or, ***three to God*** and ***seven to neighbor***?

Lower right: Still today, some define God's will as "Do unto others as you would have them do unto you," and "Love your neighbor as you love yourself." Jesus went way beyond that. He taught, "Love one another *as I have loved you*," John 13:12–17. And to show them what He meant, ***Jesus washed their feet***. He did that which no Jew would do; washing feet was a task reserved for Gentile slaves.

When Jesus said, "I have not come to destroy the Law and the prophets" (Matthew 5:17), He did not mean "I endorse every law-code in your sacred writings (all 613 of them!) and fulfill all the predictions those writings contain." He meant, "I have come to explain and live out My Father's original design for humanity and to make clear what the Old Testament taught and meant about My Father's forgiving grace and mercy, and what His will was and is for His covenant people." To understand these things is to understand the heart and soul of Matthew's Gospel.

Ministry in Jerusalem

1 After Jesus arrives at Bethphage on the Mount of Olives, He sends two of His disciples to bring Him an ass on which to ride into Jerusalem. Matthew reports that they bring Him both an ass and a colt, the foal of an ass. Although it is possible that they actually brought Him two beasts, it is also possible that Matthew's narrative incorporates the use of Hebrew parallelism in which the writer *repeats* the reference to the central thought of Jesus' need of an animal. Mark 11:1–7, Luke 19:29–35, and John 12:14 refer to only one animal; in John's narrative, Jesus is referred to as the one who seeks and finds the animal.

2 After Jesus enters Jerusalem, He attacks the Temple system, 21:10–13. Within the Court of the Gentiles, animals for sacrifice are sold—as are also doves for those who cannot afford a more expensive offering; see Leviticus 5:7. Only the coinage of Tyre can be used for these purchases; other money has to be changed for that currency. After attacking the system, Jesus *heals* the blind and the lame within the Temple precincts, 21:14. Jesus then leaves Jerusalem to spend the night in Bethany, 21:17. (After David attacked and captured Jerusalem, he had the "blind and the lame" *killed*, 2 Samuel 5:6–10.)

Jesus' attack on the Temple angers the chief priests and scribes. These two groups are referred to in Matthew's nativity narrative (2:4) and also in his first and third passion predictions, 16:21, 20:18. As Jesus' passion approaches, they show up once again to show their hostility toward Him.

3 Next morning, Jesus returns to Jerusalem, 21:18. On the way into the city, He goes to a fig tree by the side of the road, and when He finds no figs on the tree He curses it—and it immediately withers away, 21:19–22. As **ILLUSTRATION 43E** pointed out, Matthew's sequence of events in relation to the cursing of the fig tree is different from that in Mark 11:11–20. However, in both cases, Jesus' action in relation to the fig tree is a sign of the judgment that is to come upon a people that, with all their apparent piety, lack the fruit of good deeds and will soon bear the punishment for their fruitlessness.

4 When Jesus eventually enters the Temple there takes place a series of controversies that resemble those reported in Mark's Gospel. The series is interrupted by three parables of judgment on Israel, 21:28–32; 21:33–46, 22:1–14.

a. The chief priests, elders, and people question Jesus concerning His authority. Jesus responds with a counter-question concerning the authority on which John the Baptist based his actions, 21:23–27. Jesus' opponents did not heed the message of John the Baptist, and they will not heed Jesus' message either. In the brief *first parable* reported in 21: 28–32, the two sons represent *first* the religious leaders and *second* the religious outcasts who responded to John's call to repentance.

b. Jesus tells a *second parable* about the owner of a vineyard sending his representatives to collect his produce from those laboring in the vineyard. The laborers kill these servants. When the owner then sends his own son, the laborers kill him as well. The message is that just as God's people have shut their ears to the message of God's prophets down through the centuries (and even killed them!), so they will also put to death God's final messenger, His own Son, 21:33–41. However, they will pay a price for their actions. God will give His Kingdom to others—to believing Israelites and Gentiles who will produce the fruits of His Kingdom, 21:42–44. And again, the chief priests and Pharisees are furious. Although they want to arrest Jesus, they fear how the crowds might react to such an action.

c. Jesus then tells a *third parable*—that of the Marriage Feast, 22:1–14. Its message is that although the religious and political elite refuse to participate in the Messianic Banquet that God has prepared for them, God will nevertheless provide guests for that banquet. What God has prepared will not go to waste! And those who refuse God's invitation and even kill His messengers will themselves suffer the loss of their city and their own lives (which is precisely

what took place in A.D. 70 when the Romans destroyed a rebellious Jerusalem and Judah). The reference to one of the guests not wearing a wedding garment (22:11–13) points to those who desire to participate in God's banquet—but on their own terms. They show no desire to repent of their former way of life—an essential condition for admission into God's Kingdom.

5 In Matthew's next episode, Jesus has to deal with the question of whether or not God's people should pay taxes to the Roman occupying powers, 22:15–22. Should they not pay taxes only to the Temple system—and so to God? Although they expect Jesus to deal with the issue as one of "either-or," His response stresses "both-and." The readiness of Jesus' opponents to hand over a Roman coin indicates their use of Roman currency and their acceptance of the financial advantages of the Roman administration. Jesus' opponents should be less concerned about what they pay to Rome and more concerned about paying to God the good deeds that are due to Him.

a. Jesus then finds Himself having to deal with the Sadducees and their denial of the resurrection of the body and life after death, 22:23–33.

b. Next come the Pharisees, 22:34–40. They seek Jesus' opinion concerning the greatest commandment in the law. (For a devout Jew, all the commandments were to be kept with equal care, but there is evidence in Jewish sources of concern in relation to the question put to Jesus.) Jesus responds by quoting not merely one commandment but two (Deuteronomy 6:4,5, Leviticus 19:18), and welding them together as one—something that had not been done prior to Jesus' appearing on the scene.

c. Jesus then questions the Pharisees with regard to their messianic expectations, 22:41–44. He points out that although the Pharisees were waiting for a *human* descendant of David ("lord"), the One who has come is David's LORD (*God*). Now, no more questions!

6 In ch. 23, Jesus first denounces some of the scribes and Pharisees for making life difficult for ordinary people while flaunting their so-called piety and righteousness to others, 23:1–12. Jesus then unleashes a series of seven "woes" against them, 23:13,15,16,23,25,27,29. The chapter concludes with Jesus grieving over the fact that although He came to gather God's people into His community as a hen gathers her chickens under her wings (to protect them from harm and destruction), they refuse to come to Him, 23:37–39. Jesus' reference is to the Roman destruction that will eventually overtake Jerusalem and those within its walls in A.D. 70. The sub-sentence is that if Jesus' hearers would listen to Him, and believe and embrace His message, that destruction would not take place!

DISCOURSE 5

Matthew 24 and 25 are referred to as the "Eschatological Discourse." They deal with the coming of God's new age, with events that will precede it, and with how the disciples are to conduct themselves while waiting for it to break in. *That it will come* is certain; *when it will come* is known only to Jesus' Father.

In ch. 24, Jesus speaks of:

- The coming Destruction of Jerusalem and the Temple, 24:1,2
- The initial calamities that will serve as "signs" of what is coming. 24: 3–14
- The Great Tribulation; the coming desecration of the Temple by the Romans, 24:15–28
- The coming of the Son of Man, 24:29–31
- Lessons to be learned from a fig tree, 24:32–35
- The unknown day and hour, 24:36–44
- Servant: faithful or unfaithful, 24:45–51

Ch. 25 consists of three sections:

- In 25:1–13, Jesus tells the parable of ten young maidens waiting for the coming of a bridegroom. Five are wise. Five are foolish. The message is, "*Live expectantly!* The Heavenly Bridegroom will appear at any moment."
- In 25:14–30, Jesus tells the parable of the talents. The message is, "*Live responsibly!* While you are waiting for the Lord to reappear, manage the creation and life God is lending you as He wants you to use them."
- In 25:31–46, Jesus describes Himself as the Son of Man coming on the Last Day of history to separate humanity into two groups: sheep and goats. The message is "*Live compassionately!*" (See 45E.)

Matthew's Passion Narrative

1 After delivering the Eschatological Discourses, Jesus tells the disciples that His crucifixion will soon take place, 26:1,2. The chief priests and elders assemble in the palace of Caiphas, the High Priest, to devise a strategy for arresting Jesus so that they might have Him executed, 26:3–5.

2 When Jesus dines in the home of Simon the leper, a woman anoints His head with a jar of very costly ointment. Jesus commends the woman for her actions, and states that she is preparing Him for His coming burial, 26:6–13.

3 Judas asks the chief priests how much they will give him if he betrays Jesus, 26:14–16.

4 Jesus celebrates the Passover Meal with His disciples, and shares His new Holy Supper with them, 26:17–29. During the course of the meal, Jesus names Judas as the one who will betray Him, 26:25. He also tells the disciples that, although suffering and death lie in the immediate future for him, His message and ministry in relation to the Kingdom of God will be vindicated in the Resurrection. He will then share a new table fellowship with them at the Banquet of the Kingdom, 26:29.

5 Jesus and the disciples go to the Garden of Gethsemane on the slopes of the Mount of Olives, 26:30. Jesus tells the disciples that, this very night, they will all desert Him and Peter will deny Him three times, 26:31–35. (The third watch—or end of a three-hour time-block—of the night was called "cockcrow.")

6 Jesus engages in fervent prayer, seeking His Father's help to cope with the agony that is now only a matter of hours away, 26:36–46. While Jesus prays, the disciples sleep!

7 Judas leads a large crowd, armed with swords and clubs, to where Jesus is praying. Matthew makes no mention of Roman soldiers being among those who go to the Garden of Gethsemane to capture Jesus, 26:47. (Passover would have been a difficult time to find and arrest Jesus; Jerusalem was crowded. Judas solved the problem for those seeking Jesus' death.)

8 The entire Sanhedrin, with Caiphas presiding, participates in the first trial at night, 26:57–68. Among other things, Jesus' opponents accuse Him of blasphemy, 26:65—the punishment for which was death by stoning, Leviticus 24:10–16.

Note: According to the *Mishnah*, produced in written form about A.D. 200, to be guilty of blasphemy one had to pronounce "the Name itself," *Yahweh*. It is significant that in 26:64, Jesus does not use *Yahweh*, but a surrogate, "the Power." Also according to the Mishnah, the trial narrative contains elements contrary to the Jewish code of Law: trial on a feast day, a night session of the court, pronouncement of a verdict of condemnation at the same session at which testimony was received. However, it is debatable whether these laws were in force at the time of Jesus' trial—and if they were, it is possible that the Jewish leaders were so angry with Jesus that they were prepared to ignore them. They wanted Jesus dead—at any cost and as soon as possible.

9 Peter, who is present in the courtyard of the building in which the trial is being conducted, denies Jesus three times—and then weeps bitterly, 26:69–75.

10 Judas repents of his actions, returns the money to the chief priests and elders, and hangs himself. The money he returns is used to buy a potter's field, 27:3–10.

11 After being tried by the Jewish leaders, Jesus is tried by Pilate, the Roman procurator; only he could authorize an execution, 27:1,2, 11–26. Pilate offers the Jewish leaders a choice: free Barabbas (meaning, "son of the father") or Jesus (the true Son of the Father). Although Pilate's wife (a *Gentile* woman) tells him to have nothing to do with "that innocent man," and although he washes his hands before Jesus' accusers, he hands Jesus over for crucifixion. (According to Deuteronomy 21:1–8, when dealing with a murder when the killer is unknown, the elders of the city nearest to where the body is found must wash their hands and declare, "Our hands did not shed this blood.")

12 Roman soldiers mock and abuse Jesus, 27:27–31. (Although Jesus answers back to Satan during His temptation, He does not do so to the Roman soldiers who abuse Him.) Among other things, the soldiers place a *crown* of thorns on Jesus' head, and place a mock *scepter* in His hand, 27:29. (The term "cohort" in 27:27 usually denotes 600 soldiers.) They then lead Jesus to the place where He is to be crucified, 27:26–31. Along the way, they compel Simon of Cyrene to carry Jesus' cross—most likely, the cross bar only, 27:32. After placing Jesus on His cross, they offer Jesus a drink designed to make it easier for Him to endure the pain—but He refuses it, 26:33,34. In keeping what was usually done when executing a political rebel, the soldiers divide Jesus' clothing among themselves; Jesus is crucified naked. The soldiers put a sign above Jesus' head, "This is Jesus, the King of the Jews" (v. 37), and keep watch, v. 36. Ironically, a sign meant to mock Jesus declares the truth about Him.

13 While Jesus is on the cross, He is mocked by the two bandits (most likely, Zealots) who are crucified with him, by those who surround the cross, and by the chief priests, scribes, and elders, 27:38–44. However, when the centurions and his associates see what is taking place—including an earthquake—they are terrified and say, "Truly, this man was God's Son!" (27:54). Indeed, if God cannot get a true confession from the lips of His own people, He will get it from the lips of Gentiles!

14 As also in Mark and Luke, darkness covers the land at midday; three hours later Jesus breathes His last, 27:45–50. Like Mark, Matthew quotes only one Word from the Cross, "Eli, Eli, lema sabachthani?", 27:46. According to Matthew 27:50 (as also in John 19:30), Jesus finally gives up His spirit and dies. Several women observe what is taking place, 27:55,56.

15 After Jesus' death, the earth shakes, rocks split open, tombs are opened, and those in the tombs appear to many in Jerusalem *after* Jesus' resurrection, 27:51–53. These events reflect Ezekiel 37:1–14 and declare that, through Jesus' ministry, passion, and resurrection, the long-awaited Kingdom of God has broken into history.

The Jewish leaders looked forward to the coming of a Messiah who would defeat the Romans. They now look up at a "Messiah" who has been defeated by the Romans. How wrong they are! The Messiah has conquered the real enemy—Satan, and the kingdom and power of the demonic! The age of death is over! The true Messianic Age has begun!

16 Joseph of Arimathea (a town 5 miles or 8 kilometers north of Jerusalem)—also a disciple of Jesus—obtains Pilate's permission to take Jesus' body down from the cross, wraps the body in clean linen cloth, places it into his own new tomb (hewn out of rock), rolls a stone across the entrance of the tomb, and goes away, 27:57–60. Mary Magdalene and "the other Mary" observe *what* Joseph of Arimathea does—and *where* he does it, 27:61. They know the location of the tomb in which Jesus is buried!

17 The next day, the Chief Priests and Pharisees seek Pilate's permission to have Jesus' tomb sealed and guarded. The burial in Joseph's tomb, and the presence of Jewish (and possibly some Roman) guards, set the scene for the explosive events that follow on Easter Sunday morning, 27:62–66.

18 Throughout Matthew's passion narrative, Jesus remains the majestic Messiah of Israel. Although this theme is present also in Mark, it is given particular emphasis in Matthew. Jesus knows what awaits Him. He predicts what the Jewish leaders will do to Him, 26:12,18.

He knows who will betray Him, 26:25. He predicts that Peter will deny Him, 26:34. His captors cannot seize Him until He has confronted Judas with his treachery, 26:50. When the High Priest commands Jesus to reveal His identity, Jesus—with majestic dignity—predicts His eventual exaltation to the right hand of God, 26:64. Those who file past Jesus' cross jeer Him and ridicule His claim to be God's Son (27:39–44). However, when death comes, Roman soldiers acclaim Jesus to be the true Son of God and nature erupts to draw attention to Jesus' identity and victory, 27:51–54.

Matthew's Resurrection Narrative

1 The opening of Jesus' tomb is associated with an earthquake; those guarding the tomb are terrified by this experience, 28:1–4. As an angel of the Lord spoke to Joseph after Mary conceived (1:20–25), so too an angel of the Lord speaks to the women who go to the empty tomb on Easter Sunday morning, 28:2–7.

2 The risen Jesus meets women near the tomb, and there is a mutual greeting, 28:9,10.

3 The problem of the empty tomb is reported to the Jewish leaders, who in turn try to keep the matter quiet by resorting to bribery. They concoct a false story instead of believing in Jesus' triumph, 28:11–15. The tomb is certainly empty! According to those guarding the tomb, Jesus body has been stolen; according to Jesus' brothers and sisters, Jesus has risen from the dead!

4 Jesus meets His disciples (referred to as "brothers" in 28:10) in Galilee. Although some worship Him, others have doubts about Him, 28:16,17.

5 Jesus points to His kingly authority and sends His disciples forth to draw people from all nations into His community. His disciples are to teach all nations and to baptize them in the name of the Father, the Son, and the Holy Spirit. They are to teach His new followers to observe (not just "believe") all that He has commanded them, 28:16–20.

6 In Matthew's *first narrative*, Jesus is referred to as Emmanuel, *God with us*, 1:23. In Matthew's closing narrative, Jesus assures His disciples that *He will be with them* to the close of the age, 28:20.

45E

Jesus and the End

1 Matthew stresses the importance of taking seriously the final appearance of Jesus at the end of time. His fifth discourse (chs. 24,25) is an expansion of Mark's "Little Apocalypse" (ch. 13).

2 Jesus predicts the coming destruction of the Jerusalem Temple and the nation by the Romans, 24:1,2; 24:15–28. In 24:3–14, He speaks of troubles that will occur in the religious and political realms prior to the final appearing of the Son of Man, 24:29–31. When Jesus referred to vultures gathering on a corpse (24:28), possibly His hearers detected a reference to the eagle carried on the standards of the Roman army; the corpse of Palestinian Judaism was to be swooped on by the eagles of Rome. Although Jesus urges His followers to equip themselves to read the signs (24:32–35), He insists that only His Father in heaven knows when the end will take place, 24:36–44.

3 Several parables follow in which Jesus stresses that the faithful must be ready for His final appearing at all times. He encourages the faithful and warns the lax, 24:45–51. When the Lord reappears, some will be ready and some will be caught unprepared, 25:1–13; therefore, *live expectantly.* While waiting for the final day, the faithful are to use the life and material goods God is lending them in a responsible manner, 25:14–30; therefore, *live responsibly.* The message of 25:31–46 is, *live compassionately* (see *middle section* of **ILLUSTRATION 45E** below).

4 While anticipating the end, the faithful are to witness both to "the lost sheep of the house of Israel" (10:5,6) and to all nations, 28:19,20. Indeed, the end cannot come until Jesus' Good News of the Kingdom is proclaimed throughout the world, 24:14. Until the end comes, the new community is to confess Jesus before the world (10:32,33), demonstrate a discipleship that reflects Jesus (10:7,8), baptize in the name of the triune God (28:19,20), and teach and exhort others to do God's will. They are to be aware at all times that they are members of an eternal community in whose midst Jesus dwells, 28:20. When the end comes, the Lord will manifest His presence in glory and splendor to welcome His own into His Father's Eternal Home, Matthew 25:34.

The *upper* and *middle sections* of **ILLUSTRATION 45E** depict the message of Matthew 25:31–46—a passage that defines what will take place on the final day of history.

Upper section

Matthew 25:31-34

- Jesus will reappear in glory (***crowned, triumphant Jesus in posture of welcome***), command all the graves to give up their dead, and gather all nations before Him, v. 31.
- When Jesus gathers before Him all nations, He will separate them into two groups, placing the ***sheep at His right hand*** and the ***goats at His left hand***, vv. 32,33.
- Having done this, Jesus will speak first to the sheep at His right. He will address a word of invitation ("Come") to those who are blessed by His Father (v. 34), and invite them to inherit the kingdom prepared for them from the foundation of the world.
- Those finally received into the Father's house are welcomed ("Come", 25:34) only because they are "blessed" by Jesus' Father; they "inherit" (not "merit") the "kingdom" prepared "*for* them" (not "*by* them") before the beginning of time (when they were not present to help prepare it). God has done it all. All cause for human boasting is eliminated. Grace reigns supreme.

Middle section

Matthew 25:35-46

- Jesus will welcome His own on the basis of forgiving grace, and commend them for acts of service they have rendered to others, 25:35,36 (***servant figures***).

- They gave food to the hungry (***plate, knife, fork***), drink to the thirsty (***drinking glass***), companionship to the lonely (***person cut off from others***), and *clothing* to those lacking it. They also visited and cared for the sick (***symbol of healing, serpent around staff***), and visited the ***prisoner (behind bars)***.

  When serving people in these situations of need, they were serving none other than Jesus.
- Jesus will dismiss those who claim to know Him (Matthew 25:44, "Lord"), but do nothing to demonstrate it. Jesus does not refer to any evil that they might have done, but to the good that they failed to do. They failed to serve Jesus in His distressing disguises.
- Jesus' words serve as a reminder that Christians are to distinguish between *the basis of acceptance* (God's grace), and *the basis of commendation* (service rendered to others, and so to Jesus). No deed of service is to be done for the sake of reward, but to meet need for its own sake, Matthew 25:37–39.

Lower section

- ***Food and drink*** *(left)***:** The Gospels frequently refer to Jesus sharing a meal with His disciples and followers. His followers today are to understand that He is present with them constantly (Matthew 28:20)–in a meaningful way also at mealtime.
- ***Drop of water—symbol for baptism:*** Baptism is not about committing life to God and doing good deeds in the hope of being accepted into heaven. It is about being adopted by God into His family, being declared brothers and sisters of Jesus and sharers in all that He achieved for sinful humanity, being granted the joy of living in Jesus' forgiving presence, and inspired to reflect Jesus as forgiving Savior and Servant Lord in all thoughts, words, and deeds.
- ***Bread and cup:*** In the Lord's Supper, Jesus invites His brothers and sisters to dine with Him and of Him, and then to go forth to reflect His presence and Servant lifestyle in all they think, say, and do.
- ***Basin and towel*** *(right)***:** As Jesus washed His disciples' feet, so He calls His brothers and sisters to serve each other. Because we are "re-membered" to Him in the Eucharist, we should also seek to make Him visible in the manner in which we use life as His servant-people.

Jesus and the Bible's "Big Story"

A number of times in the sermon on the mount, Jesus refers to what had been taught by previous teachers in Judaism, and then adds, "But I say to you...," 5:21,22; 5:27,28; 5:31,32; 5:33,34; 5:38,39; 5:43,44. Jesus *speaks* the final Word of God because He *is* the Final Word of God incarnate. **ILLUSTRATION 45F** summarizes the events and theology of the biblical narrative, and shows how Jesus brings the teachings of the law and the prophets to their intended meaning.

1 ***GENESIS 1–11:*** As the human race grows, God eventually calls ***ABRAHAM*** to be the first of a people formed to carry out God's mission to humanity. The ***four blocks of blue, red, and yellow in the triangle*** (*left*) refer to the four narratives of *SIN—JUDGMENT—GRACE* in Genesis 1–11. The ***symbol below*** depicts the chaos that sin caused. (See **ILLUSTRATION 4D**.)

2 ***Major Covenants 1,2,3:*** The three major Old Testament covenants are those with ***ABRAHAM*** and ***DAVID*** (covenants of ***DIVINE COMMITMENT***), and that with Israel at Mt. ***SINAI*** (a covenant of ***HUMAN OBLIGATION***). In the covenants with Abraham and David, God makes promises about what He will do for them and their descendants *in the future*; hence, in each case the ***attached arrow points forward***. At Mt. Sinai, God makes no promises concerning future actions, but lists what He has done for His people *in the past*; hence, the ***attached arrow points backward***. The term "Obligation" in relation to the Sinai covenant does not imply that God's people have to do something to be accepted by God; rather, it implies that God calls those whom He, in forgiving grace, has declared to be His people to seek to live as His obedient people.

3 The ***circle of small circles around Sinai*** shows that God gathers a *community* around Himself at Sinai. The Old Testament scriptures began referring to this community as a ***NATION*** (Exodus 19:3–6), as the ***PEOPLE*** of God (Exodus 5:22,23), and as the ***SON*** of God, Exodus 4:21–23.

4 After making the ***Sinai covenant***, God does not depart, but resides among His people in the ***Tabernacle***. Israel is to understand itself as a community of people living around the presence of God. The ***law-code*** provides behavior guidelines for life in God's community.

5 The ***PROPHETS*** attack the nation on the basis of the Sinai covenant. They insist that unless the people repent and return to the Lord, destruction will overtake them. The people do not listen. The Northern Kingdom is exiled and destroyed in 721 B.C. Judah goes to ***EXILE IN BABYLON*** in 597 and 587 B.C. While in exile, the people ask many questions (***question marks***). In particular, what troubled the people greatly during the latter stage of their time in Babylon, and also during the *postexilic period*, was the fact that the Davidic dynasty was no more! They prayed to God to give them back their kings, Psalm 89 (***crown with question mark above it***).

6 Isaiah 40–55 spoke a message of comfort and hope to the exiles in Babylon. These chapters state that God formed Israel to be a ***LIGHT*** *to the nations*, a ***SERVANT*** *people*. When the discipline of the exile was over, God would lead His people back to the Promised Land. God would transform the nation and the land—making the land a ***NEW CREATION***, a *new Garden of Eden*, Isaiah 51:1–3.

7 ***JUDAISM*** developed slowly but surely in the centuries following the return from Babylon (***expanding lines***). Throughout the postexilic period (with the exception of the Maccabean-Hasmonean period), the nation was under foreign domination (***Roman helmet and sword***). Some zealously studied the sacred writings (***scrolls***) to discover more about why the nation had gone into exile; their goal was to avoid a repetition of the disaster. Various groups sought to hasten the coming of the Messianic Age—

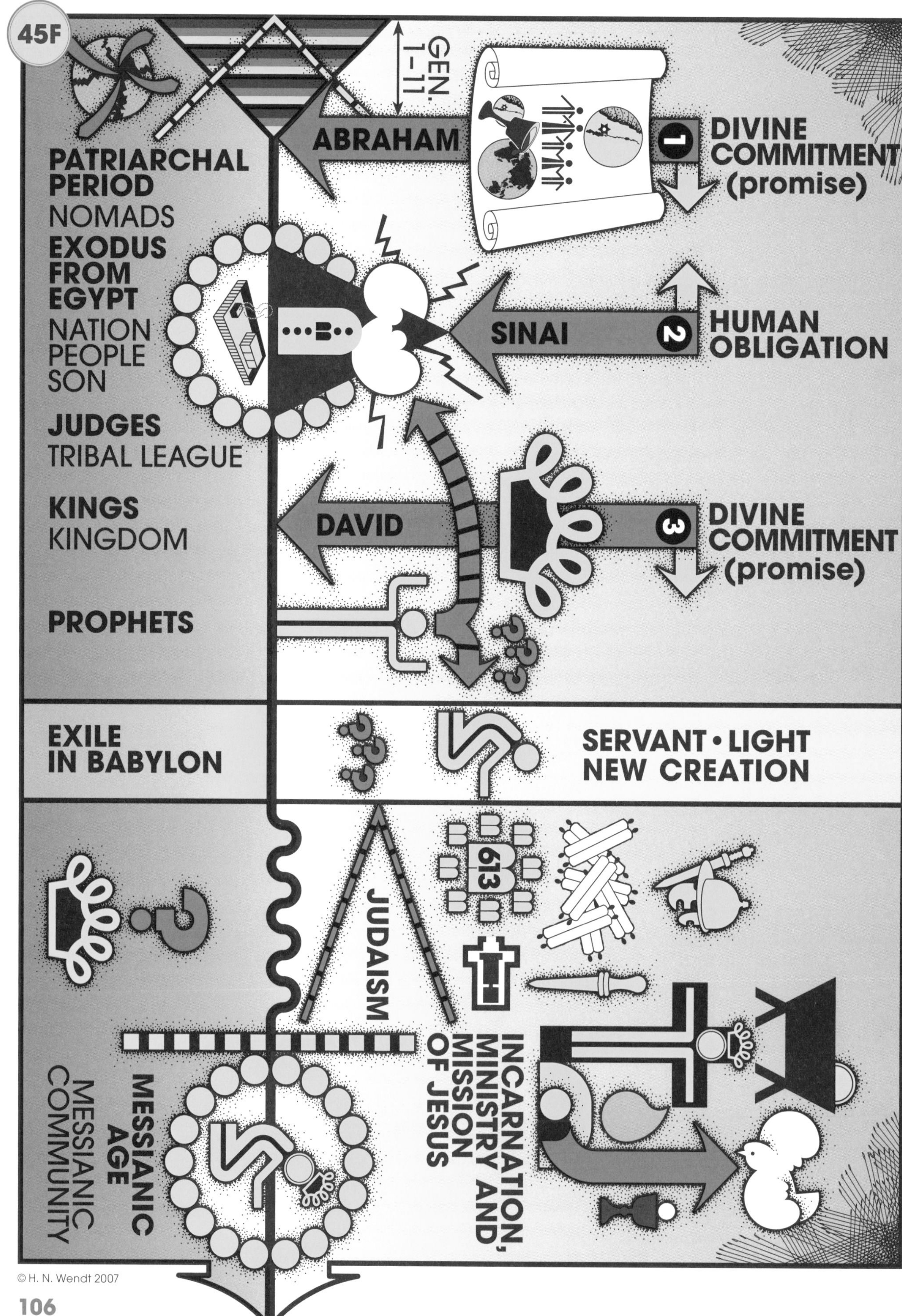
45F
GEN. 1–11
ABRAHAM
1 DIVINE COMMITMENT (promise)
PATRIARCHAL PERIOD
NOMADS
EXODUS FROM EGYPT
NATION
PEOPLE
SON
SINAI
2 HUMAN OBLIGATION
JUDGES
TRIBAL LEAGUE
KINGS
KINGDOM
DAVID
3 DIVINE COMMITMENT (promise)
PROPHETS
EXILE IN BABYLON
SERVANT • LIGHT
NEW CREATION
613
JUDAISM
INCARNATION, MINISTRY AND MISSION OF JESUS
MESSIANIC AGE
MESSIANIC COMMUNITY

some by obedience to the ***law-codes*** (*scribes and Pharisees*), some by worship rituals in the ***Temple*** (*priests*), and others by the power of the ***sword*** (*Zealots*).

8 *INCARNATION, MINISTRY AND MISSION OF JESUS*

Eventually Jesus the Messiah came in a most surprising manner and for a most surprising mission—to establish a very surprising kind of ***MESSIANIC COMMUNITY***.

- Jesus was placed in a ***manger*** in a simple home in Bethlehem,
- was declared to be *King* and *Servant* at His ***baptism***,
- gathered, taught, and commissioned a *community* of followers,
- was ***crucified***, ***died***, ***was buried in a tomb***, and ***rose from the dead***.

Jesus continues among His people as the Living Word who alone may determine and proclaim Truth (***circle of small circles around Servant-King***). Jesus remains among His people through:

- His *Holy Spirit* (***dove***)—the work of Jesus and the work of the Spirit are one and inseparable. The Spirit continues the work of Jesus.
- *Holy baptism* (***drop of water***)—through which God adopts us into His family as sons and daughters; that is, brothers and sisters of Jesus.
- His *Holy Supper* (***bread and cup***)—Jesus shares a meal with His people.

Jesus As "Fulfillment"

1 Matthew's general outline and structure suggest that he saw in Jesus a new Moses who came to carry out a new Exodus, a new rescue mission:

- to free God's people from bondage to sin, Satan, judgment, and condemnation; and,
- to lead them into the inheritance of an eternal relationship with His Father.

Soon after His ministry begins, Jesus (as did Moses) takes the disciples and others to a *mountain* and teaches them His Father's will (chs. 5–7) which He himself models throughout life. In the transfiguration, Jesus leads Peter, James, and John up a *mountain*, 17:1–9. In Matthew's final scene, Jesus meets with the disciples on a *mountain*, 28:16–20.

2 The first word Jesus speaks in the Sermon on the Mount is "Blessed," a term that occurs nine times in nine verses, 5:3–11. Jesus' definition of the term is very different from that given in Deuteronomy 28:1–14. Jesus never links being blessed to possessing and enjoying material goods. He links it only to reflecting His servant life-style. The path of life He spells out is not a plan for *effecting* fellowship with God, but a guideline for *reflecting* fellowship with God. Jesus' teachings supplant all previous teachings. He removes the yoke of the scribal demands from the neck of God's people and replaces it with His own light yoke, Matthew 11:28–30.

Although some Pharisees thanked God daily that they were not born an outcast, a Gentile, or a woman, immediately after the Sermon on the Mount, Jesus shows compassion to a leper (8:1–4), a Gentile (8:5–13), and a woman (8:14–17). All human criteria concerning worthiness must yield to the principle of supreme mercy.

3 In Matthew 5:17, Jesus says: "Do not think that I have come to abolish the law or the prophets; I have not come to abolish but to fulfill." Jesus is not saying that He has come to fulfill Old Testament prophecies in a literal, mechanical manner. Jesus is saying that He has come to bring the teaching of the law and the prophets to their original, intended meaning. Jesus' ministry and teaching are not merely an addendum to Judaism, adding to it a few details not previously dealt with. Jesus' Person and ministry constitute a radical reform movement, a new beginning to the people of God.

4 Jesus' life demonstrates, and His teaching proclaims, God's true purpose and will for humanity. Obedience involves a single-minded dedication to reflecting Jesus' behavior patterns in dealing with others, 5:44,45,48. Calculation and manipulation in determining the will of God are ruled out. Unlike the Pharisees who *teach* correctly but do not *live* correctly (5:17–20, ch. 23), Jesus' followers are to learn to know, do, and teach the will of God, 7:21–23. They are to emulate the example of their Lord whose life demonstrates the intended meaning and purpose of God's Law, God's Torah.

5 Jesus does not call His followers to debate what constitutes obedience and to perform rituals for their own sake. He calls them to focus on living compassionately: giving food to the hungry, drink to the thirsty, lodging to the stranger, clothing to the naked, help to the sick, and showing concern to the prisoner, Matthew 25:31–46. Jesus allows no room for establishing first, second, or third levels of priority in the use of life; obedience in His kingdom is to be a full-time concern. He calls His followers to devote all of life to the worship and service of God, Matthew 4:10 ("only"). The significance of the word "first" in Matthew 6:33 is understood more clearly if Jesus' message is summarized as, "Devote yourself *full-time* to seeking the things of the Kingdom of God." The word is not to be understood in terms of "priorities in life" but rather in terms of "total focus in life." The word "first" finds no mention in the parallel passage in Luke 12:31.

6 Jesus does not call His followers into a private relationship with Himself, but into the fellowship of His community. Greatness within this community is not determined by achievement for self, but by service rendered to others, 20:25–28. Each member must do nothing to harm the faith of another (18:1–9), but must forgive without limit (18:21,22), seek the straying with compassionate zeal (18:12–14), and confront the indifferent with loving firmness, 18:15–20.

7 Although both good and bad will be found in the community, the obedient are not to waste time evaluating their performance or rectifying undesirable situations. They are to sow God's mercy and will energetically and leave it to God to reap the harvest, 13:24–30. Throughout life, they are to apply themselves to learning and doing the things of God's Kingdom lest they be found among the bad weeds to be thrown into the fire on the last day, 13:47–50.

8 Although Matthew's Jesus unleashes some blistering attacks on His opponents for their hypocrisy and lack of faith, this may reflect the frustration of the early church that, although many Gentiles accepted Jesus and embraced His message and mission, the majority of Jews did not.

It is unfortunate that anti-Semitism eventually appeared and justified itself by referring to some of the statements in Matthew's Gospel. It is wise to remember that not all Jews rejected Jesus; it is more correct to refer to those who opposed Jesus as His "enemies" rather than as "the Jews."

SUMMARY

45A In His teaching ministry, Jesus declares numerous times that He has not come to destroy the Law and the Prophets, but to "fulfill" them—to bring them to their intended meaning. Although Jewish rabbis taught that God had given Noah and his descendants (non-Jews) seven commandments, God gave the descendants of Abraham 613 commandments and many oral traditions. However, Jesus gives His followers, His brothers and sisters, one central commandment: to love and serve one another as He has loved and served them—in all they think, say, and do.

45B Matthew contains some unique details. Whereas David had decreed that the blind and the lame were to be denied access to the Temple, after attacking the Temple system, Jesus heals the blind and the lame. When returning to the Temple the next day, Jesus curses a fig tree—which dies immediately. When confronted by the Chief Priests, Sadducees, elders, Pharisees and scribes, Jesus tells three parables: how two sons respond to their father's order; what wages the owner of a vineyard pays to his workers; the response of those invited to a marriage feast. When denouncing the scribes and Pharisees, Jesus proclaims seven "woes."

45C Unique details in Matthew's passion narrative are: Judas offers to lead Jewish leaders—for a price and at night—to a place when they can arrest Jesus. When Judas observes the end result of his betrayal, he hangs himself. Both Pilate's wife, and Pilate himself, declare Jesus "not guilty." Pilate washes his hands to tell Jesus' accusers that they alone are responsible for what is about to take place. After Jesus breathes His last, cosmic signs occur. Dead persons return to life—and show themselves to others after Jesus' resurrection. The Jewish leaders place guards at Jesus' tomb—to ensure that His body will not be stolen by His supporters.

45D On Easter Sunday morning, Jesus' departure from the tomb is linked to an earthquake. Those guarding His tomb are terrified. An angel tells the two Marys that Jesus has returned to life, and they are to tell the disciples to go to Galilee where they will meet the Risen Jesus. After meeting with the disciples, Jesus instructs them to witness about Him to the ends of the earth.

45E In ch. 24, Jesus describes the events that will take place prior to the coming destruction of Jerusalem, and outlines what will transpire on the Last Day. In ch. 25, He tells three parables that summon His hearers (and all humanity) to live *expectantly*, *responsibly*, and *compassionately*. Jesus assures His beloved and blessed brothers and sisters that, on that Last Day, He will welcome them into His Eternal Home where they will spend eternity in His presence. Although that welcome will be based on God's forgiving grace, Jesus will commend His family members for spending life caring for Him by caring for the needy around them. At the same time, He will reject those who claimed to know Him but failed to serve Him in all His "distressing disguises."

45F The New Testament writings present Jesus as the One in Whom all previous history and beliefs achieve their "grand finale." In Jesus, there is a new beginning to the people of God and a new beginning to the Davidic dynasty. Jesus' ministry constitutes a "reform movement" in relation to the Sinai Covenant—a clarification of God's intended mission and will for His people.

45G As Moses once ascended a mountain, Jesus gathers His new people around Him on a mountain to explain to them the true will of God for their lives. When defining the meaning of the term "blessed," Jesus does not link it to possessing and enjoying material things; He links it to knowing and reflecting His servant lifestyle.

CROSSWAYS®
5
SECTION
UNITS 41–50
The Gospels and Acts
UNIT 46
Luke (I)
Early Narratives and Ministry in Galilee
GENESIS
MATTHEW
MARK
LUKE
JOHN
2 SAMUEL
ACTS
PSALMS
ISAIAH
JEREMIAH
EZEKIEL
AMOS
ROMANS
1 CORINTHIANS
2 CORINTHIANS
GALATIANS
EPHESIANS
PHILIPPIANS
COLOSSIANS
1 THESSALONIANS
2 THESSALONIANS
1 TIMOTHY
2 TIMOTHY
TITUS
PHILEMON
HEBREWS
JAMES
1 PETER
2 PETER
1 JOHN
2 JOHN
3 JOHN
JUDE
REVELATION

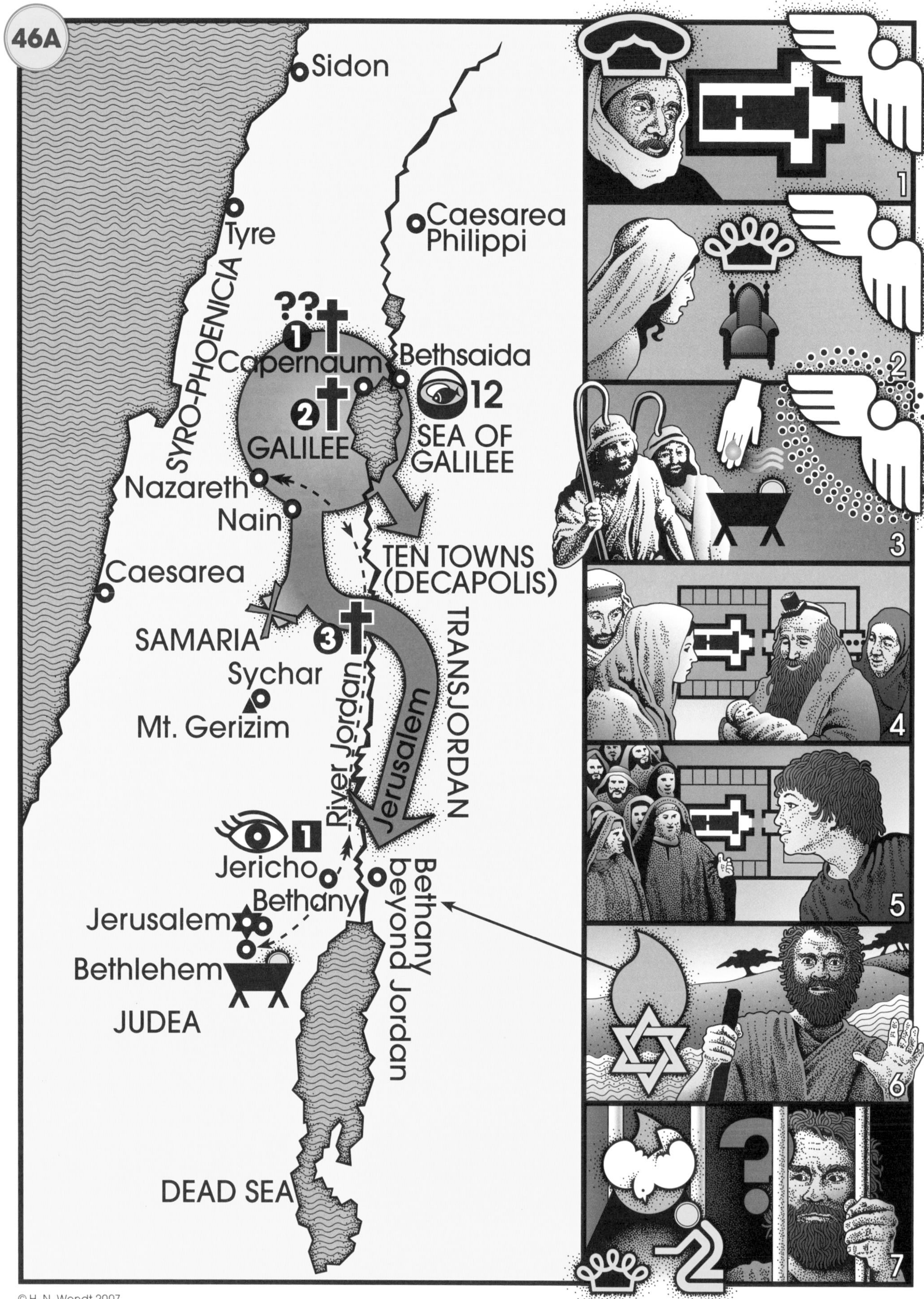
46A
Sidon
Tyre
Caesarea Philippi
SYRO-PHOENICIA
??
1
Capernaum
Bethsaida
12
2
GALILEE
SEA OF GALILEE
Nazareth
Nain
Caesarea
TEN TOWNS (DECAPOLIS)
SAMARIA
3
TRANSJORDAN
Sychar
Mt. Gerizim
River Jordan
Jerusalem
1
Jericho
Bethany
Bethany beyond Jordan
Jerusalem
Bethlehem
JUDEA
DEAD SEA
1
2
3
4
5
6
7

Luke's Geographical Outline

Compare the *left section* of **ILLUSTRATION 46A** with the *left section* of **ILLUSTRATION 42B**. (The *right section* of **ILLUSTRATION 46A** will be dealt with in 46D.)

1 Mark contains no nativity narrative. He introduces us to an adult Jesus living in ***Nazareth*** of ***GALILEE*** who goes to John the Baptist to be baptized (most likely at ***Bethany beyond Jordan***, John 1:28). However, Luke contains a number of narratives about events in the "Jesus' story" prior to His baptism by John. (These will be analyzed in the latter part of 46B.)

2 Luke's Gospel contains a lengthy section describing the ministry of John the Baptist that closes with a reference to John the Baptist being imprisoned by Herod Antipas, 3:1–20. In his Gospel, Mark does not tell us where that ministry took place—as John does in his Gospel; see John 1:28.

3 Reference is then made to Jesus being baptized, to the heavens being opened, to the Holy Spirit descending on Jesus, and to a heavenly voice declaring Him to be King and Servant, 3:21,22. Although no reference is made to John the Baptist in relation to these events, we might presume that he baptized Jesus—and that Luke's narrative does not follow a precise chronological sequence at this point.

4 Jesus carries out most of His early ministry in Galilee. He does not work in ***SYRO-PHOENICIA*** as He does in both Mark and Matthew. However, He does minister to the man possessed with demons in the ***DECAPOLIS*** region, 8:22–39.

5 Jesus feeds the 5,000, not in Galilee (Mark 6:1,6, 30–46), but in the vicinity of ***Bethsaida***, 9:10–17 (in Jewish territory ruled by Herod Phillip). As in Mark's narrative, there are ***12 baskets of left-over bread and fish***.

6 Jesus does not leave Galilee to travel north to ***Caesarea Philippi***. His first two passion predictions take place within Galilee, 9:21,22: ***❶, cross, two question marks***; 9:43–45: ***❷, cross***. As in Mark's narrative (10:1,32–34), Jesus predicts His passion for the third time after He leaves Galilee and is on His way to Jerusalem, 9:51; 18:31–33: ***❸, cross***.

7 While traveling from Galilee to Jerusalem, Jesus tells many parables. Prior to *entering* ***Jericho***, Jesus gives sight (***eye, 1***) to a (nameless) blind man, 18:35–43. (In Mark's narrative, Jesus heals blind Bartimaeus *after* leaving Jericho, 10:46–52. In Matthew's narrative, Jesus heals two (nameless) blind men after *leaving* Jericho, 20:29–34.)

8 Luke reports Jesus leaving Galilee in 9:51 and arriving in the vicinity of ***Jerusalem*** in 19:29. Jesus enters Jerusalem on a Sunday, and immediately attacks the Temple, 19:45,46. (In Mark's Gospel, Jesus attacks the Temple on the Monday after Palm Sunday, 11:11–19.)

Luke's Outline

1 Although Luke's Gospel reveals a concern for all nations, it makes no mention of Jesus preaching to Gentiles. Why? Luke's Gospel is the first volume of a two volume work, Luke-Acts. Acts continues on from where the Gospel concludes. What Jesus proclaims to the Jews in Luke, He proclaims (through the apostles and others) to the Gentiles in Acts. Luke's two volumes constitute about a quarter of the New Testament—a greater percentage than Paul's writings.

2 Luke presents Jesus as the key to understanding God's purpose in universal history. He divides history into three eras:

First era: From ancient Israel to John the Baptist (note 16:16): John's work marks the end of the era of the Law and the Prophets. Although redemptive hopes were cherished during this era, they were not realized.

Second era: The earthly ministry of Jesus (note 4:21): This is divided into three sections:

- Jesus' nativity in Bethlehem and early ministry in Galilee, 1:1–9:50.
- Jesus' journey from Galilee to Jerusalem, and His ministry along the way, 9:51–19:28.
- Jesus' ministry in Jerusalem: His passion, death, resurrection, and ascension, 19:28–24:53.

Third era: From Jesus' ascension until the end of the age (see Luke 24:50–52, Acts 1:1–5, note vv. 4,5): During this period, Jesus, seated at the Father's "right hand" (a symbol of cosmic authority), accomplishes His purposes through the power of His Holy Spirit at work among humanity.

3 Luke traces Jesus' ancestry back to Adam (3:23–38) and calls Adam "the son of God," 3:38. God is making a new beginning to the human race, and Jesus, the new Son of God, is God's instrument to bring this about. (In Matthew's Gospel, God is making a new beginning to the chosen people, Matthew 1:1.)

4 Jerusalem plays a key role in all four Gospels. However, Matthew's Gospel mentions Jerusalem ten times, Mark's Gospel mentions Jerusalem fourteen times, and Luke mentions Jerusalem thirty times in his Gospel and fifty-seven times in Acts. Luke's narrative begins and ends in the Temple, 1:5–23; 24:50–53. Furthermore, Luke reverses the second and third incidents Matthew refers to in his temptation narrative (4:1–11)—thus making the Jerusalem Temple the stage for the third incident, 4:1–13.

Scattered throughout the travel narrative (9:51–19:28) are numerous references to Jesus being on His way to Jerusalem, 9:51, 13:22, 17:11, 18:35. During the Transfiguration, Moses and Elijah (both of whom met with God on Mt. Sinai/Mt. Horeb) speak with Jesus about the "rescue mission" (Greek: exodus) He will "complete" (not "accomplish") in Jerusalem, 9:31. He sets His face to go to that "city of death" in 9:51. His death must be in Jerusalem and by Jerusalem, 13:33. Jerusalem will treat Jesus the way it treated all the prophets and, in so doing, will bring judgment on itself, 13:34.

When Jesus arrives at the outskirts of Jerusalem, He weeps, 19:41–44. He predicts the city's destruction, 21:6. At the same time, Jerusalem is the chosen center from which salvation will spread out to the world, 9:31; 18:31; 19:11; 24:47–49; Acts 1:8. Jerusalem will play a central role in God's redemptive plan.

5 Luke's prologue (1:1–4; see the reference to "Theophilus" also in Acts 1:1–5) is written in the best Greek in the New Testament. In its complex sentences, Luke acknowledges the efforts of predecessors, states his own purpose in writing, and addresses the patron to whom the work is dedicated.
He informs Theophilus that his account of Jesus' life will demonstrate that Christianity is not an evil thing, but the way of truth. When Luke sets out to defend the Christian faith, he does not argue about it. He simply lets it tell its own story.

6 Luke's story may be outlined as follows:

PROLOGUE		(1:1–4)
1		**Infancy Naratives** (1:5–2:52)
	1:5–56	Annunciations ● *The annunciation of the birth of John the Baptist, 1:5–25* ● *The annunciation of the birth of Jesus, 1:26–38* ● *The visit of Mary to Elizabeth, 1:39–56*
	1:57–2:52	The birth of John and Jesus; the childhood of Jesus ● *The birth of John the Baptist, 1:57–80* ● *The birth of Jesus, 2:1–40* ● *The boy Jesus in the Temple, 2:41–52*
2		**Preparation for the Public Ministry** (3:1–4:13)
	3:1–20	John the Baptist
	3:21,22	The baptism of Jesus
	3:23–38	The genealogy of Jesus
	4:1–13	The temptation of Jesus
3		**The Galilean Ministry** (4:14–9:50)
	4:14–44	Jesus at Nazareth and Capernaum
	5:1–6:16	From the call of Peter to the choosing of the Twelve
	6:17–9:9	The ministry proper
	9:10–50	The climax of the ministry
4		**The Travel Narrative** (9:51–19:27)
		Jesus tells many parables while on His way to Jerusalem; eleven are dealt with in Crossways International's *The Parables of Jesus.*
5		**The Jerusalem Ministry** (19:28–21:38)
	19:28–48	Jesus' entry into Jerusalem
	20:1–21:4	Controversies
	21:5–38	Discourse on the fall of Jerusalem
6		**The Passion, Resurrection, and Ascension** (22:1–24:53)
	22:1–38	The upper room
	22:39–23:56	The passion, crucifixion, and burial
	24:1–53	The resurrection and ascension

46C

Luke's Nativity Narrative

(In this section, the author uses insights gleaned from Dr. Kenneth Bailey who spent forty years teaching in seminaries in Egypt, Lebanon, Israel, and Cyprus. His insights help westerners "see" the biblical message through Middle Eastern eyes.)

Luke's nativity narrative (2:1–20) is well known around the world. Frames 1–3 of **ILLUSTRATION 46A** depict the "traditional story."

1 ***Joseph*** and a ***very pregnant Mary*** (on a ***donkey***) travel from ***Nazareth*** through *Samaria* (a direct route) to ***Bethlehem***—passing through or near *Jerusalem* along the way.

2 After arriving in Bethlehem, they seek accommodation at an ***inn***—but none is available.

3 They find, or are offered, accommodation in a ***stable***—and only just in time, for Jesus is born soon after they arrive. Joseph and Mary wrap Jesus in swaddling clothes and place Him in a ***manger***. ***Shepherds*** come to worship Jesus, and ***wise men*** (Matthew 2:1–12) bring Him gifts.

Frames 4–6 depict the "real story."

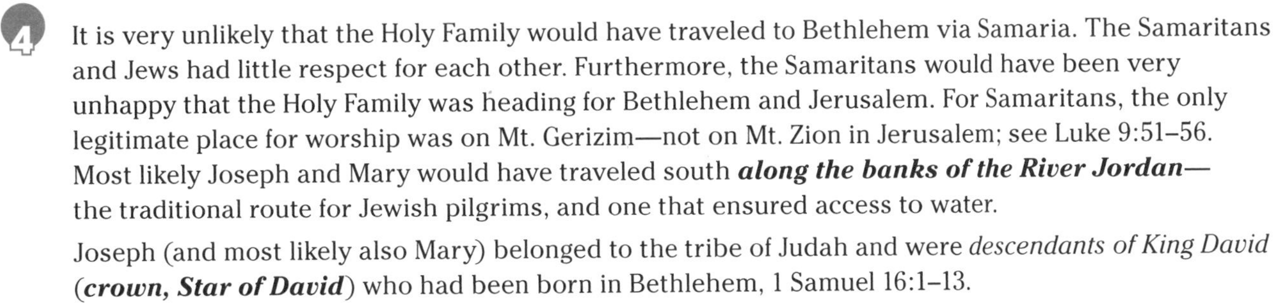

4 It is very unlikely that the Holy Family would have traveled to Bethlehem via Samaria. The Samaritans and Jews had little respect for each other. Furthermore, the Samaritans would have been very unhappy that the Holy Family was heading for Bethlehem and Jerusalem. For Samaritans, the only legitimate place for worship was on Mt. Gerizim—not on Mt. Zion in Jerusalem; see Luke 9:51–56. Most likely Joseph and Mary would have traveled south ***along the banks of the River Jordan***— the traditional route for Jewish pilgrims, and one that ensured access to water.

Joseph (and most likely also Mary) belonged to the tribe of Judah and were *descendants of King David* (***crown, Star of David***) who had been born in Bethlehem, 1 Samuel 16:1–13.

5 Although there were inns in the Palestine of Jesus' day, they were usually built on Roman roads and located about 16–18 miles—26 to 29 kilometers—apart (a day's journey for camels and donkeys carrying items for trade). Inns of that day were rather rough places that drew a rough clientele; it would have been unlikely for a man to bring his pregnant wife to such an establishment. However, Bethlehem (with a population of perhaps 150–200) was not on a Roman road, and there were no inns in Bethlehem. Furthermore, it would have been unacceptable for anyone with roots in Bethlehem to bypass relatives and seek accommodation in an inn. Joseph could have gone to any house in Bethlehem and said, "I am Joseph, son of Heli, son of Matthat, son of Levi, etc., …a descendant of David." The response would have been, "You are our kinsman! You are most welcome. Please come in. What can we do for you?" And even if there was no accommodation to be had anywhere in "the city of David" (which is unlikely), Mary had some time earlier visited her cousin Elizabeth (1:39,40) who lived but a short distance from Bethlehem. Without doubt, Elizabeth would have offered Joseph and Mary accommodation.

It is unlikely that Joseph would have taken Mary on a long journey to Bethlehem at a time when she could have given birth to Jesus at any moment. Luke reports that Joseph and Mary arrived in Bethlehem and then goes on to say, "while they were there…" suggesting that Jesus' birth took place some weeks or months later. If it was obvious when Mary arrived in Bethlehem that she was soon to have a child, it is implausible that the women of Bethlehem would have ignored Mary in her hour of need.

6 What gave rise to the "tradition" that Jesus was born in a stable? Answer: The reference in English translations to "no room in the inn," and to Jesus being placed in a manger (which gives rise to the thought of "stable"), 2:7. The word translated as "inn" (in Greek, *kataluma*) means "guest room"; it is translated this way in 22:11. Luke certainly knows the word for "inn" (*pandocheion*), and uses it in the

parable of the Good Samaritan; see 10:34. In his nativity story, Luke says that there was "no room in the guest room."

But what about the manger? In Matthew 5:15, Jesus speaks of a person lighting a lamp that gives light to *all in the house*. This could happen because many houses in Palestine in Jesus' day had one room. If a house measured 36' by 12' (11 by 3.5 meters), the family members lived in a section that measured about 30' by 12' (9 by 3.5 meters), and was about three or four feet (approximately one meter) above ground level. The remaining section, about 12' by 6' (3.5 by 2 meters), was at ground level. Each night any animals the family owned were brought into the house to spend the night in the smaller, ground-level section. They could not be stolen while there, and they contributed their body heat to the home, especially in winter. They were taken out first thing in the morning, and the space set aside for them was cleaned. Set into the upper-platform level were one or more mangers (food basins) where the animals could feed. Hence, the house where Jesus was born would have had built-in mangers.

When families could afford to do so, they added a guest room (often at a second floor level so that they did not have to buy more land). However, in some cases a house had two sections at ground level. Most likely, Joseph and Mary were welcomed into a house that had a guest room that was already occupied. If so, it was socially unacceptable for the host to ask those occupying the guest room to leave it; see Sirach 29:24–28. When Mary's time came to give birth to Jesus, the women of the house and village would have come to her aid and made available an ample supply of bedding and hot water. During the delivery process, the men of the house would have left the house for as long as necessary.

Early Narratives

See **ILLUSTRATION 46A**, *right section*

After his introductory prologue (1:1–4), Luke presents his readers with a series of narratives—many of which contain the spirit of "surprise."

Frame 1

While the aged ***priest Zechariah*** is burning incense in the Holy Place in the ***Jerusalem Temple***, the ***angel*** Gabriel appears to him and tells him that his aged wife, Elizabeth, is to conceive and bear a son. Because Elizabeth has borne no children, she is looked on as virtually an outcast, 1:25; childless women were often mocked! Zechariah entertains doubts about whether this prediction will come to pass, and loses his power of speech. Elizabeth conceives and remains in seclusion for five months, 1:24.

Frame 2

Six months after Elizabeth conceives, the ***angel*** Gabriel appears to ***Mary*** in Nazareth of Galilee, and tells her that she is to bear a son, 1:26–38. Mary, a virgin, is betrothed to Joseph—but they are not yet living together and the marriage has naturally not been consummated. Mary is to name her son "Jesus." Jesus will be a descendant of King David (***crown***) and will be given the ***throne*** of David. The meeting between the angel Gabriel and Mary takes place at a time when Caesar Augustus in Rome is at the height of his power. (Augustus died in A.D. 14, and was succeeded by the ruthless Tiberius—who was already worshiped as a god in the eastern part of the Roman Empire.)

Mary visits Elizabeth, her cousin, who lives to the south of Jerusalem near Bethlehem, 1:39–46. Elizabeth knows that Mary is pregnant, and greets her as "the mother of my Lord." Mary offers words of praise to God, 1:46–55. After staying with Elizabeth for three months, Mary returns to Nazareth, 1:56. Elizabeth gives birth to a son—who, although he should have been named after his father, is called "John" (eventually, John the Baptist). Zechariah then speaks words of prophecy, 1:67–80.

Frame 3

After Jesus is born in Bethlehem, an ***angel*** of the Lord appears at night to ***shepherds*** who are watching over their flocks. The angel tells them to go to *Bethlehem*, the city of David, where they will find the *Messiah*, the *Anointed One* (***hand, oil***), wrapped in bands of cloth and lying in a ***manger***. (Here note 2 Samuel 5:6–10 which refers to *Jerusalem* as the city of David. However, in the Gospel narratives the Old Testament "city of David" becomes the city of Jesus' opponents and enemies.) A ***heavenly host*** then praises and glorifies God. It is significant that although shepherds were seen as outcasts and forbidden entry into the Jerusalem Temple, they were the first to hear God's Good News! The glory of God is out of the Temple and surrounds the infant Jesus, God's Messiah!

Frame  4

Jesus is circumcised on the eighth day. Forty days after His birth, ***Joseph*** and ***Mary*** take Jesus to the ***Temple*** where He is honored by words from ***Simeon*** and ***Anna***, two devout, elderly persons, 2:21–38. The significance of their statements is debated.

Although *Simeon* refers to Jesus' coming ministry as a "light for revelation to the Gentiles," most likely the statement reflects a traditional Jewish hope based on Isaiah ch. 60. According to that hope, the day would come when the Jewish people would play the central role in world affairs, and the Gentiles—sitting in darkness—would have to acknowledge the supremacy of the Jews. The eventual "surprise" for the people of Jesus' day was that Jesus' ministry was not about obtaining glory for Israel, but was about calling humanity to serving—and suffering. Simeon does state that Jesus' mission would prove to be a stumbling block for many in Israel and would cause Mary deep pain, 2:28–35.

After *Anna* sees the infant Messiah, she speaks about Him to all who were looking for the redemption of *Jerusalem*, 2:36–38. However, Jesus has not come to free Jerusalem from Roman control. He has come to free God's people, and humanity at large, from control by the powers of Satan, sin, and death.

Some time later, the Holy Family returns to Nazareth in Galilee—their home town.

Frame 5

Joseph and Mary continue to visit Jerusalem and the ***Temple*** each year to celebrate the Passover, and take Jesus with them, 2:41–52. On one such visit, when the " Galilee group" sets out to return home, Joseph and Mary (referred to as His parents, 2:41, 43, 48) do so without knowing that the 12-year-old Jesus is not with them. After they return to Jerusalem and the Temple, they find *Jesus in dialogue with rabbis*. When Mary tells Jesus that His remaining in the Temple has caused them ("*your father* and I") deep anxiety, Jesus responds that they surely must have known that He would be in "*His Father's* house." *Jesus declares that His true Father is the God of the Jerusalem Temple.*

Frame 

Luke describes the ministry of ***John the Baptist*** in some detail, 3:1–20. John carries out his work in the vicinity of the ***River Jordan*** (3:3, possibly at Bethany beyond Jordan, John 1:28), and crowds come out to be baptized by him (***drop of water***), 3:7. John exhorts them not to put any trust in their genetic link to Abraham, 3:7–9. Rather, they are to share whatever clothing and food they have with the poor and needy. He exhorts tax-collectors to be honest; they were looked on as traitors and collaborators with the Romans. He exhorts soldiers to refrain from exploitation and brutality, and to be satisfied with their wages. Any Jew who chose the life of a soldier excluded himself from the covenant people; he ran the risk of being called to serve on a Sabbath.

John insists that he is not the expected Messiah, and that when the Messiah finally comes, he—John—will not be worthy to untie the thongs of his sandals (a task reserved for slaves). It is significant that John baptized Jews (***Star of David***)—even though Jews were traditionally not baptized. *Jews* baptized *Gentiles* who wished to convert to Judaism. By baptizing Jews, John was, in effect, declaring that something was wrong with the current practices of Judaism.

Frame 

John the Baptist, prison bars, question mark (*right section*): Matthew 14:1–9 and Mark 6:17–29 describe the events that result in the imprisonment and beheading of John the Baptist by Herod Antipas. John had rebuked Herod for marrying Herodias, his brother's wife, 3:18–20.

Herodias wanted John dead! In Matthew 11:2–6, we read of an imprisoned John the Baptist sending some of his followers to Jesus to ask, "Are you the one who is to come, or are we to wait for another?" Most likely John feels that if Jesus really is the Messiah, He will rescue John from prison. Jesus responds by referring to Isaiah 35:5,6—a passage that describes the things that will take place when the Messianic Age breaks in. Jesus does those things—things that point to Him as the Messiah. However, the fact that Jesus is the Messiah does not imply that He will rescue John from prison. (After all, Jesus Himself will eventually face death on a cross!) Luke reference to these events is brief, 9:7–9.

Left section: Luke 3:21,22 reports Jesus' baptism (***drop of water***), during which the Holy Spirit descends on Him in the form of a ***dove***. Furthermore, a heavenly voice declares Jesus to be *King* (***crown***, Psalm 2:7) and *Servant* (***servant figure***, Isaiah 42:1). Luke refers to Jesus' baptism in a section that *follows* reference to John's imprisonment by Herod Antipas, 3:19,20.

Jesus' Ministry in Galilee

1 Luke's temptation narrative is given in 4:1–13. It reverses the second and third of the three episodes Matthew lists in his narrative, Matthew 4:1–11. Luke's *opening scene* takes place in the Temple (1:8–10), the *third temptation* takes place in the Temple (4:9–12), and the setting for Luke's *final narrative* is the Temple, 24:53. The religious and political powers that call for Jesus' crucifixion have links to that structure and to the system carried out within its walls.

2 After His baptism and temptation, Jesus returns to Galilee, begins to teach in synagogues, and is initially praised by everyone, 4:14,15. But the tone changes. On one occasion, Jesus is invited to preach in the synagogue in His home town, Nazareth, 4:16–30. He begins by reading Isaiah 61:1,2 and a section of 58:6 ("to let the oppressed go free")—passages that pointed to the coming of the Messiah and to conditions that would prevail during the Messianic Age. After reading them, He states, "Today this scripture has been fulfilled in your hearing." Indeed, in Jesus, the Messianic Age has come! Some are puzzled by what Jesus says. Some become angry and ask how it is possible that a mere "son of Joseph" can say such things and make such a claim.

Jesus' opponents understand that Jesus read selectively—which He was entitled to do according to rabbinic tradition. However, they are furious that He makes *no reference* to the following hopes expressed in Isaiah 60:1–61:6:

a. God's glory will embrace His so-called Chosen people forever, 60:2. Oppression by other nations will cease, 61:1.

b. Rulers and people of other nations will come to the Holy Land, bringing with them their wealth—across the oceans in ships and across the land on camels, 60:3, 5b, 6, 11, 61:6b. Indeed, God's people will suck into their own hands the wealth of the Gentiles as a child sucks milk from its mother's breasts, 60:16a.

c. God will pour out His vengeance on any Gentile nation that will not serve the Jewish people, 60:12, 61:2a. Gentiles will rebuild any Jewish structures that they have reduced to rubble (60:10a), using the best of timbers from Lebanon in the process, 60:13; see also 60:17. They will also free God's people from having to do menial tasks such as caring for animals and farming the land, 61:5. Possibly the suggestion is also that God's people will be spared having to do menial tasks so that they might devote life to studying the Torah, their scriptures.

d. Diaspora Jews scattered around the Mediterranean world will return to the Holy Land, bringing their silver and gold with them, 60:9.

e. God's people will live in their land in peace and security, 60:18. The gates that lead into their towns and cities will always remain open, 60:11a. The people will all be righteous, possess the land forever, and increase greatly in numbers, 60:21,22a.

When Jesus' hearers express their rage toward Him, He responds with words indicating that, although His hearers believe that they, as Jews, are God's genetically special people, in Old Testament times God used Elijah and Elisha to minister to *Gentiles*, to *non-Jews*. Elijah ministered to the widow of Zarephath; Elisha ministered to Naaman, a leper from Syria. If Jesus' audience rejects what He has to say, God will turn His attention to the Gentiles once again. At this, Jesus' hearers become enraged, drive Him out of Nazareth, and make plans to kill Him by throwing Him off a cliff.

3 Jesus survives, leaves Nazareth, and travels to Capernaum, 4:31. (*If* Jesus traveled there that same day, He certainly traveled farther than the Torah permitted a person to do on a Sabbath.) While teaching in a synagogue there, Jesus casts a demon out of a man in His audience. Those present are amazed by what they see, and news about Jesus begins to spread far and wide, 4:31–38. Next—and still on the Sabbath—Jesus heals Simon Peter's mother-in-law, 4:38,39. When the sun sets (and the Sabbath is

over!), people flock to Jesus seeking to be healed and to be freed from demonic control, 4:40,41. It is significant that when Jesus exorcises demons, they—the enemy—recognize who Jesus is, even though His own people do not. It is also possible that the demons tell Jesus that they know His name and who He is to indicate that He can have no power over them—and to suggest that they have power over Him. In many parts of the world still today, to know a person's name is to have power over that person. Nonetheless, Jesus demonstrates His power over the demons by silencing them.

4 Next morning, when Jesus goes to a deserted place, the crowds go looking for Him. When they find Jesus they beg Him to remain with them. However, Jesus continues to preach in the synagogues of the region, 4:42–44.

5 There comes the day when, after preaching on the shores of the Sea of Galilee (also called the Lake of Gennesaret), Jesus sees two fishing boats and boards the one that belongs to Peter, 5:1–11. After preaching from the boat, Jesus tells Peter and his helpers to sail into deeper water and let down their nets. Initially, Peter is not very cooperative—but then relents and does what Jesus has told him to do. The end result is a catch of fish so large that those in the second boat must help Peter's crew deal with the catch. Peter is overwhelmed, and asks Jesus to depart from him—a sinful man. Jesus responds by telling Peter that within a short time Peter and his helpers will be fishing for *people*—not *fish*. In this incident, not only is the hope expressed in Ezekiel 47:1–12 being realized (a lot of fish are present in an unlikely place), but Jesus' circle of followers grows as a result, 5:11.

The significance of this event becomes more meaningful when it is understood that, in Jesus' day, fishermen fished at night—and close to shore where there were more fish. Why at night? They used nets made of dark, linen cord that fish could see during daylight hours. Today, fishing in the Sea of Galilee is done during daylight hours because the nets used are made of light-colored nylon thread that the fish cannot readily see.

6 When Jesus encounters a leper (an outcast!), He touches the man before He heals him, rendering Himself ritually unclean, 5:12–16. Jesus then tells the man to show himself to the priests—most likely so that he can be declared ritually clean and accepted back into his community.

7 Some people are so desperate to have Jesus heal their friend that they open up the roof of a house where Jesus is teaching and let the patient down on a stretcher-like bier, 5:17–26. Jesus' response is to assure the man that his sins have been forgiven—a statement that angers the scribes and Pharisees present. They maintained that forgiveness is obtained only through the Temple system in Jerusalem far to the south. Jesus then heals the man of his sickness, thereby assuring His audience that if His *healing* word has authority, so does His *forgiving* word. This implies that the "forgiveness system" is no longer confined to the Temple, but resides in Jesus.

8 Next, Jesus calls Levi, a tax-collector, to follow Him, 5:27,28. (Jews hated tax-collectors; they looked on them as collaborators working for the Roman occupying power.) In the celebration that follows at Levi's house, Jesus points out to His opponents that something radically new has broken into Judaism (5:29–39), and the only ones who will come to Jesus for help and healing are those who know that they are spiritually sick. When the Pharisees and their scribes ask Jesus why His disciples do not fast and pray as did the disciples of John the Baptist, Jesus responds by telling them that the "new" He is bringing cannot be attached to the "old"—even as a piece of new cloth cannot be attached to an old decaying garment, and new wine cannot be poured into old wineskins.

9 Some Jewish teachers taught that, if only all Jews would keep two successive Sabbaths properly, the Messiah would come. When Jesus breaks two Sabbaths in a row, His opponents are infuriated, 6:1–11. Mark states that they seek ways to kill Jesus, Mark 2:23–3:6; note v. 6.

10 In Luke 6:12–16, Jesus calls His disciples, and in 6:17–49 delivers the *Sermon on the Plain*—Luke's counterpart to Matthew's *Sermon on the Mount* (Matthew 5–7). In His preaching, Jesus radically reinterprets many of the cherished notions of Judaism! For example, Jesus interprets the terms "blessed" and "woe" in ways that differ greatly from the way they that were interpreted in His day; see Leviticus 26, Deuteronomy 28.

Although Jesus' hearers were prone (as are people today!) to interpret blessedness as "Blessed are those who are rich, full now, laughing, and well spoken of," Jesus responds that the rich have received their consolation, the well-fed will be hungry, those who laugh will mourn and weep, and those well-spoken of are to remember that their ancestors also spoke well of the false prophets. By way of contrast, Jesus says: "Blessed are you who are poor, for yours is the kingdom of God. Blessed are you who are hungry now, for you will be filled. Blessed are you who weep now, for you will laugh. Blessed are you when people hate you, and when they exclude you, revile you and defame you on account of the Son of Man. Rejoice in that day and leap for joy, for surely your reward is great in heaven; for that is what their ancestors did to the prophets," 6:20–23. Jesus never links "being blessed" to what a person acquires and enjoys. He links it only to reflecting His own mind and manner.

11 After offering His Sermon on the Plain, Jesus returns to Capernaum, and meets with some Jewish elders who ask Him to heal the servant of a Roman (Gentile) centurion—a person deserving of help in that he loves the Jewish people and has built a synagogue for them, 7:1–10. When Jesus is on His way to the centurion's house, He is met by some of the officer's servants who tell Jesus that their master suggests that Jesus need not trouble Himself by going all the way to the house. Just speak the healing word from a distance! Jesus does so. The servant is healed. Jesus heals the "far off" servant of a Gentile defined by Jerusalem's religious leaders as one "far off."

12 Jesus then travels to Nain where He restores to life the only son of a widow, 7:11–17. Jesus does more than restore the son to the woman. He also ensures her future financial security. When her husband died, her son became the legal owner of his father's possessions. If the son remains dead, all possessions will be handed over to a brother of the deceased father. Furthermore, by touching the bier on which the deceased son lies, Jesus renders Himself ritually unclean—at least, according to the nation's religious leaders.

13 What follows in 7:18–35 reflects Matthew 11:1–19. When an imprisoned John the Baptist (see 3:10–20) sends two of his disciples to Jesus to ask if He is indeed the Messiah (possibly hoping that Jesus will free him from prison), Jesus responds by referring to the "Isaianic signs" that He has been doing; see Isaiah 35:5,6. If Jesus is doing these things, He must be the Messiah. Jesus then addresses the crowds and tells them that if they went out to hear John with the hope that doing so would provide them with coins and soft, royal robes, they were misguided. (Note: Out of deference to Jewish leaders, some of the Herods did not place a facial image on their coins—only symbols of reeds shaking in the wind.)

14 Jesus is then invited to participate in a meal hosted by a Pharisee, 7:36–50. However, the Pharisee does not greet Jesus with a kiss, and makes no provisions for the washing of His feet and the anointing of His head with perfumed oil (all important, traditional gestures). When a woman, who with others

has entered the Pharisee's home to watch the banquet, sees how Jesus has been shamed and insulted, she washes His feet with her tears, dries them with her hair, and anoints His head with ointment that she has brought with her in a jar. (Note that in Jesus' day, women kept their heads covered, and the first one to see a woman's hair was her husband on their wedding night.) Jesus rebukes the Pharisee for publicly insulting him, and then declares the woman forgiven. (Most likely the woman was of low repute and from the lower class.)

15 Together with His twelve disciples, Jesus then travels through the villages and towns in the region, preaching His message of "Good News" and casting out demons. (Women accompany Jesus and His disciples, *and fund them*, 8:2,3. The women follow Jesus all the way to the cross, 23:55,56.) Along the way, He tells His hearers the Parable of the Sower, and explains how His message is to serve as a light that all are to see, and a light that will judge all. When told that His mothers and brothers want to see Him, but cannot do so because of the crowds, He responds by saying that His mother and brothers are those who hear and do God's word, 8:1–21.

16 When, at Jesus' request, the disciples are taking Jesus to the "other side" of the sea of Galilee, Jesus falls asleep, 8:22–25. When a threatening windstorm bursts in, the frightened disciples wake Jesus and ask Him to save them from perishing. Jesus commands the wind and the waves to be still—and they do. The disciples are afraid and amazed, and wonder who Jesus really is.

17 The narrative in 8:26–39 contains significant details. When the boat in which Jesus is being transported arrives in the Gentile region of the Decapolis, it seems that only Jesus gets out of the boat. (Most likely His disciples do not want to get Gentile dust on their feet, or walk in a region where pigs were kept.) Jesus is met by a man who is naked and demon-possessed. The man uses significant words (v. 28) when asking Jesus for help and healing. After Jesus throws a legion of demons out of the man, the demons enter a large herd of pigs (ritually unclean animals for Jews) that plunge themselves into the Sea of Galilee and drown. (This event echoes that in which Pharaoh's forces were drowned while pursuing the fleeing Israelites at the time of the Exodus.) When other swine-herders in the region see what Jesus has done, they beg Him to leave—most likely because of the fear they experience at having lost their source of livelihood—their pigs. Although the man whom Jesus exorcised wants to join Jesus' community, Jesus tells him to return home and tell people in the region what Jesus has done for him. Again, reference is made to Jesus—and only Jesus—climbing back into the boat for the return journey.

18 When Jesus returns to the west bank of the Sea of Galilee, He restores to life the 12-year-old daughter of Jairus, a leader of the local synagogue—and touches her ritually unclean body before doing so, 8:40–42, 49–56. The two sections of the narrative serve as "book ends" for a second narrative in which Jesus permits a woman who has been menstruating for twelve years to touch His outer cloak in hope of being healed, 8:42b–48. And she is healed—immediately! Jesus then forces her to confess publicly that she is the one who touched Him. Although the woman and the crowd expect Jesus to rebuke this ritually unclean woman for touching Him, He does not. Instead, He addresses her as "daughter," commends her for her faith, and bids her go in peace!

19 Jesus then gives His disciples authority and power to deal with demons, to heal the sick, and proclaim the Good News. They are to "travel light" when doing so. The disciples then do what Jesus has asked them to do—with encouraging results, 9:1–6. They eventually share their joy with Jesus, 9:20.

20 When Herod Antipas, the ruler of Galilee (and Perea) hears reports about Jesus' ministry, he is perplexed and tries to see Jesus, 9:7–9. (He eventually meets Jesus—during the course of His trial in Jerusalem, 23:6–12.)

21 Jesus then travels to Bethsaida on the northeast shore of the Sea of Galilee where He teaches and heals, 9:10,11. As the day draws to a close, Jesus feeds 5,000 men by multiplying the disciples' five loaves and two fish, 9:12–17. (No mention is made of women or children participating in this feeding account.) And as in Mark 6:30–44 and Matthew 14:13–21, there are 12 baskets of leftovers, 9:17.

22 When Jesus prays alone, with only the disciples nearby, He asks the disciples two questions: Who do the *people* think He is? Who do the *disciples* think He is? Peter responds that although the crowds do not see Jesus to be the Messiah, the disciples do, 9:18–20. When Jesus then predicts His coming passion, crucifixion, and resurrection in Jerusalem, Peter does not raise his voice in protest, 9:21,22 (as he does in Mark 8:31–33). Jesus then shares with His disciples what following Him will imply for their lives; they will find life by losing it—by giving it away in the service of others, 9:23–27.

23 Although Luke's transfiguration narrative (9:28–36) resembles those in Mark 9:2–8 and Matthew 17:1–8, it contains an important additional detail. When Moses and Elijah meet with Jesus on the Mount of Transfiguration, they speak with Him about His coming (in Greek) *exodus*—meaning "rescue event" (not "departure")—that He will (in Greek) *complete* (not "accomplish"), 9:30,31. The voice from the cloud declares Jesus to be a descendant of David (Psalm 2:7, "This is My Son, my Chosen"), and the long-awaited new prophet, new Moses, Deuteronomy 18:15 ("listen to Him").

24 Next day and immediately after coming down from the mountain, Jesus encounters a man whose son is troubled by (apparently) epileptic seizures and demon possession. The man tells Jesus that he had asked His disciples to heal the boy, but they were unable to do so. However, Jesus immediately heals the boy and restores him to his father, 9:37–43a.

25 Jesus then predicts His passion for the second time, 9:43b–45. The disciples respond by arguing about which of them will be "the greatest" in Jesus' coming Kingdom. Jesus then draws a child close to Himself and tells the disciples that those who see themselves to be the least in His Kingdom are in reality the greatest, 9:46–50. Whoever welcomes a child in Jesus' name is really welcoming Jesus—but more! They are really welcoming the God who sent Jesus among them.

Jesus then sets His face to go to Jerusalem, 9:51.

SUMMARY

46A Luke's geographical outline differs from those in Mark and Matthew. Although Jesus does heal a demon-possessed man in the Decapolis, He does not work in Syro-Phoenicia nor does He take the disciples to the vicinity of Caesarea Philippi. He remains in Galilee. However, He feeds the 5,000 in the vicinity of Bethsaida—not in Galilee itself. His first passion prediction is made in Galilee—not in the vicinity of Caesarea Philippi. He heals a blind man on the way *into* Jericho—not after leaving Jericho as in Mark and Matthew (Matthew speaks of Jesus healing two blind men after leaving Jericho).

46B While Luke speaks of Jesus expressing concern for the Gentiles, he makes little reference to Jesus ministering to Gentiles. However, in his second writing (Acts of the Apostles), Luke describes the apostles taking God's Good News to the ends of the earth (as understood at that time)—to Rome. Luke traces Jesus' ancestry all the way back to Adam—and sees in Jesus' Person and ministry a new beginning to the human race. Luke refers to Jerusalem 30 times in his Gospel, and 57 times in Acts. Ten of Luke's 24 chapters describe events that took place while Jesus was traveling from Galilee to Jerusalem.

46C Luke's nativity narrative provides information not contained in Matthew's account. Joseph and a pregnant Mary travel from Galilee to Bethlehem. The infant Jesus is visited by outcast shepherds—not by wise men (as in Matthew). Neither Luke nor Matthew refer to Jesus being born in a stable. Luke makes it clear that He was born in a house (as Matthew also states). The suggestion that His parents took up residence in a stable because there was no room for them in the inn is invalid. The word translated as "inn" means "guest room."

46D In his opening chapters, Luke refers to the aged Zechariah and Elizabeth being blessed with a son—John (later, "the Baptist"). Luke also tells of the angel Gabriel informing Mary that she will conceive miraculously and give birth to the Christ-child. God reveals His glory to outcast shepherds—who are the first to visit the infant Jesus. When Jesus is taken to the Jerusalem Temple 40 days after His birth, the aged Simeon and Anna make statements about His future ministry. Joseph and Mary return to Nazareth—but continue to take Jesus with them to the Temple each year for Passover observance (at least, until He is 12 years of age). Luke alone refers to a 12-year-old Jesus meeting with rabbis in the vicinity of the Temple.

46E Dramatic things take place during Jesus' ministry in Galilee. After He preaches His first sermon in His home town, Nazareth, His hearers plot to throw Him off a cliff. Many of the things He says and does resemble things referred to in Mark and Luke. However, in Luke's account, Jesus offers a sermon on a plain—not on a mountain (as in Matthew). Luke alone reports Jesus restoring to life the dead son of a widowed mother in Nain. While dining in the home of a Pharisee, Jesus finds Himself having to deal with insults. However, a woman of low repute does to Jesus what His host should have done—but refused to do. She washes His feet with her tears, dries them with her hair, and anoints them with perfumed oil. In Luke's transfiguration narrative, Moses and Elijah speak with Jesus about His coming "exodus" (not "departure") that He will "complete" (not "accomplish") in Jerusalem. And the voice from the cloud refers to Jesus as both the long-expected descendant of David, and the long-awaited new Moses. Many of the parables Jesus tells while traveling to Jerusalem are found only in Luke.

UNITS 41-50

The Gospels and Acts

UNIT 47

Luke (II)

From Galilee to Jerusalem

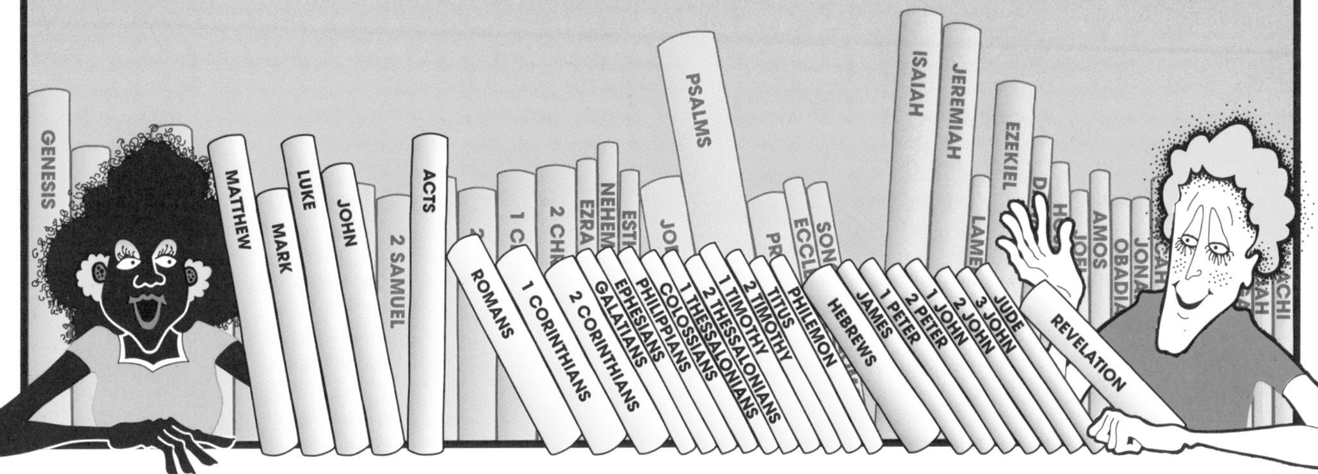

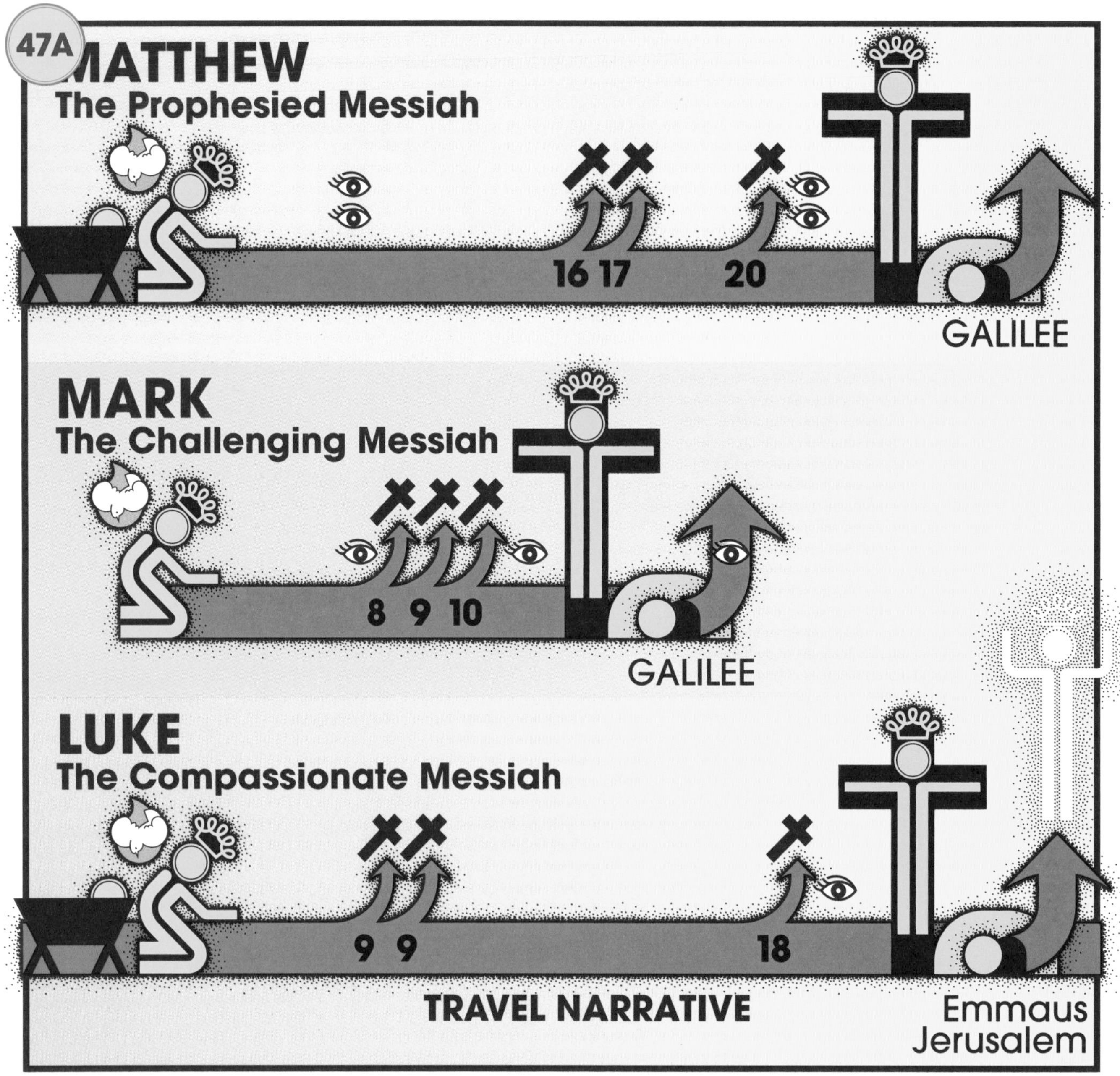

47A
MATTHEW
The Prophesied Messiah
16 17
20
GALILEE
MARK
The Challenging Messiah
8 9 10
GALILEE
LUKE
The Compassionate Messiah
9 9
18
TRAVEL NARRATIVE
Emmaus
Jerusalem

MARK
MATTHEW
LUKE
M
L
Q

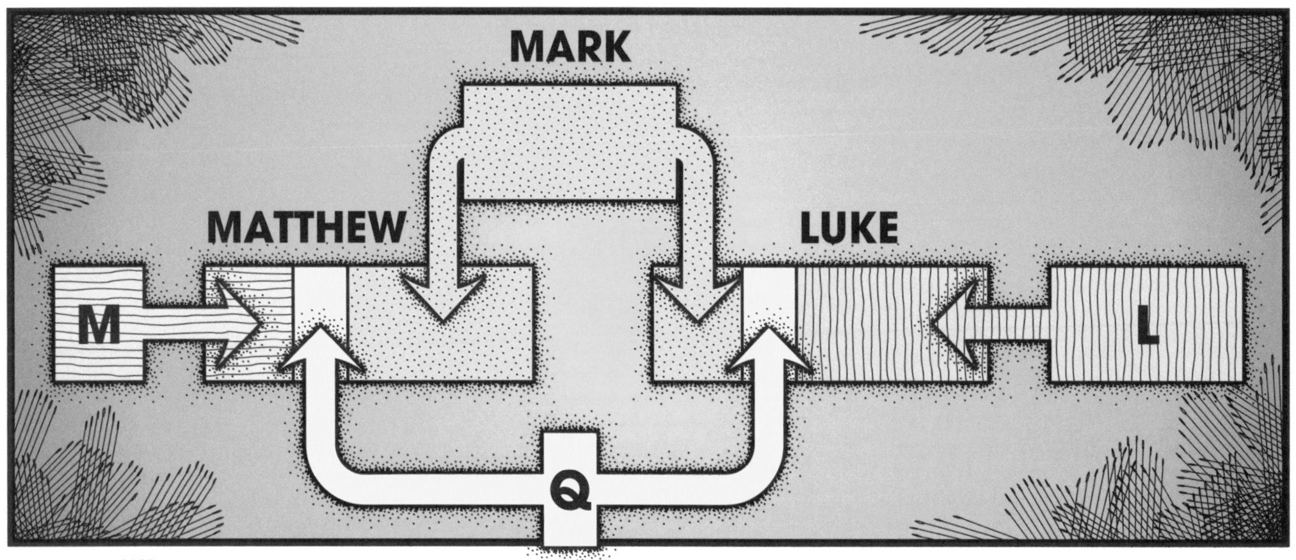

The Synoptic Gospels—a Comparison 47A

The plural term "Gospels" would not have been understood in the Apostolic Age, nor for several generations after that. The first four books of the New Testament are four accounts of the one Gospel. The plural form came to be used only in the middle of the second century. The traditional titles of the four records indicate that in them we have the Gospel, or "good news," about the ministry of Jesus the Messiah "according to" each of four evangelists. The comments that follow have to do with Matthew, Mark, and Luke—writings traditionally referred to as the *Synoptic Gospels*. The term *synoptic* is made up of two Greek words meaning "together" and "seeing"; it denotes that the first three Gospels can be lined up, seen together, and compared.

ILLUSTRATION 47A (*upper section*) depicts the relationship between the Synoptic Gospels in terms of length and narrative structure.

1 The length of each Gospel is drawn to scale. Luke's is the longest.

2 All three Gospels describe Jesus' *baptism* (***drop of water***) and the *Holy Spirit* descending on Him in the form of a ***dove***.

3 ***Manger:*** Matthew and Luke contain an infancy narrative; Mark does not.

4 ***Three arrows rising from center line; a cross above each arrow:*** Each of the first three Gospels contains three passion predictions. The numbers beneath the crosses indicate the chapters in which they occur. Luke inserts a lengthy narrative (referred to as Luke's ***TRAVEL NARRATIVE***) between the second and third predictions.

5 ***Eyes:*** In Matthew and Mark, the three passion predictions are bracketed by incidents in which Jesus gives sight to the blind. In Matthew's narrative, Jesus heals two blind men on each occasion. (Note: Matthew often presents significant figures in pairs.) In Mark, He heals one blind man on each occasion. In Luke, Jesus heals only one blind man on His way into Jericho.

6 ***Cross and empty tomb:*** Each Gospel contains a passion and resurrection narrative. Some see each Gospel as a passion-resurrection narrative with a lengthy introduction.

7 ***Place-names beneath open tomb:*** In Matthew and Mark, a heavenly messenger tells the disciples that they will see Jesus in ***GALILEE***. In Luke, the risen Jesus appears to two disciples on the way to ***Emmaus***, and then to a gathering of the disciples in Jerusalem. Luke's narrative gives the impression that Jesus ascends soon after appearing to the disciples on Easter Sunday.

8 ***Jesus ascending:*** Only Luke reports Jesus' ascension. Mark 16:1–8 makes no reference to Jesus' ascension. Matthew concludes his Gospel with Jesus assuring His disciples that He will remain with His brothers and sisters until the close of the age, 28:20.

Although all three Gospels proclaim the "good news" that, in Jesus the Messiah, the Kingdom of God broke into history, specific themes surface in each.

- ***MATTHEW—The Prophesied Messiah:*** The focus is on Jesus as the *fulfillment of Old Testament hopes*. However, although Jesus fulfills Old Testament hopes and prophecies, He radically reinterprets them.
- ***MARK—The Challenging Messiah:*** The *challenge Jesus constitutes* to the Jewish people and His disciples is highlighted. Although the Jewish people were waiting for a messiah who would give them *dominion over the world*, Jesus called them to *serve the world*.
- ***LUKE—The Compassionate Messiah:*** *Jesus' compassionate nature* in dealing with humanity is emphasized—in particular, the disenfranchised, the unclean, the lowly, and the outcasts.

ILLUSTRATION 47A (*lower section*) depicts the relationship among the Synoptic Gospels. Biblical scholars suggest the following:

1. ***MARK*** was written first.
2. Both ***MATTHEW*** and ***LUKE*** made extensive use of Mark (Matthew more than Luke).
3. Both Matthew and Luke made use of another source referred to as "***Q***" (German, *Quelle*, meaning "source")—a collection of Jesus' sayings.
4. Matthew adds his own special material referred to as "***M***," and Luke adds his own special material referred to as "***L***." The "L" materials are more extensive than the "M" materials.

To what degree the original sources were oral or written is debated. What finally matters is that God's people saturate themselves in the text of the Gospels as we now have them, and understand, believe, and do what they teach. Their focus throughout is on Jesus the Messiah as forgiving Savior and Servant Lord.

From Galilee to Jerusalem

Luke 9:51-19:28

1 When beginning His journey from Galilee to Jerusalem, Jesus initially sets out to travel via Samaria. However, the Samaritans refuse to permit Him to travel through their territory! For them, God's people should worship on *Mt. Gerizim in Samaria*—not on *Mt. Zion in Jerusalem*, 9:51–56.

2 Jesus tells the first of a series of parables that He will share during His journey south, 9:57–62. (Eleven of these parables are analyzed in Crossways International's *The Parables of Jesus*.)

3 Jesus sends 70 of His disciples out in teams of two to bear witness to Him. Prior to their departure, Jesus commands them to travel light and to expect to encounter opposition—but not to be concerned by it, 10:1–12. Those who accept the disciples' message and ministry accept Jesus, but those who reject the disciples' message and ministry reject Jesus and the One Who sent Him, 10:16.

4 Jesus utters "woes" against those living in the Jewish cities of Chorazin and Bethsaida, 10:13–16. He states that if the Gentiles living in the Phoenician cities of Tyre and Sidon had seen what He is doing, they would have repented long ago in sackcloth and ashes, 10:13–15.

5 Eventually the 70 disciples return to Jesus, full of joy concerning the impact their ministry is making on those to whom they ministered, 10:17–24.

6 Jesus is confronted by a Jewish lawyer who wishes to discuss what constitutes obedience to the Law. Jesus responds by telling him the parable of the Good Samaritan—and challenges him to change his question from "Who is my neighbor?" to "How am I to function as a neighbor to others—regardless of their ethnic origins?" (10:25–37).

7 Jesus dines in the home of Mary and Martha, 10:38–42. While Martha busies herself preparing the meal, Mary sits at Jesus' feet to listen to His teaching—an action that says, "Jesus, may I become one of Your students?" Jesus states that Mary has chosen the "better part" and accepts her, a woman, as a student. Jesus' actions are radical in that, at that time, only males could sit at the feet of a rabbi; girls and women were taught by their mothers at home.

8 After sharing His pattern for prayer with His disciples (the Lord's Prayer, 11:1–4), Jesus tells them the parable of the Friend at Midnight, 11:5–13. The parable has a humorous side to it. Jesus' hearers know that no person will refuse a fellow-villager's request for the best of food in order to share the best possible meal with a recent arrival in the village (even at midnight!). The reputation of the entire village is at stake when it comes to offering hospitality to a visitor. Similarly, Jesus' Father will heed prayers offered to Him at any hour of the day or night. (Note: The word in verse 11:8 translated as "persistence" would be better translated as "sense of honor.")

9 When Jesus carries out an exorcism (11:14–23), some of those who observe His action state that He does such things with the help of the devil. Jesus responds by telling them that if they are correct, then a civil war is taking place within the kingdom of the demonic. The truth is, however, that Jesus does all things with the help of His Father in Heaven—and through His ministry the Kingdom of God is breaking in. Furthermore, it is one thing to throw out a demon. But if that demon's presence is not replaced with God's presence and power, the demon will return—bringing seven other demons with him, 11:24–26. When a woman responds by hailing Jesus as "blessed," He responds by stating that the ones who are blessed are those who hear the Word of God and believe and obey it, 10:27,28.

10 Jesus then tells His hearers that the Assyrian people of Nineveh were more ready to hear God's Word proclaimed by Jonah than are many of those around Him, 11:29–32. Although the Queen of Sheba was ready to travel a considerable distance to listen to Solomon's wisdom, Jesus' hearers do not seem to

understand that, in Him, one greater than Solomon has come among them. Indeed, on the last day of history the people of Nineveh will utter words of judgment on many in Israel—for in Jesus one greater than Jonah has come.

11 After Jesus makes use of a simile of light and darkness to encourage His hearers to take into themselves the light of God's truth, a Pharisee invites Jesus to dine at his home—and is amazed to see that Jesus does not observe the prescribed ritual washing before the meal. Jesus responds that the Pharisees focus on irrelevant externals, but ignore the things that matter. Jesus' response angers the scribes and Pharisees, and they discuss ways to trap Jesus in something that He might say, 11:33–54.

12 In 12:1–15, Jesus warns His hearers about the leaven (hypocrisy) of the Pharisees, exhorts them to stand firm when persecuted, and shares insights about the Holy Spirit.

13 In the parable of the Rich Fool (12:13–21) Jesus shares powerful insights about the concept of ownership. Jesus points out that when we mere humans sow seed, the seed and the soil belong to God, and God grants the increase. Furthermore, we do not even own the body in which we reside. God lends it to us—and God can demand that we return to Him what belongs to Him at any moment. In the section that follows (12:22–34), Jesus teaches His hearers the importance of dependence on God. They are to focus on understanding, believing, and doing the things of God's Kingdom—and leave it to God to supply their daily *needs* (not *greeds*).

14 In 12:35–59, Jesus shares sayings about the "end time" and His final reappearing. He speaks of His message as a refining and purifying fire that will meet with acceptance or rejection, and will be a source of conflict and dissension even within families.

15 There follows another call to repentance, 13:1–5. Jesus points out that those whom Pilate once put to death, and those on whom the Tower of Siloam fell, were not great sinners singled out for punishment. Death can overtake a person at any time—so, be ready and prepared at all times. (Nothing is known about these two incidents apart from Luke's reference.)

16 In the parable of the Fig Tree (13:6–9), Jesus exhorts His hearers to take seriously His call as the "divine Vine-dresser" to bear fruit in God's Kingdom. God can and does "prune" people's lives to ensure that they bear fruit. If they do not bear God's kind of fruit in their lives, there will be serious consequences.

17 When, in a synagogue and on a Sabbath, Jesus heals a woman who has been crippled for eighteen years, the leader of the synagogue protests. Jesus responds by asking whether it is more important to refrain from work on a Sabbath, or to show mercy to a long-time sufferer on a Sabbath. His response humiliates His opponents and wins Him the approval of the congregation, 13:10–17.

18 After telling the parables of the Mustard Seed (13:18,19) and the Yeast (13:20,21), Jesus passes through surrounding towns and villages and exhorts His hearers to strive to walk through the narrow door of life—to walk *Jesus' way* rather than the *world's way*, 13:22–30. After all, many who believe that they are "first" in God's Kingdom will eventually discover that they are "last."

19 When some Pharisees warn Jesus that Herod (Antipas of Galilee) is plotting to kill Him, Jesus tells them to tell Herod ("that fox," see 9:58) that He must and will persist in His ministry, no matter what Herod thinks and does. Jesus then laments over the fate that awaits Him in Jerusalem, and the fate that will eventually overtake Jerusalem, 13:34,35. If only those living within its walls would let Jesus gather them under His protective wings!

20 While dining at the home of an important Pharisee on a Sabbath, Jesus heals a man suffering from dropsy, 14:1–6. Prior to healing the man, and anticipating the protests that His actions will inspire,

Jesus tells those present that if they themselves are prepared to save a child or an ox that falls into a pit on a Sabbath, why should Jesus not heal, on a Sabbath, a man who has been suffering for many years?

21 Jesus then tells those present that when they are invited to a banquet, they should seek the lowest place—not the highest, 14:7–14. Next, Jesus tells the parable of the Great Banquet (14:15–24) in which He says that His Father has prepared a great banquet and has invited many. Although there are those who refuse to attend (after having initially accepted the invitation), the Heavenly Host will ensure that what He has prepared will not go to waste—even if it is consumed by those whom the religious leaders think of as the lowest of the low. Sayings on discipleship follow, 14:25–35. Jesus points out that His call to radical discipleship is to be taken very seriously. Those who dismiss it or seek to accept it on their own terms will pay a price!

22 In ch. 15, Jesus tells three well-known parables: The Lost Sheep, the Lost Coin, and the Two Lost Sons. In each case, the focus is on who does the finding: the shepherd, the woman, and the father. Similarly, while some think of themselves as having "found the Lord," the truth is that the Lord is never lost—He is the One who does the finding. Jesus tells these three parables to respond to the murmurings of the scribes and Pharisees that He receives sinners and eats with them. Jesus' response is: "You are right! I do receive sinners and eat with them. More—I run to meet them, hug them, kiss them, have shoes placed on their feet, and then throw a party! I wish that you too would come to My party. But if you will not, what will you eventually do to Me?" Eventually they will cry, "Crucify Him! Crucify Him!"

23 In the parable of the Dishonest Steward (16:1–13), Jesus tells a story about a manager who, after being dismissed from his position as manager, knows how to manipulate things to benefit himself. He ingratiates himself to the tenants he was supervising to ensure his future security in terms of accommodation and food supplies. If only God's people would manage what belongs to God in such a way that when life is done God might welcome them into His Eternal Home and provide their needs to all eternity; see also Matthew 25:31–46. (The message of the parable has nothing to do with "salvation by works.") As the manager had only a small window of time to ensure that his future needs would be met, we mere morals have only a small window of time in which to lay hold of God's forgiving grace.

24 After offering sayings about the Pharisees (16:14,15), the Law (16:16,17), and divorce (16:18), Jesus tells the parable of the Rich Man and Lazarus. 16:19–31. In this life, the rich man has so much but cares so little for those who have so little—or nothing. In the life to come, things are reversed! Lazarus has so much, and the rich man finds himself in a desperate plight—with no way out!

25 Jesus then teaches about the importance of forgiving others without limit. His followers are to forgive what others are, and focus on helping them become what God wants, 17:1–4. Jesus' followers are to devote life to developing their faith and level of discipleship, 17:5,6. They are to seek to do all that God asks—and even if they achieve that, they are to understand that they have done nothing beyond what God created them to do, 17:7–10.

26 When Jesus heals ten lepers (17:11–18), and tells them to show themselves to the priests (so that their healing might be validated), only one returns to thank Jesus for healing him. And that man is a Samaritan—one despised by the Jewish people!

27 Next, Jesus exhorts His hearers to be ready at all times for the breaking in of the Kingdom of God, 17:20–37. He reminds them that their attention can be diverted by the busy routines of everyday life—such as eating, drinking, marrying and giving in marriage, buying, selling, planting, and building (as in the days of Noah and Lot), 17:26–29. God's people are at all times to look beyond the trivial to the eternal—to the present reality of living in the Kingdom of God.

28 In the parable of the Persistent Widow, Jesus points out that His brothers and sisters do not have to worry about how to get God to listen to their prayers, 18:1–8. God's ears are open at all times, and no bribing is necessary! In 18:9–14 , Jesus tells how a Pharisee's concern in worship is to tell God how good he is, while a Tax Collector's concern is to tell God how bad and undeserving he is. The latter gets God's attention—the former does not!

29 After exhorting His hearers to accept His message in an open, child-like manner (18:15–17), Jesus enters into dialog with a man who wants to know what he must do to inherit eternal life, 18:18–23. When the man assures Jesus that he has (supposedly) kept all the commandments, Jesus tells him to transfer ownership of all that he calls "his" to God, the real Owner, and learn to use all material goods to serve the needy. Jesus' advice troubles the man—for he is wealthy! Jesus continues by exhorting His hearers and disciples to take seriously what He has just taught—as difficult as it might sound, 18:24–30.

30 Jesus then predicts His coming passion for the third time, 18:31–34. Although the disciples do not really understand what Jesus is saying to them, they do not protest or ask for things relating to status and power (as they do in Mark's Gospel, 9:33–37, 10:35–37).

31 The two events that follow are profound, 18:35–19:10. As Jesus approaches Jericho, a crowd heads north out of the city to meet Him. The city's leaders know that Jesus is coming to their city and most likely have prepared accommodation and a meal for Jesus—hoping to discuss religion and politics until the early hours of the morning. When a blind beggar asks what is happening and is told that Jesus is passing by on His way to Jericho, he twice calls out, "Jesus, Son of David, have pity on me!" Although he cannot see with his *eyes*, he can see with his *heart*. Jesus restores his sight, and the man follows Jesus. Jesus then reaches Jericho—but does not stop. He bypasses the waiting meal and accommodation.

One of those living in Jericho is a despised tax-collector—a collaborator with the Romans! Although he wants to see Jesus, he faces some problems. Because he is short in stature, he cannot stand at the back of the crowds that greet Jesus as He passes through the city. Nor can he stand out front—the people hate him and might attack and stab him. So he runs ahead of the "Jesus procession" and climbs a sycamore tree—a tree with the largest leaves of any tree in the Middle East—but a tree considered to be ritually unclean. Why? Its fruit is not very tasty. Usually only birds eat it—and leave their dropping around the base of the tree. Furthermore, in Jesus' day a sycamore had to be planted at least 17 yards (15 meters) from the edge of a town. Zacchaeus, an "unclean" tax-collector, climbs that unclean tree—possibly hoping that nobody will see him do so, and that, after seeing Jesus pass by, he can eventually climb down and creep home unobserved.

Possibly some of Jericho's citizens see Zacchaeus climb the tree, gather around its base, and abuse him verbally. When Jesus sees what is taking place, He goes to the tree. The people expect Jesus to deliver Zacchaeus a verbal blast. He does not! He tells Zacchaeus that although He had intended to continue on to Jerusalem, He has changed His mind and wants to spend the night in Zacchaeus' house (which He knows is seen as ritually unclean by the scribes and Pharisees). The audience is appalled! But after Jesus has dined with Zacchaeus and his associates, Zacchaeus tells Jesus that he will give half his goods to the poor, and will restore fourfold to anyone whom he has cheated in any way. (Note that Zacchaeus is saying that until he met Jesus, he was nothing better than an animal thief, Exodus 22:1.) Jesus then assures those present that Zacchaeus is also a descendant of Abraham—and assures him of his place in God's family, God's true people!

32 Jesus then tells the parable of the Ten Gold Coins, in which He teaches that His followers are to see themselves as merely managers of creation and life—managers who must eventually give account to the Creator and Owner of all things, 19:11–17.

Ministry in Jerusalem

1 After arriving on the Mount of Olives, Jesus makes arrangements for His entry into Jerusalem—again, on a donkey, 19:28–40. Although Luke refers to the crowds spreading cloaks on the road along which Jesus travels, he makes no mention of the waving of palm branches. Surprisingly, the crowds greet Jesus as the coming *King*, v. 38 (only in Luke). And the Pharisees are angry, vv. 39,40.

2 As Jesus approaches the city, He weeps over it—knowing what will eventually overtake it in A.D. 66–70 when the Romans will destroy the city and its Temple, 19:41–44. Although David wept when *leaving Jerusalem* as a result of Absalom's revolt (2 Samuel 15:30), Jesus weeps as He *enters* the city, 19:41. *Those within its walls do not understand the true nature of the Kingdom of God. Jesus' Kingdom is, in effect, the very opposite of the kingdom David established.*

3 After entering Jerusalem, Jesus attacks the Temple, teaches within its walls, and angers the chief priest, the scribes, and leaders of the people to the point that they contemplate how they might have Jesus put to death, 19:45–48.

4 Most of the confrontations Luke describes after Jesus' entry into Jerusalem are parallel to those reported in Mark and Matthew.

a. The chief priest, scribes, and elders question Jesus about His authority, 20:1–8. Jesus responds by hanging them on the horns of a dilemma concerning the origin of John the Baptist's ministry and baptism.
b. Jesus tells his hearers a parable about an absentee landlord and tenant farmers, 20:9–19. The fate that overtakes the landlord's son (he was killed by the tenants) points to Jesus' approaching death at the hands of the religious and political leaders.
c. The Jewish leaders question Jesus concerning their obligation to pay taxes to the Roman occupying power, 20:20–26.
d. The Sadducees confront Jesus concerning belief in the resurrection of the body, 20:27–40.
e. Jesus reminds His hearers and opponents that David referred to his coming descendant as LORD, 20:41–44. The One Who has come is more than mere flesh and blood. He is God incarnate—in flesh!
f. Jesus warns his hearers about the practices of the scribes who seek the notice and applause of people, but show no compassion for the helpless and needy, 20:45–47. Indeed, they rob the helpless and needy!
g. In 21:1–4, we read of Jesus commending a widow for giving generously to the Temple treasury. She gives her all, while those who have much give little.

5 In 21:5–28, Luke offers a series of Jesus' sayings and teachings:

a. Jesus foretells the coming destruction of the Jerusalem Temple, 21:5,6.
b. Jesus describes signs that will remind His people of the coming end to history, 21:7–11.
c. The disciples must expect that they themselves will have to endure many painful things prior to the end, 21:12–19.
d. Jesus describes some of the painful things that the people will have to suffer as a result of revolting against Rome, 21:20–24.
e. The things people will have to experience as they walk through life serve as reminders of the coming Final Day to history, 21:25–28. They are not to despair, but always to look forward to that day of Final Rescue.
f. God's people are to read what takes place in the growth of figs on a fig tree as a reminder of how they are to read the unfolding course of history, 21:29–33. They are not to let themselves be sidetracked by the cares of daily life, or by the temptations to indulge themselves in what the world around them offers, 21:34–36.
g. Apparently, there were many who wanted to hear what Jesus had to say, 21:37,38.

Luke's Passion Narrative

1 The chief priests and scribes seek ways to have Jesus put to death, 21:1,2. Judas offers to work with them to devise a plan whereby he will hand Jesus over to them—for a price, 21:3–6.

2 Jesus sends Peter and John to make arrangements for the use of a guest room in which Jesus and the disciples might celebrate the coming Passover, 22:7–13. (Note that the Greek word used for "guest room" is the same as that used in the Christmas story, where reference is made to there being no room in the "guest room"—not "inn," 2:7.)

3 While Jesus celebrates the Passover Meal with His disciples, He inaugurates His Holy Supper, 22:14–20. He also foretells His coming betrayal, 22:21–23.

4 When the disciples argue among themselves concerning who will be the greatest in Jesus' coming Kingdom, Jesus has to do some corrective teaching, 22:24–30. He predicts Peter's coming denial of his Lord (22:31–34), and tells the disciples what material supplies they are to take with them when they undertake their coming ministry, 22:35–38.

5 Jesus then takes the disciples to the Mount of Olives (no mention is made of the Garden of Gethsemane), where He prays and endures great agony—even to the point of sweating blood, 22:39–46.

6 Judas leads a crowd to Jesus to capture Him. Judas kisses Jesus in the process. When one of His disciples cuts off an ear from one of Jesus' captors, Jesus immediately heals the man, and insists, "Disciples—no violence!" (22:47–53). Luke describes Peter's three-fold denial of his Lord (22:54–62), after which Jesus is ridiculed and beaten by His captors, 22:63–65.

7 Trial scenes follow:

- Jesus is tried by the elders, chief priests, and scribes, 22:66–71.
- The Jewish leaders take Him to Pilate, 23:1–5. Despite the charges made by the Jewish leaders, Pilate states, "Not guilty!"
- Pilate sends Jesus to Herod Antipas, 23:6–11. However, Jesus refuses to answer any of Herod's questions. Again, Jesus is subjected to mockery and abuse. Herod sends Jesus back to Pilate, and Herod and Pilate become friends!
- Although Pilate again insists that he finds nothing in Jesus to support the charges being leveled against Him by the Jewish leaders, he eventually releases Barabbas and hands Jesus over for crucifixion, 23:13–25.

8 Those leading Jesus to the place of execution order Simon of Cyrene to carry Jesus' cross (most likely, the cross beam only), 23:26. Along the way, Jesus addresses the weeping and wailing women of Jerusalem and points to the fate that will eventually overtake those living in Jerusalem, 23:27–32. Jesus is nailed to His cross between two criminals, 23:33.

9 Jesus speaks three "words" from the cross:

- *Father, forgive them; they know not what they do.* (23:34)
- *I say to you, today you will be with me in Paradise.* (23:43)
- *Father, into Your hands I commend My spirit.* (23:46)

10 As in Mark and Matthew, darkness spreads across the land from midday until 3 p.m., 23:44,45. The veil of the Temple is torn down the middle, 23:45b. The Roman centurion declares Jesus to be innocent, 23:47. People grieve deeply, 23:48. However, some of Jesus' friends and some women who have followed Him from Galilee to Jerusalem watch what is taking place, 23:49.

11 Joseph of Arimathea obtains permission from Pilate to remove Jesus' body from the cross, and provides Him with decent burial in a new tomb, 23:50–53. The women from Galilee watch these proceedings, and then return home to prepare the needed spices and oils to embalm Jesus' body after the Sabbath is over, 23:55,56.

Jesus Is Risen!

1 When the women return to Jesus' tomb on the Sunday morning, they find it open—but there is no body of Jesus! Two men in dazzling garments appear and tell them that Jesus has returned to life—even as He said He would during His ministry in Galilee. The women leave the tomb and tell the amazing news to the eleven disciples and others. Apparently their message is met with disbelief. However, Peter rushes to the tomb to check things out for himself, 24:1–12.

2 Jesus appears to two (unnamed) disciples on the way to Emmaus, 24:13–35. The disciples do not recognize Jesus. They had been looking forward to a Messiah who would rescue them *from* suffering; they have to learn that they have a Messiah who rescues and redeems them *through* suffering. Jesus explains to them their own "big story" from Moses and the Prophets, and then accepts their invitation to dine with them in Emmaus. During the course of the meal, their eyes are opened—and Jesus disappears. The two disciples rush back to Jerusalem where they share their experience with the eleven and others with them.

3 When Jesus suddenly appears in their midst, He does not rebuke them for their unbelief. He addresses them with, "Peace be with you," and does things to assure them that they are indeed seeing their Lord—risen and alive; He eats with them, and invites them to examine the wounds in His body, 24:35b–43. Jesus again makes use of the Law and the Prophets (i.e., the Hebrew scriptures of that time) to help those present understand the implications of the events of the past few days, 24:44–49.

4 Jesus leads the group to Bethany on the Mount of Olives, blesses them, and withdraws His visible presence. The group honors Jesus, returns to Jerusalem with great joy, and praises God continually in the Temple, 24:50–53.

ILLUSTRATION

47F

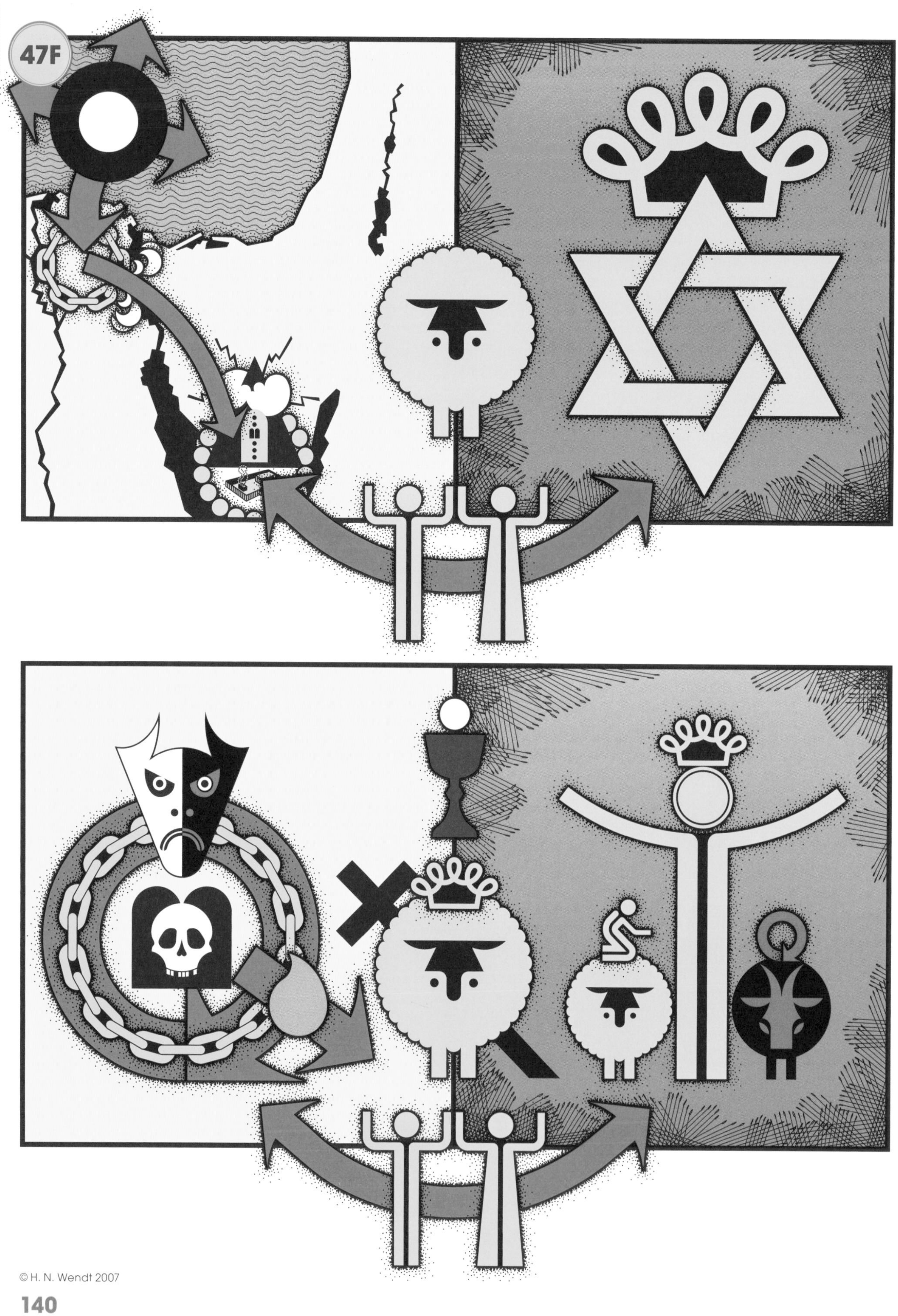

© H. N. Wendt 2007

The Messianic Banquet

Luke in particular makes frequent reference to Jesus eating with others—both friend and foe. The implications of eating together had a profound significance in Jesus' day, and continues to do so throughout the Middle East still today. The *upper section* of **ILLUSTRATION 47F** depicts the Jewish understanding of the significance of participating in a Passover meal. The *lower section* focuses on the what the New Testament teaches about the implications of participating in the Lord's Supper.

The narratives that describe Israel's forty years in the wilderness speak of God providing the people with food and drink; see Unit 10. After the nation entered the land, it celebrated a Passover at Gilgal, at which time the manna ceased to fall from the skies, Joshua 3:10–12. From this point on, the people ate food grown within the land.

Upper section

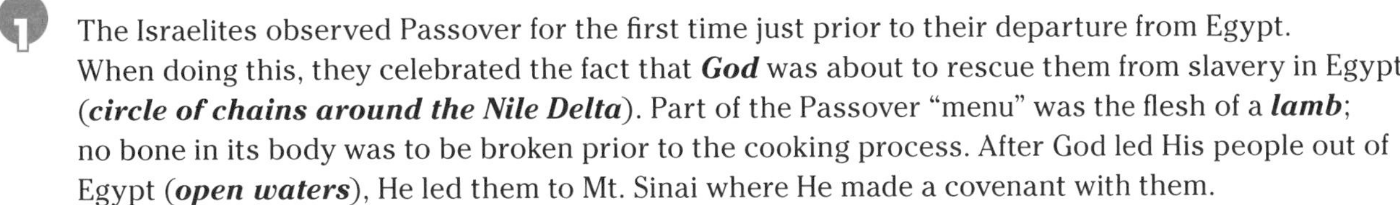

1. The Israelites observed Passover for the first time just prior to their departure from Egypt. When doing this, they celebrated the fact that ***God*** was about to rescue them from slavery in Egypt (***circle of chains around the Nile Delta***). Part of the Passover "menu" was the flesh of a ***lamb***; no bone in its body was to be broken prior to the cooking process. After God led His people out of Egypt (***open waters***), He led them to Mt. Sinai where He made a covenant with them.

2. Jewish people have continued to observe Passover down through the centuries. When doing so, they do not merely *recall* the Exodus event; they celebrate the fact that *they too participated in it* (***arrow pointing backward from male and female figures to the first Exodus***).

3. After the Babylonians finally destroyed Judah, Jerusalem, and the Temple in 587 B.C. and took thousands of its leading citizens into exile in Babylon, the Judeans found themselves without a king. However, in the centuries that followed their return from Babylon to Judah, they looked forward (***arrow pointing forward***) to the day when God would restore the Davidic dynasty (***crown; Star of David***) in Jerusalem, and the Messianic Age would begin.

4. What would things be like during the Messianic Age? Among other things, the people would enjoy an abundance of food and wine, and a prosperous lifestyle. The Messiah would create happiness among the poor and afflicted, and would gather all God's people into a banqueting community; see also Isaiah 55:1,2.

   Isaiah wrote (25:6):

   > *On this mountain the Lord of hosts will make for all peoples a feast of rich food, a feast of well-aged wines, of rich food filled with marrow, of well-aged wines strained clear.*

   Amos wrote (9:13):

   > *The time is surely coming, says the Lord, when the one who plows shall overtake the one who reaps, and the treader of grapes the one who sows the seed; the mountains shall drip sweet wine, and all the hills shall flow with it.*

   Joel wrote (3:18):

   > *In that day the mountains shall drip sweet wine, the hills shall flow with milk, and all the stream beds of Judah shall flow with water; a fountain shall come forth from the house of the Lord and water the Wadi Shittim.*

   In the pseudepigraphical work, 2 Baruch 29:5,6, and 9 we read:

   > *On one vine will be a thousand branches, and one branch will produce a thousand clusters, and one cluster will produce a thousand grapes, and one grape will produce a cor* (about 55 gallons, or 200 liters) *of wine. And those who are hungry will enjoy themselves and they will, moreover, see marvels every day.*
   >
   > *And it will happen at that time that the treasury of manna will come down again from on high, and they will eat of it those years because these are they who will have arrived at the consummation of time.*

Lower section

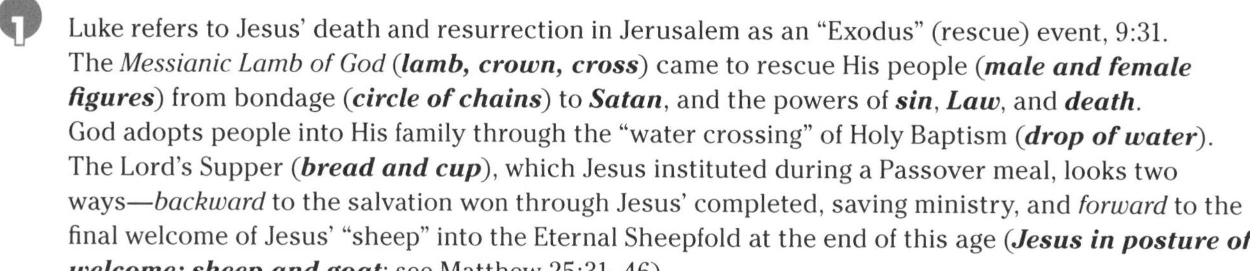

1. Luke refers to Jesus' death and resurrection in Jerusalem as an "Exodus" (rescue) event, 9:31. The *Messianic Lamb of God* (***lamb, crown, cross***) came to rescue His people (***male and female figures***) from bondage (***circle of chains***) to ***Satan***, and the powers of ***sin***, ***Law***, and ***death***. God adopts people into His family through the "water crossing" of Holy Baptism (***drop of water***). The Lord's Supper (***bread and cup***), which Jesus instituted during a Passover meal, looks two ways—*backward* to the salvation won through Jesus' completed, saving ministry, and *forward* to the final welcome of Jesus' "sheep" into the Eternal Sheepfold at the end of this age (***Jesus in posture of welcome; sheep and goat***; see Matthew 25:31–46).

2. Issues relating to sharing a meal together play an important role in the Gospel narratives—in particular, Luke. During Jesus' ministry, Jewish leaders invite Jesus to eat with them: Simon the Pharisee, Luke 7:36–50; a Pharisee, 11:37–52; and a ruler from among the Pharisees, 14:1–24. They also criticize Him for eating with others and call Him a glutton and a drunkard, 5:29–32; 7:33–50; 15:1,2. At the Last Supper (22:1–38), even the disciples argue about who will be the greatest in Jesus' kingdom, 22:24–27. After all, prior to Jesus' crucifixion and resurrection even the disciples fail to understand the nature of the Messianic Age and Banquet that is in progress throughout Jesus' ministry.

3. In Luke 12:37, Jesus says He will gird Himself and serve His people at table. In Luke 14:1–14, Jesus points out that only the poor, maimed, blind, and lame have the proper disposition to accept the invitation He sends out. People will be gathered from all corners of the earth to sit at table with the Old Testament saints, 13:28,29. At the time of the final consummation of the Kingdom, the disciples will eat and drink with Jesus in the Kingdom of God, 22:30.

4. According to Revelation 19:9, the Grand Finale to the Messianic Banquet will take place in the life to come when Jesus' brothers and sisters will celebrate the eternal Marriage Supper of the Lamb of God.

Key Themes in Luke

1 Luke traces Jesus' ancestry back to Adam (3:23–38) and calls Adam "the son of God," 3:38. God is making a new beginning to the *human race* (not just the *chosen people*, as in Matthew), and the new Son of God is God's instrument to bring this about.

2 Luke expresses a *universal concern* in relation to salvation. He alone includes in the quotation from Isaiah, "and all flesh shall see the salvation of God," 3:6, see Isaiah 40:3–5. The Samaritans are mentioned favorably, 9:51–56; 10:30–37; 17:11–19. The widow of Zarephath and Naaman, the Syrian leper, demonstrated faith while Israel often did not, 4:25–27. As in Matthew and Mark, a Roman centurion makes an admirable confession of faith beneath the cross, 23:47. The lists of officials in 2:lff. and 3:lff indicate that Jesus' ministry will have universal repercussions.

3 *Jesus loves to be in the company of those the Jewish religious elite avoid:* the poor, Samaritans, lepers, publicans, soldiers, public sinners in disgrace, and uneducated shepherds. Jesus invites Himself to the house of a tax collector for a meal, thus violating Jewish laws of ceremonial purity, 19:1–10.

4 Luke is the Gospel of the *great pardons*. Jesus deals with a "sinful" woman in a most compassionate way, 7:36–50. Jesus tells Zacchaeus that He wants to dine with him, 19:1–10. At Calvary, Jesus prays for His executioners (23:34), and makes a sublime promise to one of the thieves executed with Him, 23:39–43.

5 Matthew's Gospel is somber and majestic. Mark's is urgent. Luke stresses the joy of those who believe the gracious word of pardon the Father speaks to them through His Son. This is especially evident in the parables of the joyous shepherd, the joyous woman, and the joyous father, ch. 15.

6 Jesus always has time to show *understanding and sympathy*. He pauses on the way to Calvary to speak with the weeping women, 23:27–31. He heals the servant whose ear Peter cut off, 22:51. After Peter's denial, He pauses to look at him, 22:61.

7 The Gospel reflects a pronounced concern for the *well-being of women*, who at that time enjoyed no legal rights whatsoever. Jesus comes into repeated contact with them and treats them with dignity and understanding: Elizabeth; Anna the prophetess; the widow at Nain (7:11–17); the woman in Simon's house (7:36–50); Mary Magdalene, out of whom He cast seven demons; Joanna, the wife of Herod's steward; Chuza (8:2,3); Mary and Martha (10:38–42); and the weeping daughters of Jerusalem (23:27–31).

8 *The disciples must leave all things to follow Jesus and be totally dedicated to Him*, 5:11; 9:62; 14:26. They must sell what they have and give alms, 12:33. They will have to carry their cross throughout life, 9:23. However, they are asked to suffer nothing different from their Master, who must also suffer, 9:22, 13:33, 17:25, 22:37, 24:7,26,44. Money and earthly possessions pose a threat to discipleship, 12:13–34; ch. 16.

9 Detachment from the demands and standards of the world is possible only because Jesus and His disciples remain continuously dedicated to God in *prayer*. Jesus prays before every important step in His ministry: before His baptism, 3:21; before choosing the twelve, 6:12; before Peter's declaration that He is the Messiah, 9:18; at the Transfiguration, 9:28; before teaching the disciples how to pray, 11:1; in Gethsemane, 22:41. Jesus insisted that His followers be people of prayer, also, 6:28; 10:2; 11:1–13; 18:1–8; 21:36.

10 Luke refers repeatedly to the *work of the Spirit*, 1:15,35; 2:25–27; 3:16,22; 4:1,14,18; 10:21; 11:13; 12:10,12. The Spirit is now given not only to special individuals like the judges of old, but to John the Baptist (1:15) and his parents, 1:41,67. Jesus' conception is brought about by the Spirit (1:35), and He Himself is filled with the Spirit, 4:1. The "good things" God will surely give those who ask Him (Matthew 7:11) become "the Holy Spirit" in Luke 11:13. What the Spirit does in the life of Jesus, the Spirit continues to do in the life of the Church (Acts).

11 The *blame for Jesus' crucifixion* is laid at the feet of the Jewish leaders, 20:20,26; 23:2,5,18–25. Although the Roman authorities are involved in the events of the passion history, they are not blamed for what transpires.

12 *Luke omits scenes of violence and disrespect:* the murder of John the Baptist, Mark 6:14–29; the impatient remarks of the disciples, Mark, 4:35–41, Luke 8:22–25; the outrages committed during the passion, Mark 14:65, 15:15–19; the suggestion that Jesus had gone out of His mind, Mark 3:21. On the cross, Jesus utters no cry of dereliction, but simply commits His spirit into His Father's hands, 23:46.

13 Matthew mentions *Jerusalem* ten times, Mark fourteen times, and Luke thirty times in his Gospel and fifty-seven times in Acts. The activity outlined in Luke's Gospel begins and ends in the Temple, 1:5–23; 24:50–53. Scattered throughout the travel narrative (9:51–19:28) are numerous references to Jesus being on His way to Jerusalem, 9:51, 13:22, 17:11, 18:35. During the Transfiguration, Jesus speaks with His disciples about the "exodus" (rescue event) that He will "complete" in Jerusalem, 9:31. He sets His face to go there, 9:51. His death must be in Jerusalem, and at the hands of those within Jerusalem, 13:33. Jerusalem will treat Jesus the way it treated all the prophets, and in so doing will bring judgment on itself, 13:34. When Jesus arrives at the outskirts of the city, He weeps, 19:41–44. He predicts its destruction, 21:6. God will eventually withdraw His presence from Jerusalem and the Temple, 13:35. At the same time, Jerusalem is the chosen center from which salvation will spread out to the world, 9:31; 18:31; 19:11; 24:47–49; Acts 1:8.

SUMMARY

47A Studying the respective narratives in the four Gospels is like looking at the life of Jesus through four different lenses. Although the narratives in the first three Gospels resemble each other, there are differences. Mark contains no nativity narrative. Matthew often refers to "two" of this and that, rather than "one"—as in Mark and Luke. While Matthew, Mark, and John speak of the risen Jesus meeting with the disciples in Galilee, Luke speaks of Him ascending into heaven from the Mount of Olives in Jerusalem on Easter Sunday. Although Matthew and Luke in particular resemble Mark in content, both seem to have drawn on a collection of Jesus' sayings (whether oral or written) and each contains unique material.

47B When setting out to travel from Galilee to Jerusalem, Jesus is forbidden permission to travel south through Samaria. Luke's "travel narrative" contains unique elements—such as:

- Parables found only in Luke (e.g., The Good Samaritan; The Rich Fool; The Great Banquet; The Lost Sheep; The Lost Coin; The Two Lost Sons; The Dishonest Steward; The Persistent Widow; The Pharisee and the Publican; The Rich Man and Lazarus);
- Jesus dines in the home of Mary and Martha, and accepts Mary as a student;
- A Pharisee who hosts a meal for Jesus notes that He does not observe purification rituals;
- Jesus dines with Zacchaeus—a despised tax-collector and collaborator with the Romans.

47C After Jesus arrives on the Mount of Olives, He looks across the city of Jerusalem and weeps. Although David wept as he *left* Jerusalem, Jesus weeps as He *enters* Jerusalem. Many of the confrontations that Jesus has to deal with after attacking the Temple system resemble those reported in the other three Gospels.

47D There are numerous parallels between Luke's passion narrative and those of Matthew and Mark. However, Jesus prays on the Mount of Olives—not in the Garden of Gethsemane. Only Luke makes reference to Pilate sending Jesus to Herod Antipas for questioning; however, Jesus answers none of the questions Herod put to Him. Only Luke the physician refers to Jesus healing the man whose ear Peter cut off. In Luke, Jesus utters three very moving "words" from the cross—not one, as in Matthew and Mark.

47E After Jesus returns to life, only Luke refers to Jesus walking with two disciples on the way to Emmaus. The setting for the final scene in Luke is the Mount of Olives—not Galilee. Only Luke refers to Jesus' actual ascension.

47F Luke makes frequent reference to Jesus eating with people—both friend and foe.

47G Other unique Lucan emphases are:

- Luke traces Jesus' ancestry back beyond Abraham (as in Matthew) to Adam;
- Luke expresses a concern in relation to universal salvation;
- Jesus loves to be in the company of those the Jewish elite despise;

- Luke focuses on Jesus offering “great pardons”;
- The spirit of joy emerges frequently in Luke’s narrative;
- Jesus shows great concern for the welfare of women;
- Luke refers repeatedly to the work of the Holy Spirit in relation to Jesus’ ministry;

UNITS 41–50

The Gospels and Acts

UNIT 48

John (I)

Jesus, the Word Made Flesh; Jesus' Identity; John as "Trial Narrative"

48A

Jesus: The Word Become Flesh

The eagle flies higher than any other bird. It is said to be the only creature that can look directly into the sun and not be dazzled or blinded by it. Throughout the centuries, the Church has used the eagle as a symbol for the Gospel according to St. John. The choice is appropriate, for John's Gospel soars to sublime heights. Its opening verse says, "In the beginning was the Word," and in 1:14 John writes, "And the Word became flesh and lived among us." **ILLUSTRATION 48A** helps explain the profound significance of John's understanding of Jesus as the Final Word of God.

1 ***Six spirals; cloud, symbols for God and the Written Word:*** When God "speaks," what God says goes forth with divine power (***spirals***) to cause things to happen in *creation* and *history.*

2 ***First spiral at left:*** "In the beginning" (Genesis 1:1), God spoke, and the word He spoke went forth with power to bring *creation* into existence. God's word still sustains and directs creation.

3 ***Second spiral at left:*** God's word called Abraham and made a covenant with him, and later formed a ***covenant community*** out of Abraham's descendants at ***Mt. Sinai***. God's Word continues to direct *history.*

4 ***Torah scrolls, Mt. Sinai, Sinai covenant, prophet*** (*lower left corner*)***:*** The Old Testament prophets spoke to the people of their day from within the framework of the Sinai covenant. They told the people that disaster would overtake them if they persisted in ignoring God and His will for their lives (as revealed in the Torah/Law).

5 **Three "mountain peaks"** (*to right of the prophet and covenant community*)***; lines of vision to each peak:*** The hopes and dreams of the prophets might be compared with the experience of people today driving toward, and up into, a mountain range. When they reach what they thought was the top, they see an even higher line of peaks, and then another, and must climb them also to reach the top. They could never have seen the final line of peaks from the plain below.
Similarly, although an Old Testament prophet could see how the word he spoke might address the present and immediate future, he did not always know how God might finally use the word he spoke. One might say that God kept the words a prophet spoke in storage, and then put them into the mouths of later prophets so that they might address later situations; compare Micah 3:5 and Jeremiah 6:13,14, 8:10,11; Jeremiah 31:15 and Matthew 2:18.

6 ***Jesus as Servant-King; crowned Jesus on cross; open tomb; rising arrow; dove*** (Holy Spirit)***:*** Hebrews 1:1–3 says that, although God spoke in various ways throughout history, God spoke in a final and dramatic manner through His Son, Jesus the Messiah. In John 1:14, the evangelist tells us that, in Jesus, the Word clothed itself in flesh and became a flesh-and-blood Person.

7 In John's day, the term "Word" (or *Logos*) was widely used in philosophical discussion.

a. The pagan world thought of *Logos* as the controlling power that permeated the created order. The pagan philosophers urged humanity to discover what *Logos* is, and to live in harmony with it. By living in harmony with *Logos*, tranquility and order would result.

b. The Jews spoke about wisdom as the divine blueprint for creation and life. Wisdom was equated with the Torah, the first five books of Moses—the first thing God created. After wisdom came into existence, it advised God concerning all subsequent creative acts. Eventually, wisdom was personified. The Old Testament understands "the word of God" as God's revelation of Himself, whether in creation, in deeds of power and grace, or in prophecy.

8 When John calls Jesus "the Word," he states that Jesus reveals, and is, the divine Word, wisdom, plan, and blueprint. Jesus is God incarnate, God come-into-flesh. Jesus is the ultimate Word and revelation of God. As God previously revealed Himself through involvement in Israel's history and the words of the prophets, God now reveals Himself in a Person. When *Jesus* is substituted for *Word* in vv. 1–14, the profundity of John's message in relation to Jesus becomes clear.

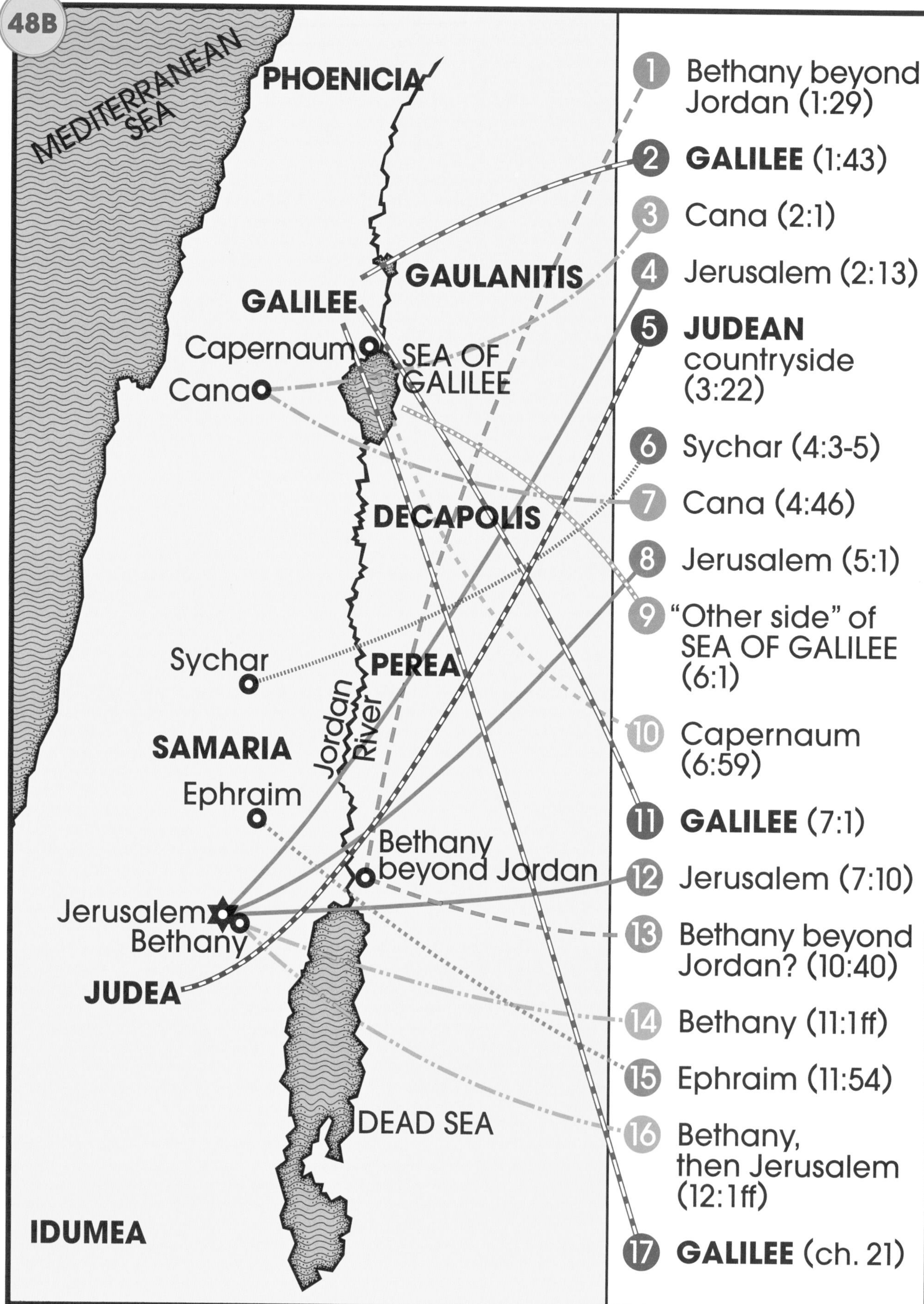
48B
MEDITERRANEAN SEA
PHOENICIA
GAULANITIS
GALILEE
Capernaum
SEA OF GALILEE
Cana
DECAPOLIS
Sychar
PEREA
Jordan River
SAMARIA
Ephraim
Bethany beyond Jordan
Jerusalem
Bethany
JUDEA
DEAD SEA
IDUMEA
1 Bethany beyond Jordan (1:29)
2 GALILEE (1:43)
3 Cana (2:1)
4 Jerusalem (2:13)
5 JUDEAN countryside (3:22)
6 Sychar (4:3-5)
7 Cana (4:46)
8 Jerusalem (5:1)
9 "Other side" of SEA OF GALILEE (6:1)
10 Capernaum (6:59)
11 GALILEE (7:1)
12 Jerusalem (7:10)
13 Bethany beyond Jordan? (10:40)
14 Bethany (11:1ff)
15 Ephraim (11:54)
16 Bethany, then Jerusalem (12:1ff)
17 GALILEE (ch. 21)

Jesus' Geographical Movements

ILLUSTRATION 42B outlines Jesus' geographical movements in the Gospels of Mark and Matthew. **ILLUSTRATION 46A** depicts His geographical movements in Luke's Gospel. **ILLUSTRATION 48B** depicts His geographical movements in John's narrative.

1. As the Gospel begins, Jesus goes to where John the Baptist is working—***Bethany beyond Jordan*** just to the northeast of the ***DEAD SEA***, 1:28,29.
2. Jesus goes to ***GALILEE***, 1:43.
3. He attends a wedding in ***Cana*** (2:1) and then goes to ***Capernaum***, 2:12.
4. He goes to ***Jerusalem*** where He attacks the Temple system, 2:13.
5. Jesus works in the countryside of ***JUDEA***, 3:22.
6. He leaves Judea for Galilee (4:3), and while traveling through ***SAMARIA*** meets with a Samaritan woman at Jacob's well in the city of ***Sychar***, 4:5.
7. He continues on to Galilee (4:43) and goes to ***Cana***, 4:46.
8. He goes back to ***Jerusalem***, 5:1.
9. He crosses to the other side of the ***SEA OF GALILEE***, although no mention is made of any return from Jerusalem, 6:1.
10. He teaches in a synagogue in ***Capernaum***, 6:59.
11. He goes about in ***GALILEE***, 7:1.
12. He goes to ***Jerusalem*** (7:10) and spends time in the Temple, 7:14, 10:22.
13. He crosses to the East Bank of the River Jordan (possibly ***Bethany beyond Jordan?***), 10:40.
14. He goes to ***Bethany*** (11:1–53) where He raises Lazarus from the dead.
15. He goes to ***Ephraim***, about 15 miles (24 kilometers) to the north of Jerusalem, 11:54.
16. He returns to ***Bethany*** (12:1) and enters ***Jerusalem***, 12:12.
17. He meets with seven of the disciples on the shores of the ***SEA OF GALILEE***, ch. 21.

The illustration points to the fact that John's chronological and geographical patterns are different from those of the first three Gospels which—for example—refer to Jesus attending only *one* Passover. John refers to Jesus participating in *three* Passover observances; compare Mark 14:1,12,14,16 with John 2:13,23, 6:4, 11:55, 12:1, 13:1. However, is John talking about *three different Passover observances*, or is he merely talking about *the institution of Passover* as such?

Some believe that John is indeed concerned with chronology, and that his Gospel incorporates traditions older than those found in Matthew, Mark, and Luke. Others argue that John moves from theme to theme with a certain indifference to those finer points of chronology that occupy the minds of western historians today. They argue that John intended his Gospel to be a series of sermons about truths Jesus taught, rather than a biography. They point out that at times it is difficult to determine where Jesus finishes speaking, and where the evangelist adds his own words. To illustrate, where should quotation marks be placed in 3:10–21? Comments about these matters will be made in the materials that follow.

ILLUSTRATION
48C
WORD
OF GOD
LAMB OF GOD
TEACHER
MESSIAH
SON OF GOD
KING OF ISRAEL
SON OF MAN
LORD AND
GOD

Jesus' Identity—No Secrets

ILLUSTRATION 48C depicts some of the titles and functions ascribed to Jesus in John 1; these culminate in Thomas' profession of faith in 20:28. The ***symbol for God*** appears at *top left.* The ***crown*** (*top right*) denotes Jesus' Kingship. The *nature of Jesus' Kingship* (Jesus washes the disciples' feet, John 13:1–17) is depicted at ***lower right*** (see also **ILLUSTRATION 43D**). Points 1–5 relate directly to **ILLUSTRATION 48D**; points 6–10 relate to other themes encountered in John ch. 1.

1 ***WORD OF GOD:*** "And the Word became flesh and dwelt among us," 1:14. The word translated as "dwelt" literally means "tented" or "tabernacled." John declares that God is now "encamped" among His people, not invisibly in the Holy of Holies that only the High Priest could enter one day each year, but in the person of Jesus the Messiah. The invisible God becomes visible in the divine-human Word. The written Word bears witness to the Incarnate Word. God's Final, Living Word is Jesus the Messiah.

2 ***Titles on descending arrow:*** John's opening chapter contains a list of titles that state who Jesus is and define His mission. These are:

- ***WORD OF GOD***, 1:1,14
- ***LAMB OF GOD***, 1:29,36
- ***TEACHER*** (Rabbi), 1:38
- ***MESSIAH***, 1:41
- ***SON OF GOD***, 1:49
- ***KING OF ISRAEL***, 1:49
- ***SON OF MAN***, 1:51; see Daniel 7:13

3 ***Fig tree:*** In 1:48 Jesus says to Nathanael, "I saw you under the fig tree before Philip called you." During previous centuries the hope was that, when the Messiah came, people would experience the peace and joy of sitting under their own vine and fig tree, Micah 4:4; 1 Kings 4:25; Isaiah 36:16. If Nathanael is sitting under a fig tree, the Messianic Age has broken in!

4 ***Triumphant Jesus; angels; square stone cancelled out:*** Many find Jesus' statement in 1:51 somewhat puzzling: "Very truly, I tell you, you will see heaven opened, and the angels of God ascending and descending upon the Son of Man." The Holy of Holies in the postexilic and Herodian Temples was empty—apart from a low, flat stone built into the floor at its center. (The Ark of the Covenant was most likely destroyed by the Babylonians in 587 B.C.) This stone was called the "Foundation Stone" (*eben shetiyah*). It was about 18 inches square and two inches high (45 centimeters square and 5 cm high). Jewish *tradition* held that Jacob was using this stone as a pillow when, in a dream, he saw a ladder reaching up to heaven with angels ascending and descending on it, and heard God speak to him, Genesis 28. When those who returned from Babylon rebuilt the Jerusalem Temple, they found themselves needing a symbol of God's presence. Again according to *tradition*, they went to Bethel, found this stone, and placed it in the Holy of Holies.

In Jesus' day, the rabbis ascribed numerous functions to this stone. It was "the navel of the earth," the point from which the world grew in the initial creative process. It was the point of contact between heaven and earth, between God and humanity. It held the subterranean waters in check and prevented them from flooding the earth. It was also that place where, on the annual Day of Atonement, blood was sprinkled to atone for the nation's sin. However, Jesus declared that He replaced that stone and the Holy of Holies, and their functions. This is but the first of numerous replacements that surface in the ensuing chapters.

5 The series of titles ascribed to Jesus in John's first chapter reaches its grand finale in John 20 when Thomas falls down before the Risen Jesus and proclaims, "My Lord and my God!" (***LORD AND GOD***)

6 In Mark 1–8, Jesus does not state in *words* who He is, and discourages any reference to His being the Messiah until His *actions* have demonstrated what kind of Messiah He has come to be. About halfway through the Gospel, He asks the disciples who the *crowds* think He is, and then who *they themselves* think He is, Mark 8:27–30.

John approaches the question of Jesus' identity quite differently. From the very outset, he declares who Jesus is, and why He has come. In doing so, John draws heavily on Old Testament and intertestamental concepts.

7 The expression "In the beginning" (1:1) reflects Genesis 1:1. John's desire is to declare that Jesus' life and mission brought about a new beginning to creation, history, and humanity.

8 Some interpreters detect hints of a seven-day scheme in 1:29,35,43; 2:1. If there is a "next day" (1:29), there must have been a previous day; hence, the reference in 1:29 is to *Day Two*. (*Day One* is hinted at in 1:1, which reflects Genesis 1:1.) The reference in 1:35 is to *Day Three*, that in 1:43 is to *Day Four*, and that in 2:1 is to Day Seven (three days after Day Four). If this seven-day structure is intentional, it would seem that Jesus' goal is to free God's people from bondage to a rather legal religious system and to introduce them to God's final, eternal Sabbath rest. (The implications of the previous sentence will be analyzed in Unit 49.)

9 John states that those who come to faith in Jesus undergo a new birth. This is not a second physical birth, but has to do with being born into the family of God. This birth takes place through the will of God when, in forgiving grace and through His crucified and risen Son, He gathers people back into the divine family and teaches them to walk as His beloved children, 1:12,13. Tragically, when Jesus came to His own creation, it did not recognize Him. Many of those who claimed to be the people of God refused to welcome Him, 1:10,11. Even so, some did come to faith—and to membership in the eternal family, 1:12,13.

10 Jesus, the eternal Word, did not arrive unannounced. John the Baptist heralded His coming, 1:6–8,15,19–28. John insisted that his own role was merely to prepare the way for the great final Exodus (*rescue*) that was soon to take place, 1:23. The evangelist locates John's ministry on the East Bank of the River Jordan (1:28), indicating that he called his Jewish hearers out of the land and made it necessary for them to enter it again through a water-crossing—at about the same spot where, long before under Joshua's leadership, their ancestors entered the land to undertake the conquest.

John: A Trial Narrative

John's trial, passion, and resurrection narratives will be analyzed in Unit 49. The comments that follow point to the overarching theme of *trial* that weaves its way through all of John's Gospel.

THE JEWISH TRIAL

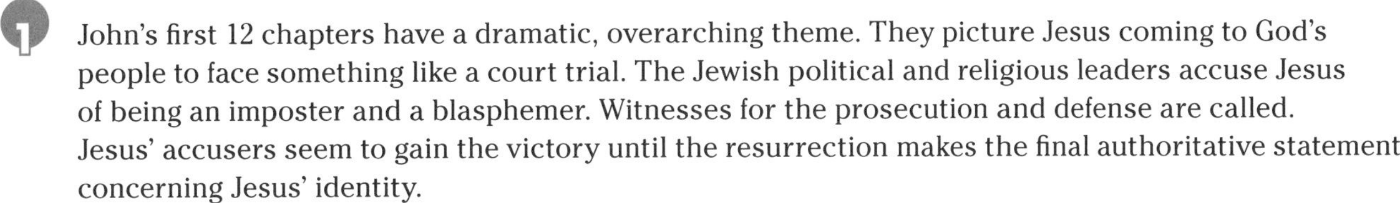

1 John's first 12 chapters have a dramatic, overarching theme. They picture Jesus coming to God's people to face something like a court trial. The Jewish political and religious leaders accuse Jesus of being an imposter and a blasphemer. Witnesses for the prosecution and defense are called. Jesus' accusers seem to gain the victory until the resurrection makes the final authoritative statement concerning Jesus' identity.

2 The spirit of "trial" emerges more clearly when the following details are considered. Although Jesus' opponents make the final decision to have Him put to death *after* He raises Lazarus (ch. 11), they oppose Him *throughout His ministry.* The opposition hinted at in 1:11 reveals itself in specific situations as the narrative unfolds.

- Jesus' opponents want to kill Him for healing on the Sabbath and making Himself equal with God, 5:18.
- When Jesus refers to Himself as the bread from heaven (6:33,35–40), many do not accept what He says and desert Him, 6:60,66.
- When Jesus goes to Jerusalem to attend the Feast of Booths or Tabernacles, some want to arrest and kill Him, 7:19,25,43,44. They accuse Him of being a Samaritan and demon-possessed (8:48,49), and try to stone Him, 8:59.
- Those who endorse Jesus' ministry are thrown out of the synagogue, 9:22.
- When Jesus refers to Himself as the Good Shepherd, the One in whom Ezekiel 34 is fulfilled, His opponents are divided, insist that He is demon-possessed, throw stones at Him, and try to arrest Him, 10:19,20,31,39.

3 Chs. 13–17 describe events in the Upper Room where, in a sense, the *disciples are on trial by Jesus.* Do they really understand His message? Do they understand what claiming Jesus as Lord and Messiah implies for their daily life? The first stages of Peter's denial are outlined in 18:15–18. The latter details of Peter's denial are given in 18:25–27.

4 Jesus and the disciples proceed from the Upper Room to the Garden of Gethsemane, where Jesus is captured. Those who seize and bind Jesus take Him to Annas. Annas had been High Priest until A.D. 15, when he was deposed by the Romans. Five of his sons succeeded him as High Priest, and Caiaphas (the present High Priest) is his son-in-law. The High Priest then questions Jesus; he must still be Annas; see 18:19,24,28. (A High Priest retained his title through life.) What transpires between Annas and Jesus is not a trial, but a conversation in which Annas questions Jesus about His disciples and His teaching. Annas then sends Jesus bound to Caiaphas. However, there is no reference to any conversation between Caiaphas and Jesus, or to any kind of trial by the Jewish Sanhedrin, 18:24.

5 Why has John omitted any reference to a formal Jewish trial *within his passion narrative*? The answer becomes clear when the events outlined in chs. 11 and 12 are understood. When Jesus goes to the aid of Lazarus, He is met by Martha and Mary. Both profess faith in Jesus' power. Martha expresses her conviction that Lazarus will return to life in the resurrection on the Last Day, and thus expresses the traditional hope of *some* Jewish people at that time. Jesus assures her that hopes concerning death and resurrection have been transformed and fulfilled, for He is present, 11:25–27. *Jesus is the resurrection and the life!* Shortly afterwards, Jesus restores Lazarus to life, 11:43,44.

The response to Jesus' action is immediate. Some rejoice, but some inform the Pharisees what Jesus has done. The Pharisees believe that the resurrection of the body will take place at the close of the

Age when the Messiah comes. Jesus' actions are scandalous and cause the Pharisees much distress. Has the Messianic Age come, and is Jesus the Messiah? Impossible! Jesus must go! The Jewish trial follows, 11:47–53. The members of the Sanhedrin determine that, rather than risk losing their nation and Temple, Jesus must be eliminated. Accordingly, Jesus is tried *in absentia* and condemned to death, 11:53,57. Furthermore, a decision is made to kill Lazarus as well; after all, Lazarus was "Exhibit A" in the recent disturbing resurrection event, 12:9–11. However, John makes no reference to Lazarus being put to death.

THE ROMAN TRIAL

John's description of Jesus' trial by Pilate is recorded in 18:28–19:16. It will be analyzed in some detail in Unit 49. However, some preliminary comments follow.

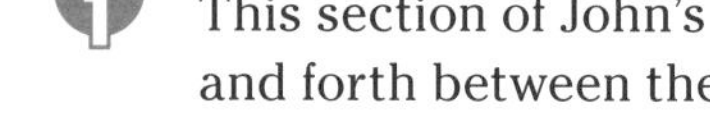

1. This section of John's narrative consists of seven sections, or seven "scenes," with Pilate going back and forth between the Jewish religious leaders and Jesus.

2. Pilate asks Jesus a series of questions:
    - *Are you the King of the Jews?* (18:33)
    - *What have you done?* (18:35)
    - *So you are a King?* (18:37)
    - *What is truth?* (18:38)
    - *Where are you from?* (19:9)
    - *Do you refuse to speak to me?* (19:10)
    - *Do you not know that I have power to release you and power to crucify you?* (19:10)

3. The irony throughout this section of the trial narrative is that it is really *Jesus* who is trying *Pilate*. *Jesus* is challenging *Pilate* to grapple with a series of questions:
    - *What kind of a King do you think I am?*
    - *Where do you think I am from?*
    - *What do You think My ministry is all about?*
    - *Do you understand that I am 'the truth'?*
    - *Are you willing to hear the truth that I speak?*
    - *Do you understand that I am the One who has power over you, and that you could do nothing to Me unless I permitted you?*

We, God's people, must remember that John challenges us today to understand that, in a very real sense, humanity continues to be on trial by Jesus and that Jesus confronts each and every one of us with the same questions. Furthermore, the Gospel itself supplies clues as to how we might answer these questions.

Although John makes no mention of the fall into sin (Genesis 3), he uses terms like "darkness" and "light" to declare that fallen humanity loves the darkness of ignorance and sin rather than the light of God's saving truth; see also 3:19,20. Terms used in Genesis 1 to refer to the physical creation are used to describe spiritual phenomena. Although the world put the Son of God to death, it was not able to snuff out the light that He brought. Jesus' light now shines more brightly, and the Word rings out more clearly. Darkness implies those ways of thinking, acting, and speaking that are not in keeping with the "light" God has revealed in Jesus. "Darkness" describes conditions where God is perceived as absent, and "light" refers to conditions where God's presence is recognized; see also Ephesians 5:1–14.

John's Outline

The outline below shows that John contains *seven* "I AM" statements, *seven* signs, and *three* passion predictions. Furthermore, Jesus' healing of the blind man in ch. 9 involves *seven* scenes, and there are *seven* scenes in Jesus' trial by Pilate.

INTRODUCTION (1:1–1:51)	1:1–18	Prologue	
	1:19–34	The witness of John the Baptist	
	1:35–51	The first disciples	
		Jesus Reveals His Glory to the World (2:1–12:50)	
1	2:1–12	The marriage at Cana	Sign 1
	2:13–25	The cleansing of the Temple	
	3:1–21	Jesus and Nicodemus (3:14, see Numbers 21:9)	Passion prediction 1
	3:22–4:3	The final witness of John the Baptist	
	4:4–26	The Samaritan woman at the well	
	4:27–42	Jesus and the Samaritans	
	4:43–54	The healing of the official's son	Sign 2
	5:1–16	The healing of the paralytic	Sign 3
	5:17–47	Jesus' witness to His sonship	
	6:1–15	The feeding of the five thousand	Sign 4
	6:16–24	Jesus walks on the water	Sign 5
	6:25–51a	Jesus as the Bread of Life	"I AM" 1
	6:51b–71	A pointer to the Lord's Supper	
	7:1–52	The speech at the Feast of Booths	
	Some manu-scripts include 7:53–8:11.	The woman taken in adultery	
	8:12–30	Jesus as the Light of the World	"I AM" 2 Passion prediction 2
	8:31–59	Abraham's true children	
	9:1–41	The healing of the blind man	Sign 6 (seven scenes)
	10:1–18	Jesus: the Good Shepherd and the door	"I AM" 3 "I AM" 4
	10:19–42	Jesus at the Feast of Dedication	
	11:1–44	The raising of Lazarus	Sign 7 "I AM" 5
	11:45–57	The plot to kill Jesus	
	12:1–8	The anointing of Jesus at Bethany	
	12:9–19	Jesus' triumphal entry	
	12:20–50	Jesus' last witness before the passion	Passion prediction 3

		Jesus Reveals His Glory to His Disciples (13:1–17:26)	
	13:1–20	The footwashing, an acted parable	
	13:21–30	Satan enters Judas, the betrayer	
	13:31–38	The glorification of the Son	
	14:1–14	Jesus as the Way, the Truth, the Life	"I AM" 6
2	14:15–31	The promise of the Counselor	
	15:1–11	Jesus as the True Vine	"I AM" 7
	15:12–27	Jesus' love and the world's hatred	
	16:1–15	The promise of the Spirit of Truth	
	16:16–33	The coming hour of sorrow, then joy	
	17:1–26	Jesus' High Priestly prayer	
		The Final Hour of Glory (18:1–20:31)	
	18:1–11	The arrest of Jesus in Gethsemane	
	18:12–27	The Jewish trial of Jesus, and Peter's denials	
	18:28–19:16	The trial before Pilate (seven scenes)	
3	19:17–37	The crucifixion of Jesus	
	19:38–42	The burial of Jesus	
	20:1–10	Peter and John at the empty tomb	
	20:11–18	Jesus appears to Mary Magdalene	
	20:19–29	Believing Thomas	
	20:30,31	The purpose of the Gospel	
		Epilogue (21:1–25)	
	21:1–14	The miraculous catch of fish	
4	21:15–19	The commissioning of Peter	
	21:20–25	The role of the Beloved Disciple	

SUMMARY

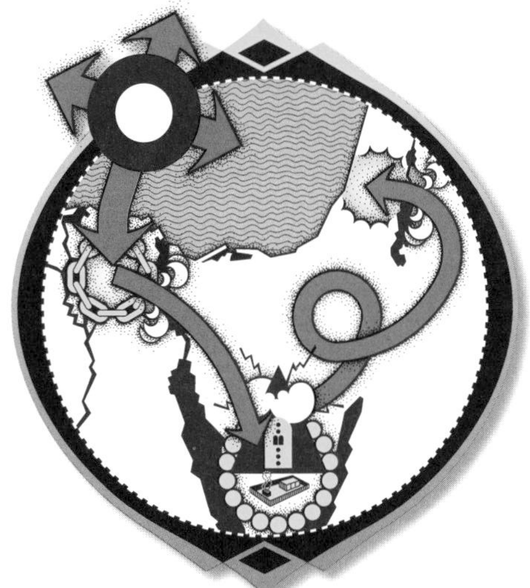

48A The Jewish people treasured the writings of Moses, and the law-codes that God revealed to them at Mt. Sinai. Within that Word were many references to the covenant that God made with them at Sinai—the covenant that became the launching point for the prophetic attack. However, the "grand finale" to Jewish history, to the concept of covenant, and to the proclamations of the prophets surface in Jesus' mission and ministry. In ch. 1, John states that "In the beginning was the Word...and the Word became flesh and lived among us." The Creator has become a flesh-and-blood Person in Jesus the Messiah—the "high point" of biblical revelation.

48B Jesus' geographical movements in John are quite different from those recorded in the Synoptic Gospels. Jesus moves back and forth between Judea and Galilee, and even speaks with a Samaritan woman. Although John refers to Passover observances in chs. 2, 6, and his passion narrative, it is doubtful that John is suggesting that Jesus' ministry lasted two or three years.

48C There is no "Messianic secret" in John's Gospel. In his opening chapter, a number of lofty, divine titles are ascribed to Jesus. When doubting Thomas finds himself face-to-face with the risen and vindicated Jesus, he professes the greatest of all titles, "My Lord and My God!"

48D The fourth Gospel takes the form of a trial narrative. As Jesus' mission unfolds, He declares that He supplants and replaces all Jewish institutions and observances—a message that angers His hearers. In John's first 12 chapters, Jesus is under scrutiny by the Jewish leaders who accuse Him of being an imposter and a blasphemer. Jesus' raising of Lazarus on the Mount of Olives is the last straw for the Jewish leaders; it moves the Sanhedrin to declare that Jesus must be put to death. If Jesus is not removed from the scene, the Roman overlords might well intervene and destroy Jerusalem, the Temple, and the Jewish nation.

In chs. 13–17, Jesus shares a meal with His disciples in an upper room. The meal is not referred to as a Passover Meal, and no reference is made to Jesus instituting His Holy Supper. Even so, Jesus challenges His disciples to think deeply when He washes their feet. No Jew would ever wash another person's feet! Only Gentile slaves washed feet! The message is that although many Jews, including the disciples, were waiting for a Messiah who would destroy their political overlords, Jesus wants them to understand that He has come to establish an upside-down, back-to-front Kingdom in which people devote life to glorifying God by serving others full-time!

In the final trial that takes place in Jerusalem, Jesus is tried by Pilate, the Roman procurator. The irony is that although it seems that Pilate is trying Jesus, the truth is that Jesus is trying Pilate—the symbol of the non-Jewish Gentile world. And by extension, the trial continues in that Jesus asks each person on Planet Earth, "Who do you think I am?" "Where do you think I have come from?" "What do you think I have done?"

48E In John, everything that Jesus says and does has a profound theological significance and a link to Old Testament beliefs and practices. Embedded in John's narrative are seven signs, seven "I am" statements, and three passion predictions. The narrative describing Jesus healing a blind man has seven scenes, as does also that describing Jesus' trial by Pilate. Prior to taking the disciples to an Upper Room, Jesus states that He has come to reveal and conquer humanity's real enemy, Satan and the realm of the demonic. As Jesus breathes His last, He states that He has "finished" what He came to do. By living the life of a Servant-without-limit, He has conquered the powers of Satan, sin, and death.

CROSSWAYS®
5
SECTION
UNITS 41–50
The Gospels and Acts
UNIT 49
John (II)
Jesus' Ministry, Trial, and Resurrection
GENESIS
MATTHEW
MARK
LUKE
JOHN
2 SAMUEL
ACTS
PSALMS
ISAIAH
JEREMIAH
EZEKIEL
AMOS
ROMANS
1 CORINTHIANS
2 CORINTHIANS
GALATIANS
EPHESIANS
PHILIPPIANS
COLOSSIANS
1 THESSALONIANS
2 THESSALONIANS
1 TIMOTHY
2 TIMOTHY
TITUS
PHILEMON
HEBREWS
JAMES
1 PETER
2 PETER
1 JOHN
2 JOHN
3 JOHN
JUDE
REVELATION

1
2
3
4
5
6
7
8
9
10
11
12
13
14
15
16

Jesus' Ministry—According to John

ILLUSTRATION 49A summarizes Jesus's ministry as outlined in the Gospel according to St. John.

Frame 

Temple ground plan; Foundation Stone within the Holy of Holies: In John 1:51, Jesus replaces the Holy of Holies of the Jerusalem Temple and the Foundation Stone located on the floor at its center. Jesus states that God's presence is not restricted to a room within a structure within a city within a land; Jesus Himself is the presence of God among humanity.

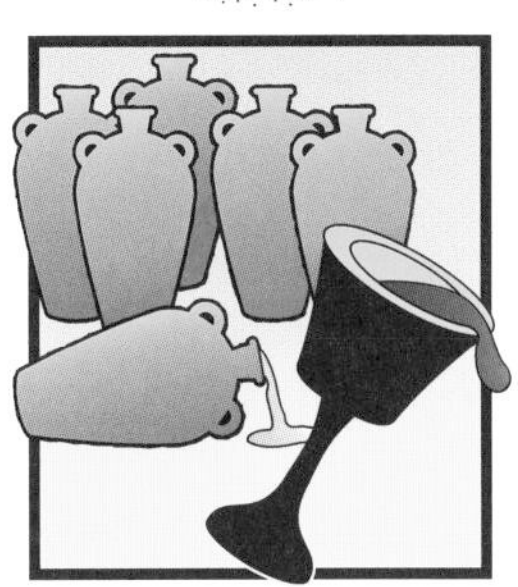

Frame 2

Water jars; chalice containing wine: John refers to Jesus' miraculous deeds as "signs" that make a theological statement in relation to Jesus' ministry. The first of these took place in Cana in Galilee, 2:1–12. Jews were in the minority in Galilee and came into repeated contact with Gentiles. After each encounter they had to make themselves ritually clean once again by means of a ceremonial washing; see Mark 7:3,4.

Jesus attends a wedding celebration at Cana in Galilee where, in the course events, the hosts run out of wine. To run out of wine at a wedding is a social disaster, and brings disgrace on the family. The couple celebrating their marriage might read the situation as one that will bring bad luck on their future life together. Jesus goes to their rescue. He tells servants at the celebration to fill six stone jars with water—up to the brim. (Water in these jars would normally have been used for purification rites. Water used for this purpose had to be in *stone* jars. After all, if jars are made out of *clay*, water poured into them can infiltrate the clay and be rendered ceremonially unclean—making it unfit for use in purification rites.) When the servants draw out the contents of the jars, they find that it has been changed. The hosts now have access to an estimated 150–225 gallons (565 to 850 liters) of very good wine!

The Old Testament suggested that, when the Messiah finally came, there would be an abundance of wine, Amos 9:13; Joel 3:18. The non-canonical 2 Baruch 29:5 said something similar.

> *The earth will also yield fruits ten thousandfold. And on one vine will be a thousand branches, and one branch will produce a thousand clusters, and one cluster will produce a thousand grapes, and one grape will produce a cor of wine.* (The measure referred to as "cor" is uncertain; estimates vary from 35 to 60 gallons, or 130 to 225 liters.)

When Jesus creates an abundance of wine at Cana, He declares that the Messianic Age has come. Furthermore, water intended for use in ritual washings is transformed into wine that makes the heart glad. Where Jesus is present, all previous purification rituals and practices are superseded. To be in Jesus' presence is to experience unending joy. Jesus alone establishes and sustains humanity's relationship with the Father.

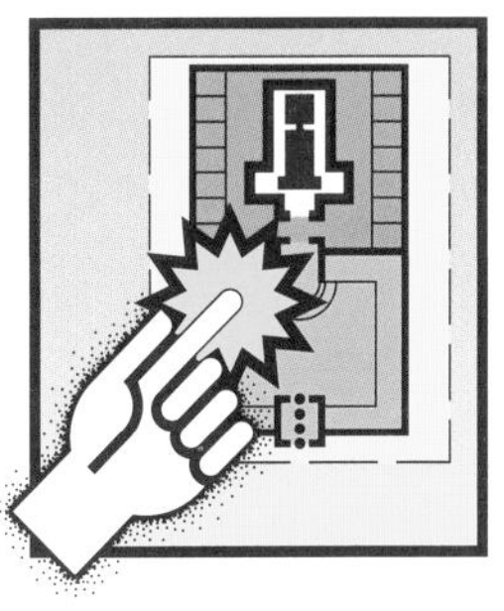

Frame 

The Temple Complex: After declaring that He replaces the Holy of Holies, the Foundation Stone (1:51), and purification rites, Jesus declares that He replaces the entire Temple complex. With what? His resurrected body and the Christian community (also His "body"). John 2:13–17 reports Jesus attacking the "Temple system"; 2:18–22 reports the ensuing conversation. Here, as elsewhere, John uses an "episode-discourse" structure.

Question mark; person beneath a Star of David; person beneath symbols for Baptism and the Holy Spirit: Nicodemus believes that a person born of a Jewish womb is automatically a child of God. Jesus informs him that admission into the family of God is by a different birth process altogether—the radical activity of God working through the Holy Spirit in the water of baptism. What matters is not a genetic link in relation to *physical birth*, but *spiritual rebirth* in relation to a person's inner life, ch. 3.

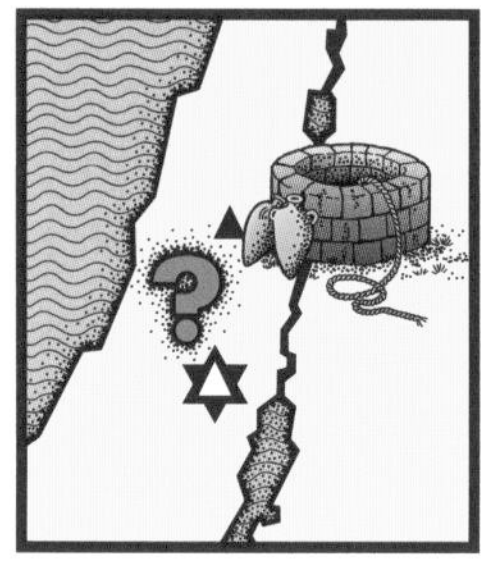

Frame 5

Star of David with Temple Mount superimposed; question mark; location of Mount Gerizim; well and water jars: John reports Jesus' conversation with a Samaritan woman in the vicinity of Sychar near Mt. Gerizim in Samaria, ch. 4. (Samaritans claimed to be the true descendants of Abraham; they had opposed the return of the Jewish exiles from Babylon.) The conversation takes place at noon. (Women usually go to a well in the morning or late afternoon when it is cooler—not at midday. This woman wants to avoid contact with other women who know about the life she has been leading.) After Jesus asks the woman to draw Him water to drink, He assures her He has *living water* to give—a statement she finds puzzling. When Jesus tells her that He knows about her numerous past and present illicit sexual relationships (He does not openly rebuke her), she changes the subject and raises the issue of the legitimacy of worship localities. The Samaritans believed that the Temple on Mt. Gerizim was the only valid place for the pure worship of God, while the Jews reserved that role for Mt. Zion in Jerusalem. Jesus declares that "the hour is coming, and is now here," (4:23) when both convictions are invalid. Jesus Himself is the focal point of all true worship, 4:23–26. The issue is *Person*, not *place*.

After her conversation with Jesus, the women leaves her water jar at the well, returns to Sychar, and tells other people about what she has experienced. She invites the people to "come and see" Jesus, and suggests that He might even be the Messiah—remarkable, for the Samaritans did not believe in the coming of a Messiah. Many Samaritans believe in Jesus because of the woman's testimony, go out to meet with Him, and invite Him to stay with them—which He does, for two days. The Samaritans then refer to Jesus as "the Savior of the world" (4:42)—a title given only to the Roman Emperor.

Frame 6

Symbol denoting Sabbath; crippled man crawling toward a pool of water: John 5 reports Jesus healing a crippled man at the pool of Bethzatha (or Bethesda) in Jerusalem. A discussion concerning Jesus' authority follows. The episode outlined in 4:46–54 can be linked to that reported in 5:1–16. The two incidents tell of Jesus healing two people: *first*, the son of a Gentile nobleman; *second*, a sick Jewish man at the pool of Bethzatha. Both healings illustrate the life-giving power of Jesus' spoken word. In healing the nobleman's son, Jesus gives new life to one at the brink of death. In healing the man at the pool of Bethzatha, Jesus gives new life to one who is otherwise helpless.

The second healing takes place on the Sabbath, 5:9b. In acting as He does, Jesus demonstrates His authority over Sabbath ordinances, and replaces them with Himself and the rest that He alone can give. Although the exchange in 5:17–18 seems puzzling, the point that emerges is clear. The Jews argued that, although God had commanded *them* to refrain from work on the Sabbath, *God* does not, and cannot, cease from activity on that day. God has to continue working to keep creation functioning. In "working" on the Sabbath, Jesus claims for Himself the authority of God, for *He is God*.

Frame 7

The Passover, Manna, and Land Expectations: As God once fed the Israelites with meat and manna in the wilderness, so Jesus feeds His people at Passover time with ***bread*** and meat (***fish***), ch. 6. As in Mark 6:43, there are 12 baskets of leftovers, John 6:13. The people are so impressed that they express their desire to make Jesus King over their land, possibly hoping to have Him lead them in a revolt against the Romans. Jesus leaves them (6:15), but soon afterward His disciples see Him walking toward them across the Sea of Galilee, 6:16–21.

Jesus' power over the forces of nature duplicates the power of God as described in the Old Testament, e.g., Psalm 89:9; 107:23–32. Jesus, therefore, must be God incarnate. Jesus is the Ruler of the *universe*. Indeed, when the crowds offer Jesus dominion over *their little land* (6:15), they are hardly offering Him any promotion; He is already Lord of the universe!

In asking Jesus for a sign, the crowds refer to the fact that God provided their forefathers with manna during the period of the wilderness wanderings. Although the manna ceased to fall after they entered the land (Joshua 5:10–12), they believed that it would fall again when the Messianic Age broke in:

> *And it will happen at that time that the treasury of manna will come down again from on high, and they will eat of it in those years because these are they who will have arrived at the consummation of time.* (2 Baruch 29:8)

However, Jesus declares that He is the True Bread of Life come down from heaven, and that He sustains life throughout time and eternity. Many of His hearers cannot accept this claim (6:60), and leave Him, 6:66. Although the circle of Jesus' adherents diminishes, the disciples remain with Him, 6:67–69.

Frame 

Simple shelter, with leafy cover: Jesus attends the Feast of Tabernacles in Jerusalem—an event mentioned only in John's Gospel, 7:1–52; 8:12–59. Tens of thousands attend, and live in simple tents or booths as a reminder of their experiences during the wilderness period. The feast also celebrates the culmination of harvest—especially of olives and grapes. Priests, carrying citrus fruit and palm branches, march around the Temple altar. They pour water from the pool of Siloam over the altar to in the hope that God will provide His people with adequate rain during the approaching year. Giant candles are lit in the Temple court—candles that cast their light far and wide over the city; the people dance in their light. The Festival lasts for eight days and begins and ends on a Sabbath. The observance is associated with the coming of the Messiah—and the hoped-for liberation from Rome. It is also associated with the Day of Judgment (also known as the Day of the Lord) when God will establish His universal Kingdom. After attending the feast, Jesus proclaims Himself to be the Water of Life (7:37–39), the Light of the World (7:14–52, 8:12–59), and the "I AM," 8:58, 18:6 (see Exodus 3:13–15; God refers to Himself as "I AM")—claims that arouse opposition and anger, 8:13, 31–33, 37, 44, 48, 59.

John 9:1–7 describes Jesus healing a blind man at the pool at Siloam, and 9:8–41 reports a discourse on judgment. When Jesus and the disciples first see the man, the disciples suggest that his blindness is a result either of his own sin or that of his parents. Jesus rejects both ideas and says the condition exists so that God might be glorified. Jesus then heals the man on the Sabbath. The Pharisees conclude that Jesus must be a sinner, for if He heals on the Sabbath, He is not from God. (There are *seven scenes* in this healing narrative: 9:1–7; 9:8–12; 9:13–17; 9:18–23; 9:24–34; 9:35–39; 9:40,41.)

Jesus' actions declare Him to be the Light of the world. He is also the Judge of those who encounter His light. The Pharisees' problem is that they call evil good, and good evil. Their concern is ritual, not human need. They slander and condemn both Jesus and the one Jesus heals. However, the ones who are judged and found wanting are the Pharisees themselves. Judgment is exercised *on* the Pharisees, not *by* the Pharisees. Those who think they can *see* are declared to be *blind*.

It is important to note the titles used by the man Jesus healed of his *physical* blindness as his *spiritual* sight grows. First, "the *man* called Jesus," 9:11. Second, "He is a *prophet*," 9:17. Third, "*Lord*, I believe," 9:38 (after which he worships Jesus). The irony is that one who is *blind* is empowered to *see* (the truth about Jesus), while those who believe that they can *see* are in reality *blind* (to God's truth and to Jesus' identity).

Frame 

Menorah above Temple ground-plan: John 10:22–42 reports Jesus attending the Feast of Hanukkah (Dedication). This eight-day feast falls in mid-December and commemorates the rededication of the Temple in 165 B.C. during the Maccabean wars (see Unit 37), and the relighting of the Temple menorah.

There grew up the custom of lighting candles in Jewish homes—an additional candle each day of the festival. The observance is also known as the Feast of Lights, not only because of the customary lighting of lamp-stands in the Temple courts, but also because the concept of "the light of liberty" played a role in its rituals—rituals that resembled those used in the Feast of Tabernacles. Jesus claims that He has been dedicated in place of the Temple and has been given authority to judge humanity.

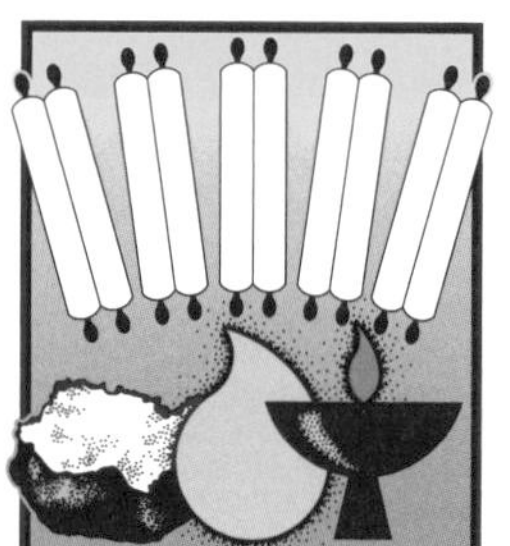

Frame 

Five scrolls; bread; drop of water; lamp: Jewish religious leaders referred to the first five books of the Hebrew scriptures (Torah, Law) as the *water* and *bread of life*, and the *light of the world*.

Jesus declares that *He* is the Water of Life (4:7–15), the Bread of Life (6:35–59), and the Light of the World, 8:12; 9:5. In so doing, Jesus declares that He is God's final revelation and ultimate Word to humanity. Jesus alone has authority to interpret divine truth, and all teaching and opinion must be filtered through His mind to determine the mind and will of God.

Frame 

Servant-King Jesus with shepherd's staff; three servant figures: In Ezekiel 34, God declares to the exiles in Babylon that He will no longer let earthly kings rule His people, but that He Himself will be their King, their Good Shepherd. Ezekiel 34:25–31, 36:8–38, and 37:15–28 describe conditions that the people hoped would prevail in the Promised Land when God finally established His Kingship over the nations of the world.

In John 10, Jesus declares Himself to be the Good Shepherd, the divine King—thus indicating that the ideal conditions of the End Time find their fulfillment in fellowship with Him. The response of the people to Jesus' claim is reported in 10:19–21,31,39; they say that Jesus is demon-possessed, prepare to stone Him, and try to arrest Him.

Frame 12

Open tomb: The straw that breaks the camel's back in Matthew, Mark, and Luke is Jesus' attack on the Temple system, e.g., Mark 11:15–18. In John, it is the raising of Lazarus—at Bethany (meaning, "The House of the Poor") on the Mount of Olives, John 11:38-44; 12:9,10. The Jews expected the resurrection to take place at the end of the age when the Messiah came, Isaiah 25:8; Daniel 12:2. In raising Lazarus from the dead, Jesus declares that the Messianic Age has broken in—*with Him.* The resurrection is a present fact and reality. Furthermore, the *future* Final Judgment has moved into the *present.* To encounter Jesus is to be judged by Him. Jesus' judgment is the Last Judgment—an ongoing and timeless judgment, 3:19. Although *Jesus* is seemingly on trial throughout His lifetime on earth, as soon as He appears, *humanity* is on trial. The fate of each person depends on his or her answer and living response to the question, "Do you believe that Jesus is the Messiah, the Son of God?" 20:31.

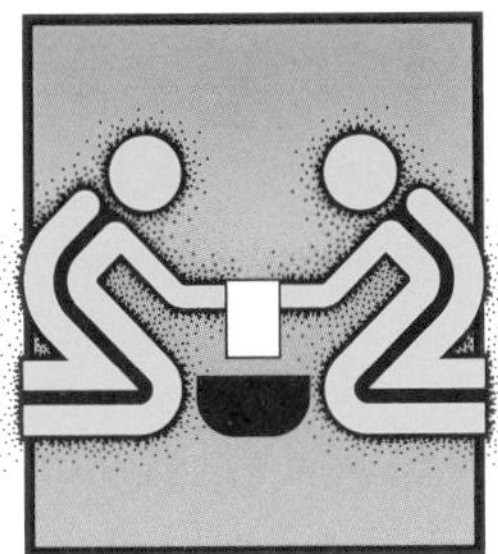

Frame 13

Servant figures facing each other; towel and basin of water: Many Jews longed for the events of the last days. When those last days came, God's will would be done, the Messiah would appear, there would be a judgment, a resurrection, a return of Jewish exiles to Israel, and a revelation of the true God to the non-Jews, some of whom would be gathered to Jerusalem to join with Israel in true worship. However, the resurrection of Lazarus is the last straw for the Jewish leaders. They reject Jesus, condemn Him, and plot His death. The leaders of the Old Israel fail to see the fulfillment of its hopes in Jesus' Person and ministry, and say a final "No!" to Him. In condemning Jesus, they condemn themselves (12:44–50), but fail to stop the Living Word from accomplishing the Divine Plan.

Although the Jewish leaders in Jerusalem reject Jesus, some *diaspora* Jews come to Jerusalem to see Jesus and to have fellowship with Him. *They* come to *see* Jesus (12:21), while the *Jewish leaders* remain obstinately *blind.* However, although some of Jesus' own people turn on Him, He does not reject them. Throughout His ministry, some have remained loyal to Him, 6:66–69. Jesus now takes them into an Upper Room (chs. 13–17) and proclaims to them in word and action the nature of His Kingship (13:1–11), and the nature of life in fellowship with Him, 13:12–20. The Living Word accomplishes His mission—and little wonder. The Word who washes His disciples' feet is also the Word who in the beginning called the universe into existence. His humble exterior cradles a sublime power!

Comments about the following three frames in **ILLUSTRATION 49A** are provided later in this unit.

Frame 14

See 49F.

Frame 15

See 49G.

Frame 16

See 49G.

Passion Predictions in John's Narrative 49B

1 Up to the end of ch. 12, Jesus is portrayed as a public figure who does miraculous "signs" for all to see. The dialogues of this section are between Jesus and inquirers, opponents, and the crowds. Jesus is portrayed as the Life and Light, the Savior and Judge of the world. However, the response to Jesus is not universal or enthusiastic. Those who wish to crown Jesus want to make Him the wrong kind of king over the wrong kind of realm, 6:15. Jesus' own people do not receive Him, 1:10–11. His signs evoke only rejection.

2 After Jesus raises Lazarus from the dead, definite plans are made to arrest Jesus and put Him to death, 11:57, 11:53. The world appears to have won its case against Jesus. Ironically, as the religious and political leaders do their very worst to Jesus, they bring about His enthronement. John's Gospel contains three Passion Predictions, 3:14,15; 8:28; 12:31–33. Each sets forth a theology of the cross.

a. The suspension of Jesus on the cross will, like the lifting up of the bronze serpent in the wilderness (Numbers 21:4–9), save those who look to Him in faith.

b. The complete truth about Jesus' Person will be revealed only at the cross. The meaning of Jesus' mysterious term, "I AM," will then become clear.

c. Jesus' statement in 12:31 is deserving of careful thought:

> *Now is the judgment of this world; now the ruler of this world will be driven out.*

Jesus states that until He appears on the scene, until He is received as the Lord of life, Satan, the prince of this world, is in control. However, when Jesus is on the cross and Satan appears to be at his most powerful, the truth is that *Jesus is at His best* and triumphs over Satan and the world. The hour of the cross and the ensuing resurrection are the climactic events in Jesus' life. They establish that new reign in which the risen King draws new subjects to Himself in forgiving mercy and grace, and teaches them to walk through life in the spirit of their King—as servants of God and others.

The Upper Room

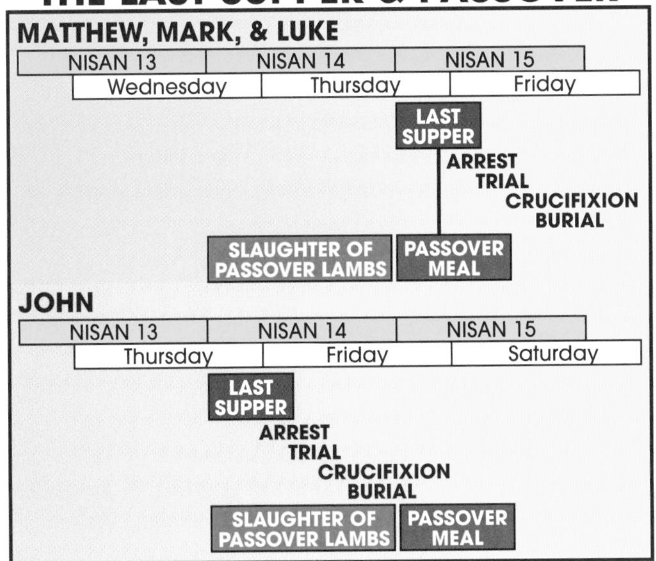

According to Matthew, Mark, and Luke the meal in the Upper Room on Maundy Thursday was a Passover Meal.

According to John's Gospel, Passover began on the Friday evening following Jesus' crucifixion.

John 13–17

1 The following themes are developed:

- The footwashing, John ch. 13.
- The death and return of Jesus, ch. 14.
- The relation between Jesus and His followers, chs. 15,16.
- Jesus' prayerful concern for His new community, ch. 17.

2 Some see Jesus' glory and believe. In chs. 13–17, John concerns himself with these people and their relationship to Jesus. The point of transition is 13:1–20, which presents a highly dramatic picture of Jesus in the Upper Room washing the disciples' feet. (No Jew would ever wash another person's feet. Only Gentile slaves washed feet.) The footwashing event is an enacted parable that illustrates the meaning of Jesus' impending death. The cross washes us clean—but there is more. Jesus' actions illustrate the nature of His kingship and the relationship that is to exist among His followers. They belong to a *community* in which they are called to forgive and serve one another. Their love for each other is the badge that reveals their identity to the world, 13:34,35. Although Leviticus 19:18 commanded the Jewish people to love their neighbor *as they love themselves*, Jesus commands the disciples to love one another *as He has loved them*, 13:15. A higher standard indeed!

3 Jesus predicts that one of the disciples will betray Him, dips a piece of bread into a dish, and gives it to Judas. (To dip bread into something and pass it to another is a sign of special friendship.) Judas, the unfaithful disciple, then departs to betray His Lord. Although Jesus *portrays* love, Judas *betrays* love.

4 The faithful are now alone with Jesus. Dialogues, monologues, and finally a prayer unfold the relation of the faithful to their Lord and God. In chs. 14–16, Jesus prepares the disciples for the hour of separation and sorrow that must come if they are to experience the presence and joy of the Spirit.

5 The High Priestly Prayer (17:1–26) speaks of the passion as the glorification of the Son, and as the climactic event that is necessary for the sanctification (*making holy*), mission, and unity of God's people. In this prayer, Jesus prays for Himself (17:1–5), for the disciples (17:6–19; that they might be protected from the "evil one," Satan, v. 15), and finally for those to whom the disciples will bear witness, 17:20–26.

The Jewish Trial

1 The term *hour* rings in the background of John's Gospel like a muffled bell, 2:4; 7:30; 8:20; 12:23; 12:27; 13:1; 17:1. It tolls *seven* times in anticipation of Jesus' coming hour of glory. Jesus also refers to His *glory*, or to His being glorified, *seven* times, 2:11; 8:49–59; 12:16–23,28; 13:31–32; 17:1–5; 17:20–24. Throughout His life, Jesus manifests a glory contrary to human understanding of the word, for He assumes the form of a Servant even to the point of giving away life on a cross—His finest hour, 17:1.

2 In John 10:11, Jesus says, "The good shepherd lays down his life for the sheep." John's passion history reflects that thought. Jesus' death is not the result of cruel fate, or of plans that go awry. From beginning to end, Jesus takes the initiative. Jesus is the master of His passion at every turn. He virtually calls down death on Himself. He is doing the work His Father sent Him to do, 17:4; 19:28–30. It happens because it must happen, 12:38; 13:18; 19:24,28,36,37. None of it takes Jesus by surprise. John indicates Jesus' foreknowledge of what was to overtake Him with, "Jesus, knowing all that was to happen to Him...," 18:4. Jesus goes to the cross voluntarily.

3 The Jewish trial (18:12–14,19–24) is virtually over by the time it begins. No mention is made of formal charges. No witnesses are summoned. No charge of blasphemy is leveled against Jesus. Jesus is questioned only about His disciples and His teaching. He is not mistreated. His judges level no accusations, but attack Him with violent gestures, 18:22. Jesus remains calm and dignified throughout. John devotes seven verses to describing Peter's denials, 18:15–18,25–27.

4 It is only during the trial before Pilate (18:28–19:16) that the Jewish leaders level charges: "If this man were not a criminal, we would not have handed him over to you," 18:30. Even then, they do not seek a *trial*; they seek Jesus' *death*. They have made up their minds about Jesus long before they capture Him and hand Him over to Pilate, 5:18; 7:1,25,30,44; 8:20,59,; 10:31,39; 11:53.

5 Prior to the trial before Pilate, John mentions the following witnesses who testify for Jesus:

- John the Baptist, 1:6–34; 3:28; 5:32–34
- Jesus Himself, 3:11,32,33; 8:13–18; 18:37
- Jesus' works or signs, 5:36; 10:25
- The Samaritan woman, 4:39
- God the Father, 5:37; 8:18
- The Scriptures, 5:39
- The man born blind, 9:1–41
- A crowd of people, 12:17
- The Holy Spirit, 15:26.
- The disciples, 15:27.
- The evangelist, 19:35; 21:24.

The Trial Before Pilate

In this final confrontation, Pilate represents the non-Jewish world. Although Pilate is supposedly trying Jesus, it is really Pilate who is on trial. The emphasis throughout the dialogues between Jesus and Pilate is Jesus' Kingship. Jesus informs Pilate that His own people rejected Him because He was the wrong kind of King for them, 18:35,36. Pilate makes one last comment against the Jewish leaders with the superscription he attaches to the cross, 19:19. This superscription attests to the world that Jesus is indeed *King!* The Jewish leaders thus finally suffer defeat.

John lists seven scenes in which Pilate moves in and out of the Praetorium—from Jesus to the Jewish leaders and back again.

Scene 1

Pilate is *outside* with the Jewish leaders who demand Jesus' death, 18:28–32. Although they will not enter Pilate's quarters (a *Gentile* location) lest possibly they be contaminated by bread with leaven in it (they are preparing to observe Passover), they ask Pilate to kill Jesus. They seek an *execution*, not a *trial.*

Scene 2

Pilate is *inside* with Jesus and discusses "kingship" with Him, 18:33–38a. When Pilate asks Jesus why the Jewish leaders are so angry with Him, Jesus responds that He turned out to be the wrong kind of King. He is, after all, a Servant-King who washes feet—the King of Truth. This puzzles Pilate.

Scene 3

Pilate is *outside* with the Jewish leaders—who choose Barabbas rather than Jesus as the one to be freed, 18:38b–40. Pilate declares that he can find no crime in Jesus, 18:38b; he repeats this in 19:4 and 19:6.

Scene 4

Pilate is *inside* with Jesus when the latter is scourged, 19:1–3. Although the treatment given Jesus is designed to mock Him, it nevertheless declares who He is: *The King of the Jews!*

Scene 5

Pilate is *outside* with the Jewish leaders and presents Jesus to them, 19:4–8. They reject Jesus, basing their position on an appeal to their sacred writings, 19:7. When Pilate hears them say that Jesus claimed to be the Son of God, he becomes more afraid than ever. Naturally Pilate, a Roman, was ready to believe that gods could show up in human form.

Scene 6

Pilate is *inside* with Jesus and asks Him where He is from. When Jesus refuses to answer Pilate, the latter discusses "power" with Him, 19:9–11. Jesus reminds Pilate that, in the final analysis, Pilate is free to do only what Jesus permits him to do.

Scene 7

Pilate is *outside* with the Jewish leaders, tries to have Jesus released, but finally hands Jesus over to them, 19:12–16a. Pilate yields to the Jewish leaders when they threaten to have him thrown out of the exclusive club known as "Friends of the Emperor." Because Pilate is an imperial procurator—one appointed by the Emperor—he belongs to that club and does not want to lose his membership in it and the privileges that come with it.

Pilate hands Jesus over for crucifixion at *midday* on the Day of Preparation for Passover (19:14)—at that very hour when people began to hand over their lambs for ritual slaughter in preparation for the Passover meal. Hence, Jesus is declared to be the final, one-for-all, once-for-all Passover Lamb who takes away the sin of the world. The Jewish leaders remain adamant in their rejection of Jesus, and ironically declare that Caesar is their king.

3 Pilate's pathetic, frenzied running to and fro expresses the turmoil in a person's soul when faced with the innocent King and his having to make up his mind about Jesus' identity and ministry. Ironically, it is Pilate, this pagan Roman ruler, who declares that Jesus is King of the Jews and insists that He be called that right to the bitter end, 19:19–22. At the same time, when Pilate presents Jesus to the Jewish leaders as King, they respond with, "We have no king but the emperor," 19:15. What irony—the Jewish leaders despised the Roman emperor!

4 One detail referred to in *Scene 7* (above) calls for special comment. According to the Synoptic Gospels, Jesus celebrates a Passover meal with His disciples in the Upper Room (Mark 14:12 and parallels). According to them, Jesus is crucified on Passover day itself, for the Jewish day began and ended at sunset. However, in John's Gospel, Jesus' last meal with His disciples in the Upper Room takes place on the day of *Preparation* for the Passover, 13:1; 18:28; 19:14,31,42. Both versions agree that the events of the Upper Room took place on a Thursday night, the crucifixion on a Friday, and the resurrection on the following Sunday. The difference lies in *Passover* as opposed to *Preparation for the Passover.* Furthermore, Mark reports that Jesus was crucified at *9 a.m.*, 15:25. John 19:14 says He was handed over for crucifixion at *midday.*

Regardless of which timetable is historically correct, John's emphasis is theological. In John's opening chapter, Jesus is twice referred to as "the Lamb of God," 1:29,36. Lambs used in the annual Passover meals were handed over in the Temple beginning at midday on the Day of Preparation—to be ritually slaughtered by the Temple priests in preparation for the Passover meal that evening. John wishes to present Jesus as the perfect, final, universal Passover Lamb who died for the sins of the world. It is with good reason that Jesus' legs were not broken, 19:33. No bones in a Passover lamb were to be broken in the preparation process, Exodus 12:46. In John, chronology serves theology.

Crucifixion—Coronation

Frame 14 **ILLUSTRATION 49B**

Crowned Jesus on cross: John's description of Jesus' journey from Pilate to Calvary is dignified. It is His coronation procession. Jesus is on His way to His enthronement—and the cross is His throne. Jesus will be lifted on to a throne of rough, splintered, blood-stained wood as other royal figures might be lifted on to their more regal thrones. Anything that might detract from the dignity of the journey and the coronation itself is omitted. There is no reference to Simon of Cyrene; Jesus carries His own cross. There is no mockery on the way to Calvary or at Calvary, no commiseration for the weeping women of Jerusalem, no darkness, no portents, and no confession of faith by a Roman centurion. All attention is directed to Jesus as King and to His strange throne—a cross!

1 Pilate's superscription, "The King of the Jews," is attached to the cross to bear witness to Jesus' authority. The Jews object to its presence, but it remains, 19:22. As in the Synoptic Gospels, Jesus is crucified between two men—most likely, political rebels being executed. Jesus' executioners divide His garments among themselves. Women observe the entire event; they are not seen as prospective combatants. Perhaps the *apparently* young John can stand beneath the cross because he is not seen as a threat.

2 Jesus' actions on the cross are regal and consistent with His behavior during His arrest and trial. From beginning to end, Jesus takes the initiative in all that happens. He is like the director of a play who also performs the role of the main character. He utters no cry of dereliction, of abandonment. He remains fully conscious and in control of Himself throughout. He entrusts His mother to the care of the youthful John, 19:25b–27. He says, "I am thirsty," 19:28,29. His final cry proclaims victory, "It is finished," 19:30. Jesus' executioners do not kill Him; *He bows His head and gives up His spirit*, 19:30b.

3 The body of a political rebel was usually denied decent burial; it was left hanging on the cross until it rotted, or was eaten by birds and dogs. But Jesus' burial has royal features. His body is anointed with a royal quantity of spices (19:39) supplied by Nicodemus, a Jewish leader and a member of the Sanhedrin, 3:1. He is buried in a new tomb (19:41,42) supplied by Joseph of Arimathea; kings were always buried in a new tomb! Both Nicodemus and Joseph of Arimathea treat Jesus as a family member by assuming care for His body. Furthermore, they render themselves ritually unclean and unable to observe Passover, and open to suspicion and possible charges for helping One seen to be a rebel.

4 Five main threads run through John's passion narrative. Jesus shows Himself to be:

- *The perfect Passover Lamb* dying for the sins of the world.
- *The Good Shepherd* freely offering His life for His own.
- *The Son* who carries out the will of His Father to the point of giving away life itself.
- *The Judge* of the world and the powers of darkness.
- *The Messianic King* enthroned in glory.

Frame 15 ILLUSTRATION 49B

Open tomb; rising arrow; female figure with hands raised in praise: Jesus' resurrection is established in 20:1–10. The presence of the linen wrappings convinces the disciples that a resurrection has taken place. After all, if the body had been stolen, the thieves would have taken the wrappings as well as the body.

In 20:11–18, Jesus Himself announces His resurrection to Mary Magdalene. Although she hopes that her pre-crucifixion association with Jesus will be resumed, Jesus declares that He will not continue to live among His people as He did prior to His crucifixion and resurrection. Jesus must withdraw His presence from *one place* so that He might be present in *every place*. Jesus must take His *visible* leave of her so that He might remain *invisibly* with *her* and *His people everywhere*. Although Jesus is about to withdraw His *visible* presence, He will nonetheless remain present among His people in a manner that fills the Universe. In His ascension, Jesus did not *withdraw* His presence; He *transformed* it.

1 Jesus' continuing presence among His people is stressed in 20:19–23 and 20:26–29. When Jesus appears among His followers, He does not "come" from anywhere. He is among them constantly, although invisibly. On several occasions, the risen Jesus reveals His presence in a visible way. His greeting on each occasion is, "Peace be with you," 20:21,26.

2 John's account compresses Jesus' resurrection and ascension, and the giving of the Spirit, 20:22. (According to John 7:39, the Holy Spirit will *appear on the scene* and *begin His work* only *after* Jesus' coronation and resurrection.) "He breathed on them" reflects Genesis 2:7. Although Jesus says He will eventually send the Spirit to His disciples, He also says that He himself will come to them (14:28), and that He and the Father will make their home with them, 14:23; see also Matthew 28:20; Romans 8:9,10; 1 Corinthians 3:16,17. When the Spirit comes, His mission will be to continue Jesus' mission, 16:14. He will teach and accomplish what Jesus would have taught and accomplished had Jesus not "gone away."

3 The series of titles begun in chapter one reaches its grand finale in 20:28, "Lord and God." Finally, John defines his purpose in writing his account—to inspire people to believe that Jesus is the Messiah, the Son of God, and believing, to have life in His name, 20:30,31.

4 Although the Gospel possibly did end at this point initially, ch. 21 describes the resources available to the post-resurrection community—the continuing presence of Jesus who dines with His brothers and sisters and defines their mission and responsibilities. The fact that these shepherds/fishermen gather a huge haul of fish points to the fact that the Messianic Age has indeed broken in (see Ezekiel 47:1–12; note v. 9) and that success will crown their witness.

Frame 16 ILLUSTRATION 49B

Crowned Jesus with arms extended in welcome; fish cooking on fire; seven men aboard a fishing boat: Finally, the risen Lord feeds them with bread and fish, an act symbolizing His continuing presence, and His feeding them through the Eucharist. *Three times* Jesus asks Peter, who had denied Him *three times*, "Do you love me?" (21:15–17). He tells the disciples that some will have to experience martyrdom (21:18,19), and that His reappearing will not take place as soon as some might wish, 21:20–23.

1 The post-resurrection appearances reported in the four Gospels are as follows:

a. In **Mark**, the messenger in the tomb instructs the women to tell the disciples that Jesus will meet them again in *Galilee*, 16:1–8. They will "see" Jesus in Galilee. The word "see" implies more than physical sight; it implies that the disciples will finally understand Who Jesus really is, and what His Kingdom is all about.

b. In **Matthew**, Jesus appears to the women near *Jerusalem* and to the disciples in *Galilee*, ch. 28.

c. In **Luke**, Jesus appears to two disciples on the way to *Emmaus* (24:13–35), then to Peter (11:34), and then to the eleven disciples and their companions in *Jerusalem*, 24:36–49. Luke reports no meetings in Galilee.

d. **John** reports Jesus appearing to Mary Magdalene (20:11–18) and the disciples (20:19–29) in *Jerusalem*. (Mary Magdalene served as His apostle to the disciples!) Finally, Jesus appears to the disciples in *Galilee*, ch. 21.

49H
POWER
POSITION
PROFIT
PLEASURE

The Kingdom of God Has Come

Note: **ILLUSTRATIONS 49H–J** help tie together the themes that surface in the four Gospels.

In Mark's Gospel, Jesus' first recorded words are, "The time is fulfilled. The Kingdom of God has come. Believe in the good news," 1:14,15. Jesus' words might be summarized as follows:

- *The time is fulfilled:* "No more waiting! No more delay! Your long–cherished hopes and dreams of a Messianic Age are now being fulfilled—by Me!"
- *The Kingdom of God has come:* "God's Kingdom is not merely something that might come one day. It is here! It has broken into history! I am the King of that Kingdom!"
- *Believe in the good news:* "When Roman citizens are told that the emperor is to pay them a visit, they hear the message as 'good news.' After all, the emperor declares that he is Lord, that He rules the world, and that he brings peace to humanity. However, I am bringing much better good news to all humanity of all time—from the elite to the least!"

Upper section of **ILLUSTRATION 49H**

The Kingdom of God

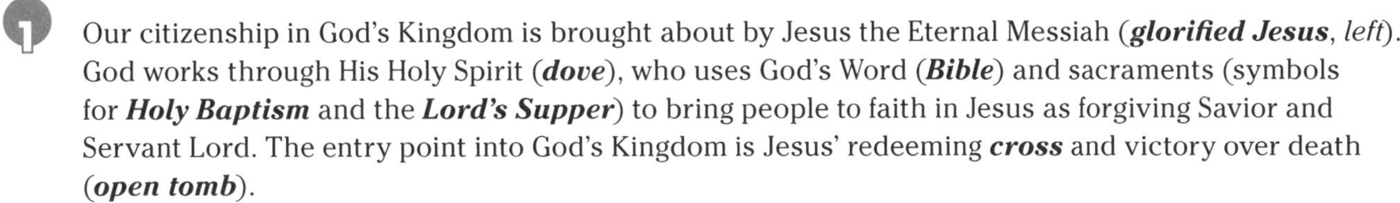

1 Our citizenship in God's Kingdom is brought about by Jesus the Eternal Messiah (***glorified Jesus***, *left*). God works through His Holy Spirit (***dove***), who uses God's Word (***Bible***) and sacraments (symbols for ***Holy Baptism*** and the ***Lord's Supper***) to bring people to faith in Jesus as forgiving Savior and Servant Lord. The entry point into God's Kingdom is Jesus' redeeming ***cross*** and victory over death (***open tomb***).

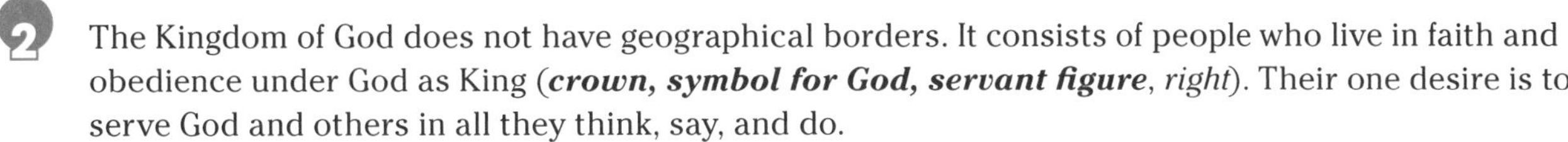

2 The Kingdom of God does not have geographical borders. It consists of people who live in faith and obedience under God as King (***crown, symbol for God, servant figure***, *right*). Their one desire is to serve God and others in all they think, say, and do.

Lower section

The Kingdom of the Devil, the World, and our Flesh

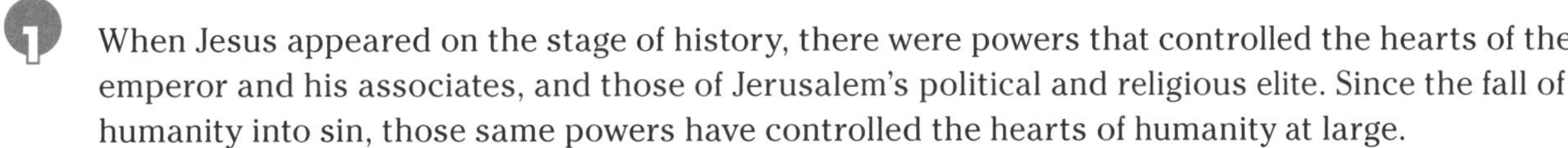

1 When Jesus appeared on the stage of history, there were powers that controlled the hearts of the emperor and his associates, and those of Jerusalem's political and religious elite. Since the fall of humanity into sin, those same powers have controlled the hearts of humanity at large.

- The biblical writings (especially the New Testament) make frequent reference to Satan (***satanic face***, *left*), 1 Chronicles 21:1; Matthew 4:1–11; 1 Peter 5:8,9; Revelation 12:9.
- On ***Planet Earth***, Satan works through the *sinful human heart* (***symbol for sin, law-code, human heart***) to seek ***POWER*** for self, ***POSITION*** for self, ***PROFIT*** for self, and ***PLEASURE*** for self.

2 Satan's message is: "Forget all this 'God stuff' (***symbol for God cancelled out***, *right*). Ask only, 'What's in it for me?'" (***symbol for sin above person in posture of indifference***).

In his temptation narrative (1:12,13), Mark makes no reference to Satan leaving Jesus. The battle between Jesus and Satan continued throughout the course of Jesus' ministry. Satan sought to stop Jesus from going to His cross. However, to break Satan's power over humanity, Jesus persisted in His servant ministry all the way to the cross, and completed His saving ministry by giving His life away, John 12:31, 19:30. At the cross, Jesus overcomes Satan, sin, and death. Although Satan remains among humanity as the "great deceiver," Jesus, in forgiving grace, invites people into fellowship with Himself and citizenship in His Eternal Kingdom.

The message of all four Gospels is: *Flee the kingdoms of this world! Embrace with joy your membership in God's Eternal Kingdom. Jesus alone can bring joy to your heart, meaning to your life, and hope in the face of death!*

491

The Final Rescue (Exodus)

ILLUSTRATION 491 focuses on the key truth that unlocks the door to understanding the central message of all four Gospels. The two upper sections of the illustration were explained in Unit 31. They remind us that as God once rescued the Israelites from Egypt (*Exodus 1*), so God carried out a second rescue (*Exodus 2*) when He delivered the Judean exiles from bondage in Babylon. Furthermore, the returning exiles hoped that as God had once called the universe into existence (*Creation 1*), God also would bring about *Creation 2* by transforming Judah into a New Eden for them to enjoy, Isaiah 51:3.

The comments that follow focus on the lower section of **ILLUSTRATION 491**.

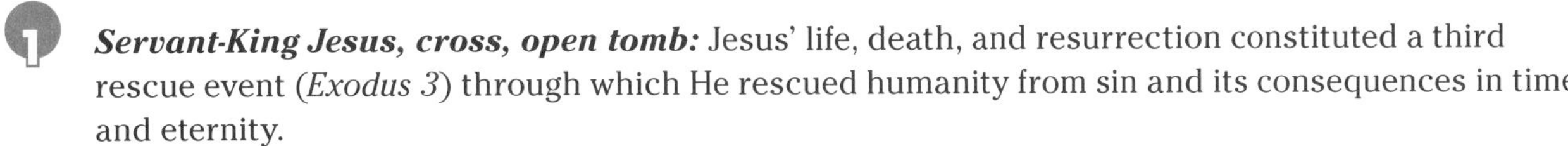

1 ***Servant-King Jesus, cross, open tomb:*** Jesus' life, death, and resurrection constituted a third rescue event (*Exodus 3*) through which He rescued humanity from sin and its consequences in time and eternity.

2 The powers and forces that hold humanity captive are:

a. ***Satanic face:*** Although Old Testament writings make reference to Satan (Job 1:6, 2:1), the sole *clear* reference to Satan as a power hostile to God occurs in 1 Chronicles 21:1. However, numerous references to Satan and demons occur in the intertestamental literature.

b. ***Symbol for sin, circle of chains:*** In the New Testament, Jesus defines the goals and strategies of the Satanic: to seduce people from living to serve God and others into serving themselves. Although people gauge success in terms of what they achieve for themselves, Jesus teaches that such people are in bondage to Satan and their own sinful flesh. True freedom, true "success," is to be measured only by Jesus' yardstick.

c. ***Law-code:*** Although the commandments in themselves are good, spiritual confusion and chaos result because people by nature tend to do the *right thing* for the *wrong reason*. The term for this is works-righteousness. Those who strive to achieve salvation by keeping the commandments are under obligation to keep not just *some* of them, but *all* of them.

d. ***Skull symbolizing death:*** Because no person can keep the commandments perfectly, and because the wages of sin is death, all people fall under judgment and condemnation. Hence, those who try to save themselves in God's sight through obedience are like people trapped in quicksand trying to save themselves; the harder they try, the more they sink into despair and death.

e. ***Drop of water—symbol for baptism:*** Jesus lived the sinless life humanity was meant to live but cannot, and also died the death humanity deserves to die so that it need not. Through the waters of baptism, God makes people partakers of, and sharers in, all that Jesus accomplished, Romans 6:3,4.

f. ***Hand, heart, servant figure:*** The *new creation* that God seeks to bring about is to create within those who come to faith in Jesus the Messiah—as forgiving Savior and Servant Lord a heart that reflects Jesus' servant heart.

49J
1
2
3
4
5
6
7
8
9
10
11
12
13
14
15

Jesus, the Final Interpreter of Scripture 49J

Those who work their way through the Old Testament writings encounter numerous threads and themes. How are these to be understood today? Are Christians today to perpetuate some or all Old Testament practices? Which ones? How is the determination to be made? The issue can be resolved only when people understand that God spoke His *final Word* in the *Living Word*, Jesus the Messiah. In Jesus, God appeared on the stage of visible history clothed in flesh. The challenge, then, is to read Jesus' lips and life.

ILLUSTRATION 49J shows how all Old Testament themes must now be funneled through the mind of Jesus the Messiah—the *Living Word* and the *Final Interpreter* of the *written Word*. In the *top left corner* is the ***symbol for God***, surrounded by a ***cloud*** *signifying the presence and glory of God*. The numbers below correspond to those in the illustration.

1 ***People of God:*** Our relationship with God is not established by ancestry (i.e., by descent from Abraham, Isaac, and Jacob), but by faith in Jesus as forgiving Savior and Servant Lord, John 3:1–16; 14:6.

2 ***Land:*** The Christian hope centers on life in God's Kingdom—wherever that life might be lived. It does not focus on life in the land of Canaan, 1 Peter 1:3–5.

3 ***Rescue:*** Jesus rescues God's people, not from Egypt, Assyria, Babylon, Persia, Greece, or Rome, but from the powers Satan, sin, and death, Romans 6:20–23.

4 ***Sinai, covenant, law-code:*** In Jesus, God clothed Himself in flesh, John 1:14. Jesus established God's New Covenant with humanity (Mark 14:22–25), and Jesus alone determines what His brothers and sisters are to believe and how they are to live, Matthew 11:29,30.

5 ***False gods:*** Swiss theologian John Calvin said that the human mind is an idol factory. Anything that sidetracks us from living to serve God and others is idolatry, Ephesians 5:5. Our "god" is whatever we devote life to.

6 ***Ark of the Covenant, sword:*** Jesus alone is the link between heaven and earth, John 1:51. "Holy war" has nothing to do with battling other nations. Rather, Jesus calls and empowers us to fight the real enemy: Satan and the demonic powers, Ephesians 6:10–18.

7 ***Crown:*** Jesus, the final descendant of David, is the eternal King of the universe, Hebrews 1:8.

8 ***Jerusalem:*** God's people are already citizens of the Eternal Jerusalem, Revelation 21:9–21. They look forward to finally entering that Eternal City in the life to come.

9 ***Temple:*** God's Temple now consists of "living stones"—people joined by grace through faith to Jesus as Savior and Lord, and in servanthood to each other, 1 Peter 2:5; Ephesians 2:19–22.

10 ***Altar of Sacrifice:*** God does not want us to give Him dead animals, but our living bodies—to be used throughout life to His glory in the service of others, Romans 12:1.

11 ***Lamp*** (*Wisdom*), ***scroll:*** Jesus is the wisdom of God (1 Corinthians 1:24) and the Word of God, Hebrews 1:1,2. In Jesus, one greater than Solomon has come, Matthew 12:42.

12 ***Rule over the nations:*** In the latter part of the Old Testament period, some Jews hoped that the day would come when they would rule the nations. In Daniel 7:11–14, the "son of man" (RSV) is a term for the Jewish people, "the saints of the Most High." However, Jesus is God's "Son of Man," the first of God's new and true people, and Lord of the nations, Ephesians 1:15–23.

13 ***Death and the grave:*** Jesus has overcome death and the power of the grave, and will one day command the realm of the dead to yield up its dead, John 5:25–29; 1 Corinthians 15.

14 ***Praying hands:*** Although the Old Testament writings contain many examples of prayer, Jesus' brothers and sisters look to Him for guidance in prayer, and as the model for prayer, Matthew 6:5–13.

15 ***Funnel, Servant-King Jesus the Messiah, open tomb, dove:*** Jesus the Messiah is Lord of Time and Eternity. **Jesus alone determines what Christians are to believe and how they are to live. Jesus is the model for the godly life.** God's people (***two servant figures facing each other***) are to direct all questions concerning what they are to believe and how they are to live to Jesus. Jesus alone provides humanity with God's "final word," God's "final opinion."

SUMMARY

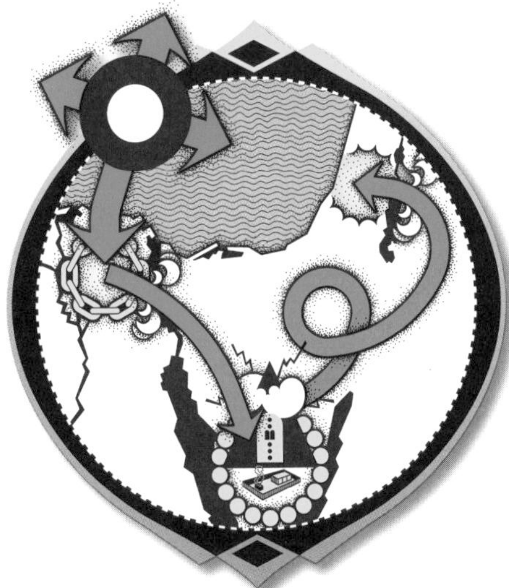

49A The theme of *replacement* plays a central role in John's Gospel. It surfaces first in ch. 1 where Jesus is declared to be the incarnate Word of God Who replaces Jewish scriptures. It reaches its high point in chs. 13–17 when Jesus forms a New Israel out of the disciples. In between, Jesus reinterprets numerous Old Testament beliefs and replaces numerous Old Testament practices.

49B John's term "hour" points forward to events associated with Jesus' cross. Jesus must experience crucifixion and death to enter the eternal glory that He has shared with His Father from eternity.

John's passion narrative stresses the Kingship of Jesus. Throughout, Jesus remains calm, regal, and dignified. Little mention is made of the Jewish trial in the actual passion narrative; Jewish leaders judge Jesus throughout John's first twelve chapters. Pilate represents the confused Gentile world trying to make up its mind about Jesus. Although the narrative gives the impression that Pilate is trying Jesus, the truth is that Pilate himself is being tried and judged.

49C The footwashing event described in ch. 13 is found only in John's Gospel. Jesus' followers are to serve each other as Jesus has served them. They are not merely to love others *as they love themselves.* They are to love others *as Jesus has loved them.*

49D Throughout John's passion narrative, Jesus is in control; He is doing what His Father wants Him to do. Nothing takes Jesus by surprise. The only references to Jewish involvement in Jesus' trial are the following: Annas (who had been High Priest until A.D. 15) asks Jesus several questions and then sends Him to his son-in-law, Caiaphas—who asks Jesus no questions, but sends Him to Pilate. Throughout the passion narrative, the Jewish leaders do not seek a fair trial; they seek Jesus' death—and only Pilate can bring that to pass.

49E Pilate is perplexed concerning the charges laid against Jesus. He goes back and forth between the Jewish leaders to Jesus—trying to make up his mind what to do with Jesus. Although he declares Jesus innocent of the charges leveled against Him, the Jewish leaders tell Pilate that if he does not carry out their wishes, they will get him thrown out of the exclusive club known as "Friends of the Emperor." Pilate hands Jesus over at midday—at the very hour when lambs begin to be led to slaughter in the Temple for the observance of Passover—which in John will begin on Friday evening (not on Thursday evening as in Matthew, Mark, and Luke).

49F The sign placed above Jesus' head, "The King of the Jews," while meant to be a taunt, expresses a profound truth. Eventually Jesus is buried in a new tomb and anointed with a 100 pounds (45 kilograms) of myrrh and aloes (both required when burying a king). Both Nicodemus and Joseph of Arimathea place their life on the line by attending to Jesus' burial.

49G The first one to learn of Jesus' return to life is Mary Magdalene. Jesus then appears to the disciples on two successive nights, and finally on the shores of the Sea of Galilee.

49H When Jesus breathes His last, He has not been conquered by Satan. Rather, He has conquered the powers of Satan, the world order, sinful flesh, and death.

49I A key element in the message of all four Gospels is that through His Messianic ministry, Jesus has carried out a Final Exodus, the final rescue of God's people.

49J Although many themes, beliefs, and traditions surface in the Old Testament writings, all must be funneled through the mind of Jesus. Jesus is the incarnation and Final Interpreter of God's truth.

CROSS WAYS®
5
SECTION
UNITS 41–50
The Gospels and Acts
UNIT 50
The Acts of the Apostles
From Jew to Gentile;
From Jerusalem to Rome
GENESIS
MATTHEW
MARK
LUKE
JOHN
2 SAMUEL
ACTS
PSALMS
ISAIAH
JEREMIAH
EZEKIEL
EZRA
AMOS
ROMANS
1 CORINTHIANS
2 CORINTHIANS
GALATIANS
EPHESIANS
PHILIPPIANS
COLOSSIANS
1 THESSALONIANS
2 THESSALONIANS
1 TIMOTHY
2 TIMOTHY
TITUS
PHILEMON
HEBREWS
JAMES
1 PETER
2 PETER
1 JOHN
2 JOHN
3 JOHN
JUDE
REVELATION

The Age of the Spirit

ILLUSTRATION 50A sums up the New Testament series of events in relation to Jesus' past, present, and future Messianic ministry.

1 The Gospel accounts tell us that God the Father (***symbol for God***) sent His Son (***Servant-King Jesus***) to walk the way of a servant-without-limit to show forth the *divine glory* (John 1:14)—a glory that reached its *grand finale* in the *crucifixion* (***cross***) when the Servant-King was at His best, John 17:1–5.

2 The Father vindicated Jesus' Person, ministry, and glory by raising Him from the dead (***open tomb***). After Jesus rose from the dead, He did not continue to live visibly among the disciples as He had during His previous ministry. For a period of forty days after His resurrection, Jesus continued to appear and disappear among His followers, Acts 1:3. He paid them several brief "visible visits" to let them know that He remained among them.

3 Although Acts 1:9 speaks of Jesus ***rising from the earth into a cloud*** (*denoting the divine presence*), that action did not represent a *withdrawal* of presence, but a *transformation* of presence. Jesus remained among the disciples—and remains among us—*invisibly*. Jesus' ascension said to the disciples, "No more little visible visits, but I am not going away. However, you will see me again when I *reappear* on the Last Day!"

4 ***Dove:*** In John's Gospel in particular, Jesus assures His followers that He will continue His presence and work through the Holy Spirit. The work of the risen Jesus and the work of the Holy Spirit are one and inseparable, John 14:16,25,26; 16:7,12–14. Jesus also states that He will perpetuate His work through His own continuing presence and power (14:18), and through the continuing presence of both the Father and the Son, 14:23.

According to Luke, all events associated with Jesus' ministry were under the direction of the Holy Spirit who filled John the Baptist (Luke 1:15), empowered Mary to conceive and bear Jesus (1:35), filled Mary when she greeted Elizabeth (1:41), inspired Zechariah and Simeon to prophecy (1:67; 2:27), descended on Jesus at His baptism (3:22), and directed and empowered Him throughout His ministry, 4:1,14.

5 The Holy Spirit uses the *written Word* (***Bible***) to teach the truths that Jesus would have us to believe and do if He were still among us visibly. In Holy Baptism (***drop of water***), God adopts people into His family as His forgiven sons and daughters, as Jesus' forgiven brothers and sisters. In the Lord's Supper (***bread and cup***), God invites His children to share in a meal that is a foretaste of things to come, Revelation 19:9.

6 Jesus promises His brothers and sisters that, as they share His glory here on earth (by believing on Him, proclaiming Him, and reflecting His servant lifestyle), they will one day share His glory in the presence of the Father in Heaven (***arrow rises into cloud***).

7 In the Acts narrative, the Holy Spirit empowers the apostles to communicate in other languages (2:1–13), to heal the sick (3:1–10), and to defy the authorities and to bear witness to Jesus, ch. 4. The Spirit empowers Stephen to witness and to endure martyrdom (7:54–60), and plays a role in Saul's conversion (9:17) and in the choosing of special workers, 13:2. The Spirit validates the work done among the Samaritans (8:14–17) and Gentiles (10:44), and assists the apostles to determine their itineraries, 13:4; 16:7; 19:21. He guides and helps those who supervise the life of the community, 20:28.

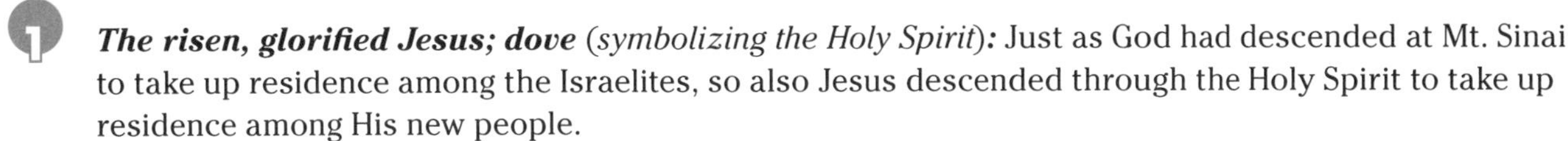

The Day of Pentecost

LLUSTRATION 50B

1 ***The risen, glorified Jesus; dove*** *(symbolizing the Holy Spirit)***:** Just as God had descended at Mt. Sinai to take up residence among the Israelites, so also Jesus descended through the Holy Spirit to take up residence among His new people.

2 ***Dotted lines signifying wind; tongue of fire:*** When God manifested the Divine Presence at Sinai, God did so through a storm cloud and fire. The continuing presence of the Risen Lord through His Spirit was accompanied by phenomena similar to those reported in Exodus 19: a noise like the rush of a violent wind, and divided tongues as of fire, Acts 2:1–4.

3 ***Community around the Risen Jesus/Holy Spirit:*** At the Tower of Babel, the nations were scattered. Part of Israel's mission in the Old Testament was to live as God's community in such a way that this fragmentation might be overcome. Furthermore, the Israelites were to witness to the nations so that they would join them in praising and serving God. Although Israel failed in its mission, the mission began again with fervor through the events described in Acts 2.

DIGGING DEEPER

1 The Gospels link Jesus' death (*rescue event*) to the celebration of Passover—an event that recalled God *rescuing* His people from slavery in Egypt. After leaving Egypt, the children of Israel spent *forty* years in the wilderness before entering the Promised Land. According to Luke's narrative in Acts, the risen Jesus remained with His disciples for *forty* days prior to His ascension into the Eternal Promised Land. After Jesus withdrew His visible presence, the disciples returned to Jerusalem, went to an Upper Room, and prayed. Peter led the move to replace Judas, Acts 1:15–25. Lots were cast in relation to the choice between Matthias and Joseph called Barsabbas. Matthias was chosen, 1:26. As there were once *twelve* tribes, there are now *twelve* apostles.

2 According to Jewish teachers, the events at Mt. Sinai took place *fifty* days after the Exodus from Egypt. Similarly, the Holy Spirit descended on the New Israel *fifty* days after Jesus' rescue event at Calvary. Although Pentecost was originally a harvest festival, by the first century A.D. it also celebrated the events that took place at Mt. Sinai, and did so *fifty* days after Passover.

3 Those who gathered around Mt. Sinai after the Exodus from Egypt were Israelites. Similarly, those present in Jerusalem for the first Pentecost were *Jews* and *proselytes* (converts to Judaism—therefore also Jews) from various parts of the Mediterranean world), Acts 2:5–10. It is significant that Peter referred to Joel 2:28–32 in his preaching, for when the prophet Joel referred to the Spirit falling on "all flesh" he had in mind only the Jewish people. The effect of Peter's preaching was profound. Luke reports that the Spirit used Peter's preaching to bring 3,000 Jews and proselytes to faith in Jesus as Savior and Lord—and all were baptized!

4 A Jewish legend stated that seventy tongues of fire appeared on Mt. Sinai, representing the seventy languages of the seventy nations on earth. At Pentecost, although those present in Jerusalem came from lands to the east and west, and from North Africa—and spoke different languages—all understood the message Peter spoke to them. God was making a powerful beginning to reversing the events at the Tower of Babel and reuniting humanity—beginning with Abraham's descendants.

5 Later, the Spirit fell also on the *Gentiles*, Acts 10:1–48—and continued to do so through the witness of the apostles.

ILLUSTRATION

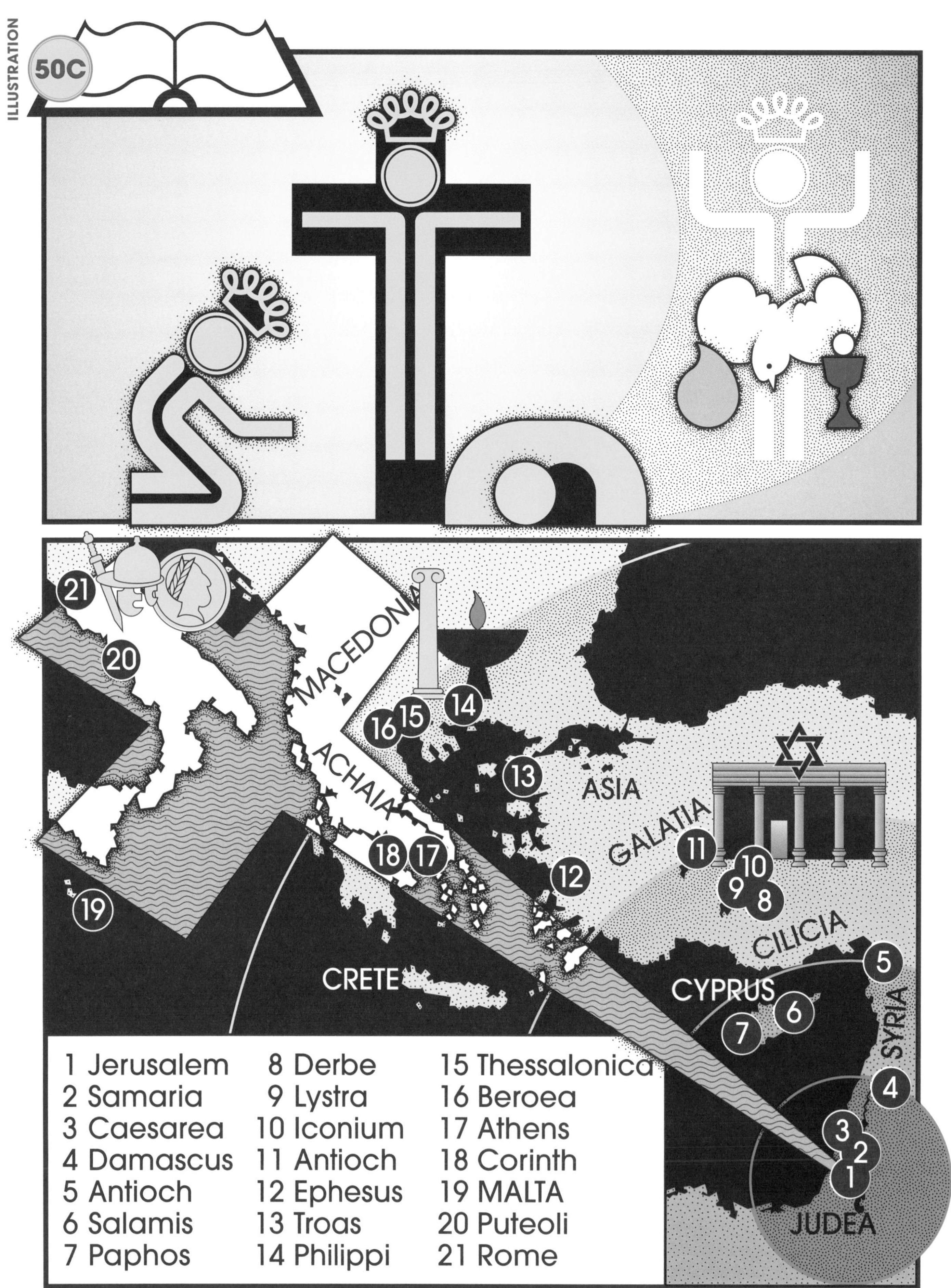

To the Ends of the Earth

During the days that followed Jesus' ascension, the disciples would have done a lot of soul-searching. The fact that Jesus was still alive but no longer visibly present among them challenged them to re-think their understanding of Jesus' Person and ministry, and the mission to which He had called them. **ILLUSTRATION 50C** depicts the message Jesus had shared with them concerning His person and mission, and the extent to which they shared it in the years that followed.

Upper section

The Jewish people and the disciples had looked forward to the coming of a political messiah-deliverer who would free them Roman domination. However, the Messiah who came shocked them with regard to His Person and ministry.

1 Yes, He was a *King* descended from the line of David. However, He came to live the life of a *Servant-without-limit* (***Servant-King***).

2 There came the day when Jerusalem's political and religious leaders manipulated the Romans into crucifying Jesus (***cross***). However, although they did their worst to Jesus, He did His best for them—and for humanity.

3 When the disciples saw Jesus being crucified, they would have thought "It's all over." However, Jesus' Father restored His Son to life (***open tomb***), and vindicated His saving, servant ministry.

4 In the ascension, Jesus did not *withdraw* His presence; He *transformed* it (***risen, glorified Jesus***). The Holy Spirit (***dove***) continues to make known Jesus' Person, presence, saving ministry, and will for humanity. In doing this, the Holy Spirit makes use of the *audible* Word (***Bible***), the *adopting* Word (***Holy Baptism***), and the *edible* Word (***Holy Communion***).

Lower section

1 Prior to His ascension, the Risen Jesus outlined the mission mandate His disciples-become-apostles were to pursue. They were to bear witness to Him first in Jerusalem, then in Samaria, and then to the ends of the earth, Acts 1:8. Acts reports how the apostles took the message of God's Good News:

From ***Jerusalem***
to ***Samaria*** (8:1–25),
to ***JUDEA*** (8:26–40),
to ***Caesarea*** (8:40; 10:1–48),
to Phoenicia (between Judea and ***SYRIA***),
to Syrian ***Damascus*** and ***Antioch*** (9:19–22; 11:19),
to ***Salamis*** and ***Paphos*** on the island of ***CYPRUS***,
to the Roman provinces of ***CILICIA*** and ***GALATIA*** and the cities of
Derbe, Lystra, Iconium, Antioch (12:25–14:28),
to the regions of ***ASIA***, ***MACEDONIA***, and ***ACHAIA*** (16:1–18:22; 18:23–21:17)
and the cities of ***Ephesus, Troas, Philippi, Thessalonica, Beroea, Athens, and Corinth,***
and finally to ***MALTA*** (28:1),
Puteoli (28:13), then
Rome (28:16).

2 In Jesus' day, more Jews lived beyond the borders of Israel than within the borders of Israel. Philo estimated that one million people lived in Alexandria in Egypt, including a very large Jewish

population. (Although, according to Acts 18:24, Apollos had links to Alexandria, nothing is known about the history of the early church there.) During his missionary journeys, Paul usually first bore witness in ***Jewish synagogues*** scattered around the Mediterranean world. More than 150 cities of the Roman Empire are known to have had synagogues. These synagogues attracted large numbers of proselytes (converts to Judaism) and still larger number of "God-fearers"—men who observed Jewish food laws and attended synagogue meetings, but shrank from the final step of circumcision. According to the Palestinian Talmud, there were 480 synagogues in Jerusalem—with schools attached.

3 The synagogues paved the way for the Christian mission. When St. Paul entered a Greek city, he always began by preaching in its synagogue. Many of his converts were drawn from among the God-fearers—which resulted in opposition among the Jews; Paul was creaming off the best of their Gentile supporters and sympathizers!

4 Paul and other apostles also had to deal with the cultural impact of *Greek Hellenism* (***Greek column***) and the *so-called wisdom* (***lamp***) *of Gnosticism*. (Gnosticism will be studied in Unit 51.) They also had to deal with the threats posed by the *Roman imperial system* (***Roman helmet and sword, coin***).

Roman Culture, Commerce & Religion 50D

1 Policies introduced by Caesar Augustus and promoted by Vespasian and Hadrian, gave rise to economic tensions. As the Romans believed in greater gods and lesser gods, they also embraced a social hierarchy that distinguished between wealthy patrons of the Emperor and the poor who were subservient to the wealthy. And the wealthy looked on the poor with disdain and exploited them to their own economic advantage.

2 Scattered around the empire were numerous large cities—in which the wealthy enjoyed an affluent life-style and the poor lived in appalling conditions. Because those living in the cities and large towns needed food, poor farmers had to work extremely hard to supply those needs—and survive in the process. Often the ownership of land was transferred from the poor to the wealthy—who sometimes focused on marketing and exporting what the land produced rather than on meeting the needs of the poor.

3 High population densities and inadequate sewage systems resulted in high disease rates and low life expectancies. Cities were often able to maintain their population levels only because poor farmers were often forced to move from the land to the city. Although efforts were made to pacify the poor by beautifying the public sectors of cities with temples, public buildings, and monuments, these things did little to meet their needs—and social tensions resulted.

4 The imperial cult played a key role in the life of the Empire. The cult constituted a control-web through which all citizens were pressured to see themselves as connected to Rome and the emperor. Its goal was to serve as a social glue to keep those scattered across a vast empire linked to each other. For most living with the borders of the empire, the imperial cult was the only way in which the emperor was known. Few ever saw the emperor himself. People came to know him only through imperial statues, temples, inscriptions, coins, public festivals, and holidays.

5 Little distinction was made between politics and cult, court and temple, rulers and gods. The same titles were given to kings, emperors, and gods. The court of the earthly ruler and the court of the god were described in much the same way. The earthly ruler was invested with divine qualities, and the gods with earthly ones.

6 Temples played a role in the economy of Asian cities. Banks and marketplaces functioned within them. In Rome, the temple of Saturn was the headquarters of the state treasury. The temple of Artemis in Ephesus was the financial headquarters of the province of Asia. Temples were key to the economic life of both city and the empire. The best that a city had to offer was mediated through the imperial temples: worship, commerce, culture, and celebration.

7 The central "myth" that operated throughout the Roman Empire during the first century A.D. was that of Augustus. It elevated him to the position of "Augustus," a title meaning "revered"—even "divine." As they traveled around with the empire, the apostles had to deal with this and other Roman myths—and their refusal to submit to the system could cost them life itself! Tradition suggests that both Peter and Paul were martyred in Rome.

Issues in the Acts of the Apostles

1 A more appropriate title for "The Acts of the Apostles" might be, "The Acts of the Risen Jesus, working through the power of His Holy Spirit and the witness of the Apostles, from Jerusalem to Rome."

2 Luke describes the events surrounding Jesus' ascension a second time in Acts 1:1–14; see Luke 24:50–53. In the moments immediately preceding Jesus' ascension, the disciples reveal that they have not understood Jesus' message. They are still expecting Jesus to restore the Davidic kingdom.

3 Most likely during the days that follow Jesus' ascension, the disciples do much soul-searching. The fact that Jesus is no longer among them visibly forces them to re-think radically their understanding of who He is, and the mission that He has entrusted to them.

4 The title, "The Acts of the Apostles," suggests that it presents the reader with a comprehensive account of the careers of the twelve apostles. However, Acts contains:

a. An outline of *some* of ***Peter's work***. Apart from the reference in 15:7, the account of Peter's activities ceases at 12:18.

b. *One brief sentence* about the death of ***James, John's brother***, 12:2.

c. *Some information* about ***James, the brother of Jesus***, who was not a member of the original twelve, 12:17; 15:13; 21:18.

d. *Some details* about ***John's activities***, although no reference is made to anything he says, 3:1–4:31.

e. *Much information* about ***Paul***.

5 Approximately one third of Acts consists of speeches and sermons:

a. by ***Peter***, 2:14–39; 3:11–26; 4:8–12; 5:29–32; 10:34–43.

b. by ***Stephen***, 7:2–53.

c. by ***Paul***: 13:16–41, Antioch; 17:22–31, Athens; 20:18–35, Miletus; 22:1–21, Jerusalem; 24:10–21, before Felix; 26:1–23, before Agrippa; 28:17–20,25–29, Rome.

6 The speeches and sermons focus on the following:

a. Jesus is a descendant of David; the New Age dawned with His coming.

b. The Father vindicated Jesus' ministry through the mighty acts performed by the power of the Holy Spirit.

c. When Jesus came to His own people, they crucified Him. Although they did this in ignorance, their actions fulfilled the Scriptures that predicted His suffering, 2:23; 13:29.

d. God set His seal of approval on Jesus' mission by raising Him from the dead.

e. Although Jesus is now enthroned at the Father's right hand (the place of authority in the heavenly realm), He has sent His Holy Spirit to bear witness to Him.

f. God's mercy is for all humanity—both Jews and Gentiles. God shows mercy toward Gentiles by supplying their every need.

g. People everywhere are summoned to repent and embrace in faith the salvation offered freely to all in the name of Jesus—the appointed Lord, Savior, and Judge of humanity.

7 Paul tailored his approach to win his audience's ears. In the synagogue at Antioch (13:16–41), he quoted the Old Testament repeatedly, for his audience knew it and loved it. In off-the-beaten-track

Lystra, he began with references to the wind and rain, and the realm of nature, 14:15–17. In Athens, where no one in his audience knew anything about the Hebrew scriptures, Paul quoted the Greek poets, 17:22–31.

8 Regardless of whether the message is proclaimed by Peter or Paul, the appeal is the same. In Jesus, the decisive hour has struck. Everything that happened prior to His incarnation pointed to His coming. The paradox of the cross is that although it was a brutal event, it is also the key event in the purposes of God. It gives meaning and authority to the apostolic proclamation, for it offers humanity the greatest gift and warns against the greatest danger.

From Jew to Gentile

Acts 1–12

1 The setting for the first seven chapters of Acts is Jerusalem. After the Spirit is poured out on the apostles and those gathered in Jerusalem to celebrate Pentecost (2:1–13), a mission gets underway, 2:14–47. Initially the message meets with success, 2:41. The members of the new community show remarkable zeal for the Lord and great concern for each other, 2:42–47.

2 Next, after Peter and John heal a crippled beggar at the Temple's Beautiful Gate and bear witness to Jesus, they are imprisoned, questioned, and forbidden to preach. This does not deter the apostles and the new disciples. Witness to Jesus continues, goods are shared, and the needy are cared for, 3:1–4:35.

3 However, the new community also encounters difficulties. Although Barnabas makes a sizable monetary gift to support the work of the apostles (4:36,37), Ananias and Sapphira lie concerning the magnitude of their gift—and die, 5:1–11.

4 When the apostles continue to do remarkable things, the Jewish leaders imprison them—only to find the prison cell empty the next morning, 5:12–19. Rather than flee, the apostles go back to preaching in the Temple, with the result that they are once again taken into custody, questioned, threatened with death, and flogged, 5:20–42. Even so, Jewish threats and punishment are powerless to prevent the growth of the movement.

5 The new movement grows so rapidly that the apostles feel the need to appoint seven deacons to assume some of the work load, 6:1–6. Numerous Jewish priests now become disciples, 6:7. However, after Stephen, one of the deacons, does great signs and wonders among the people and witnesses with power, the Jewish leaders concoct a plot to have him discredited and tried, 6:8–15. After Stephen delivers a scathing speech against them that culminates in an attack on the Jerusalem Temple (Acts 7:1–53), the Jewish leaders react violently. They stone Stephen to death and instigate a persecution, 7:54–8:3.

6 The persecution merely furthers the cause of the Christian movement, for it results in Philip going to Samaria and preaching there, 8:4–8; see also 11:19. The Samaritans were, like the Jews, a Semitic people. Their scriptures consisted of the Pentateuch. The chief bone of contention between the Samaritans and the Jews was the question of the divinely designated worship site—Mt. Gerizim or Jerusalem? After the Gospel is proclaimed in Samaria, Peter and John visit the region, sanction the work being done in that region, and witness to numerous Samaritan villages during their return journey to Jerusalem, 8:14–17,25.

7 After the Samaritan mission, Philip persists in his efforts. On the road from Jerusalem to Gaza, he witnesses to an Ethiopian who receives the word, is baptized, and returns to his homeland with joy, 8:26–40. In response to the question, "Why was an *Ethiopian* worshiping in the Jerusalem Temple?" reference might be made to 1 Kings 10:1–13. This passage is traditionally interpreted to say that when the Queen of Sheba returned to her homeland, she carried within her a child sired by Solomon. And again according to tradition, that child eventually became the first king of Ethiopia. History records that, with the passing of the centuries, many Ethiopians came to know and worship the God of Israel.

8 Acts 8:1 introduces Saul of Tarsus in connection with Stephen's execution. Stephen's martyrdom initially increased animosity against Christianity, and resulted in Paul heading for Damascus in Syria

to deal with those "heretical Christians." While Saul was en route to Damascus, Jesus appeared to him, transformed his faith life, and began preparing him for bearing witness to both Jews and Gentiles across the Mediterranean world. The spread of Christianity proceeded—not only *in spite of*, but *because of*, human opposition.

9 Luke devotes almost two chapters to describing the conversion of Cornelius, a Gentile centurion, 10:1–11:18. He considers the incident of crucial importance, for he tells it (Acts 10) and then retells it, Acts 11. The Gospel has now been proclaimed to, and accepted by, a Gentile and his household. God has shown divine approval of this development by pouring out the Holy Spirit on the new converts, 10:44. Peter dares anyone to oppose this new stage in the Gospel's progress (10:47), and the apostolic circle in Jerusalem sets its seal of approval on what has transpired, 11:18.

10 This incident marks a pivotal point in Acts. The Holy Spirit, who guided the events of Jesus' ministry and was poured out on both Jews and proselytes, now involves the Gentiles in His mission. From now on, the Holy Spirit expands His outreach and uses Jewish communities as stepping-stones to reach the Gentile world—first in the cities of *Asia Minor*, and then on the mainland of *Europe*, ch. 16. Finally, the witness is heard even in *Rome*, 28:16–31. At this point, Luke ends his account. He has told his story. The witness that began in Jerusalem has spread to Judea, to Samaria, and to the ends of the earth, Acts 1:8.

The Life of Paul

Acts 13–28

INTRODUCING PAUL

On July 17, A.D. 180, a small group from the town of Scilli in North Africa was summoned to appear before the Roman governor of the province. They were charged with belonging to a seditious organization—the Christian Church. During the trial, a box containing the little community's library was brought into the court. The governor asked the members of the group what was in the box. They replied, "Our books, and the letters of Paul, a righteous man." The letters brought into the court were copies of originals written over a hundred years earlier. Who was this man whose letters were used as evidence to support the capital charge brought against those Scillitan martyrs? Paul!

1 Paul's birth date is not known. He is spoken of as a "young man" at the stoning of Stephen, 7:58. He was born in the Hellenistic town of Tarsus in Cilicia (in present-day Turkey), 22:3. His Jewish parents belonged to the tribe of Benjamin, Romans 11:1. He had a sister, 23:16. He and his family members were Roman citizens, 22:25–29; 23:27.

2 Tarsus was a city of culture, philosophy, and education. Paul referred to the fact that he was "a citizen of an important city," 21:39. Most likely he received his early education there; but see also 22:3. Notables such as Cicero, Julius Caesar, and Caesar Augustus had visited the town. On one occasion, Mark Antony provided a royal reception for Cleopatra there.

3 Paul referred to himself as a Jew (21:39), an Israelite (2 Corinthians 11:22), a Hebrew (Philippians 3:5), and a Pharisee, Acts 23:6, 26:5. When he was invited to appear before King Agrippa II, he said, "I have belonged to the strictest sect of our religion and lived as a Pharisee," 26:5. He received some of his education at the feet of Gamaliel (22:3), a venerated rabbi who taught in Jerusalem A.D. 20–50.

4 Paul initially involved himself in the persecution of the Christian community. Acts first mentions Paul in connection with the stoning of Stephen. He eventually obtained official sanction to capture Christians in Damascus and bring them back to Jerusalem. While on the way to Damascus, he was converted to faith in Jesus with the result that Saul, the persecutor, became Paul, the apostle.

5 In his letters the apostle calls himself Paul. Acts 13:9 is a transition point for his names. Before this verse he is called *Saul*; after it, *Paul*. The name Saul is used in the conversion accounts, both before and after the transition verse; see Acts 9:4,17; 22:7,13; 26:14. It was common enough for Jews to have two names, a Hebrew one and a Greek or Roman one. It is likely that the apostle was called Paul from birth, and that Saul was the name he used in Jewish circles.

6 After his conversion, Paul spent some time in Arabia, visited the church leaders in Jerusalem, and then returned to Tarsus. Barnabas sought him out there and enlisted his services for the work in Syrian Antioch. Paul made three major missionary journeys with Antioch as his base of operations. Between the first and second journeys he took part in the Apostolic Council in Jerusalem, at which the role of the Mosaic Law in the life of Gentile converts was discussed.

7 Soon after his return to Jerusalem at the close of the third missionary journey, Paul was mobbed and imprisoned. For security reasons, he was taken to Caesarea where he spent several years in protective custody. He eventually appealed to have his case heard by Caesar in Rome. The voyage westward ended with a shipwreck on Malta. Paul finally reached Rome and spent two years there as a prisoner. There is reason to believe that he was released, and that he worked in Macedonia—and possibly Spain—prior to martyrdom during the Neronian persecutions.

Paul's Conversion

1 While Saul the Pharisee was on the road to Damascus to persecute followers of The Way (the term used to define the early Christian movement), the Risen Lord met him—and Saul the Pharisee became Paul the Apostle. Acts describes this event three times, 9:1–19; 22:3–16; 26:4–18. Paul himself wrote about it (Galatians 1:15,16) and always associated it with his apostolic commission, 1 Corinthians 9:1; 15:8. It was the decisive event in his life in which he became a slave of Jesus the Messiah (Galatians 1:10; Romans 1:1) and one committed to be "all things to all people," 1 Corinthians 9:22.

2 On the road to Damascus, Paul was not converted from an aimless life to a life of Christian virtue, but from one kind of zealous devotion (*Judaism*) to another (*Jesus*). The vision he had on the road to Damascus was very different from all others that he experienced; see 2 Corinthians 12:lff. It was comparable with those entrusted by the Risen Lord to Peter, James, the Twelve, and the five hundred, 1 Corinthians 15:3–10. Paul knew that, in an act of sheer grace, the Risen Lord had appeared to him, the arch-persecutor, 1 Corinthians 15:9ff. Furthermore, Paul realized that to persecute Christians was to persecute Jesus Himself ("Saul, Saul, why do you persecute *Me*?" 9:4).

3 Prior to his conversion, the Christian claim that the crucified Jesus of Nazareth was Messiah and Lord was for Paul impossible even to consider. It would have been incomprehensible to Saul the Pharisee that any Messiah would have identified Himself with those low-class, second-rate Jews who constituted the Church—those farmers, fishermen, shepherds, tax-collectors, housewives, and former harlots who knew little or nothing about the Jewish Law. It was an intolerable thought that these ordinary "people of the land" should presume to call themselves the "people of God." However, on the road to Damascus the Risen Lord revealed to Paul just how wrong he had been. If Paul had been so wrong about the "people of the land," was it not possible that he was also wrong about the *Gentiles*? If God could save those Jews who knew nothing about the Jewish Law/Torah, was it not possible that God could also save the Gentiles who knew nothing about it? These thoughts would have created turmoil in Paul's mind.

The Post-Conversion Years

1 Details about Paul's life during the fourteen years after his conversion are vague. Immediately after the event, he went alone to Arabia, Galatians 1:17. It is not known why he went there, although various suggestions are made: to prepare for his ministry, to visit Mt. Sinai, or to witness for Jesus in Arabia. Paul then returned to Damascus and "confounded the Jews" by "proving that Jesus was the Messiah," 9:22. Acts mentions no witness to the Gentiles during this time. When Jewish opposition forced him to leave Damascus, he went to Jerusalem (9:23–26; 2 Corinthians 11:32), leaving behind him a group of disciples, 9:25.

2 In 22:17ff., Paul states that he received the call to preach to the Gentiles while experiencing a special vision in the Jerusalem Temple three years after his conversion; see Galatians 1:18. Some suggest that this vision took place during the visit to Jerusalem mentioned in the above paragraph. Possibly he went there to compare notes with Peter, Galatians 1:18. Barnabas helped to allay suspicion among Jewish Christians (9:26ff.), for memories of Saul the persecutor were still strong in their minds. Disputes with the Hellenists resulted in a plot to kill Paul, 9:29. His faithful supporters put him on a ship headed for Tarsus, 9:30. After his arrival there, Paul worked for fourteen years in the regions of Cilicia and Syria, 9:30; Galatians 1:21; 2:1. Nothing is known about this period in Paul's life.

3 The persecution that followed the stoning of Stephen resulted in evangelism efforts in Antioch, 11:19. News of the work there reached Jerusalem, and Barnabas was sent to survey the situation, 11:22. He sensed a need for help and went to Tarsus in search of Paul. The two men then worked together in Antioch for a year, 11:26. During this time, a prophet from Jerusalem called Agabus came to Antioch and predicted a famine in the region. This famine took place about A.D. 46 during the reign of Claudius. The church in Antioch raised funds and sent them to Jerusalem through Paul and Barnabas, 11:27–30. When Paul and Barnabas returned from Jerusalem, they brought with them John Mark (12:25), Barnabas' cousin, Colossians 4:10.

4 It is traditional to treat Paul's three missionary journeys as though he undertook three distinct journeys with Antioch as his base. However, although Antioch was the *immediate* base of operation for his journeys, the *ultimate* one was Jerusalem, for Paul's missionary work began and ended in Jerusalem.

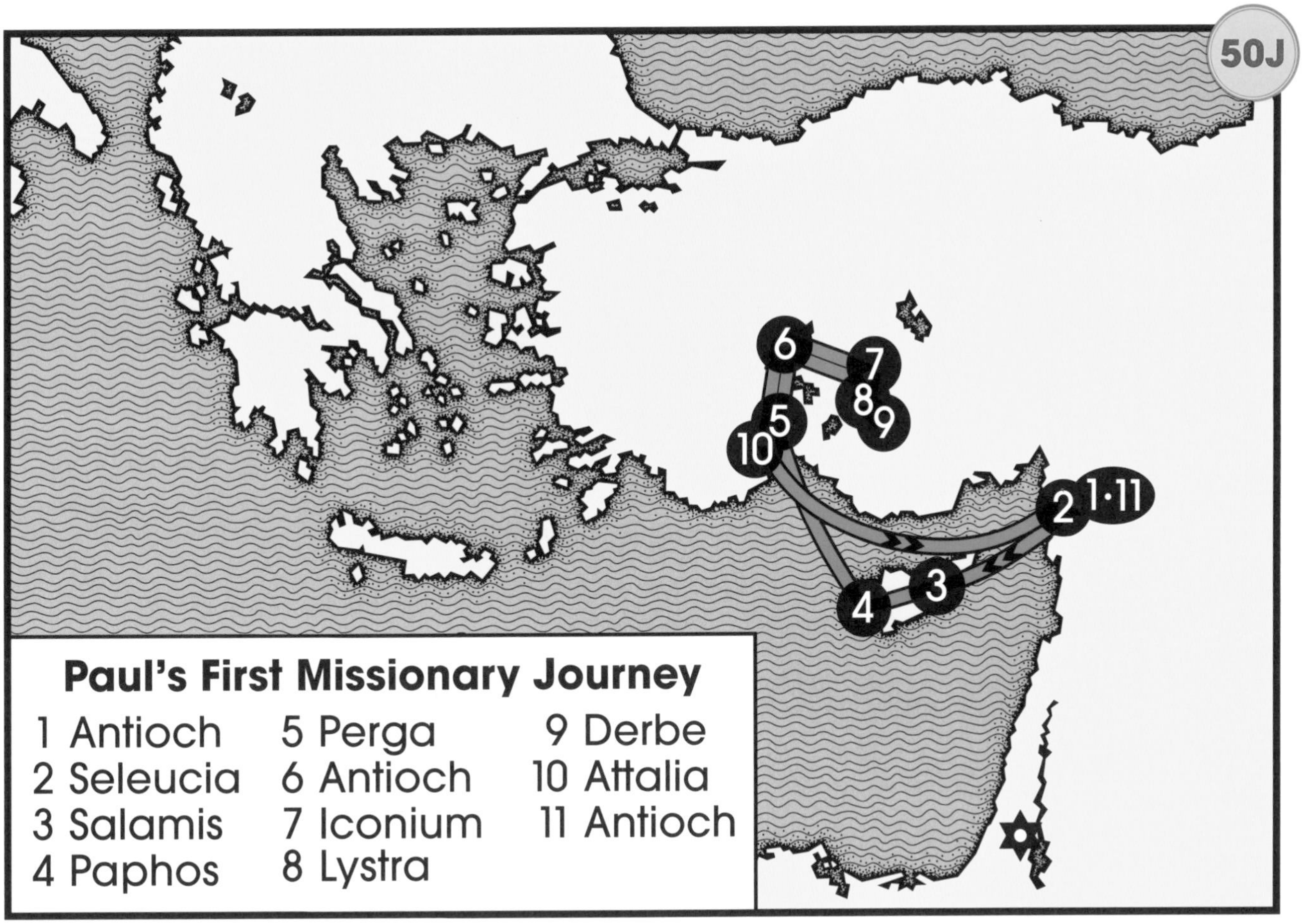

Paul's First Missionary Journey

1 Antioch
2 Seleucia
3 Salamis
4 Paphos
5 Perga
6 Antioch
7 Iconium
8 Lystra
9 Derbe
10 Attalia
11 Antioch

Paul's First Missionary Journey

Acts 13:1–14:28

ILLUSTRATION 50J depicts Paul's first missionary journey. The numbers below correspond to those on the illustration; texts quoted are from Acts. During this journey, *Barnabas and Paul* (13:2) becomes *Paul and Barnabas*, 13:43.

1. Paul and Barnabas were commissioned by the church at ***Antioch***, 13:1–3. Antioch, located on the Orontes River, was the administrative center of the Roman province of Syria. It was the third largest city of the empire—Rome being the first and Alexandria in Egypt the second.

2. Together with John Mark, the apostles set sail from Antioch's port city, ***Seleucia***, 13:4.

3. They headed for *Cyprus*. (The name comes from a Greek word for copper, for which the island was famous.) Possibly they chose to visit Cyprus because Barnabas was familiar with the island, 4:36. After arriving there, they preached in the Jewish synagogue at ***Salamis***, 13:5.

4. They then traveled to ***Paphos*** where they encountered and temporarily blinded the false prophet, Bar-Jesus. The proconsul, Sergius Paulus, believed their message, 13:6–12.

5. The group then sailed to ***Perga*** in Pamphylia, situated on the southern coast of Asia Minor. John Mark left them there and returned to Jerusalem, 13:13.

6 After Paul preached in the synagogue at ***Antioch***, many believed. However, an initial welcome was followed by a campaign of Jewish persecution and opposition—with the result that Paul and Barnabas were forced to leave the city, 13:14–52.

7 After meeting a similar reception in ***Iconium***, the apostles moved on to Lystra and Derbe, 14:1–7.

8 In ***Lystra***, after Paul healed a crippled man, the people revered Paul and Barnabas as Greek gods—Paul as Hermes and Barnabas as Zeus. After Jews from Antioch and Iconium won over the crowds, Paul was stoned and left for dead. However, after Paul recovered, he and Barnabas moved on to Derbe, 14:8–20.

9 After preaching and winning many in ***Derbe***, the apostles retraced their steps. (Had Paul and Barnabas continued on past Derbe, they would have come to Paul's home city, Tarsus, in which Paul had possibly already done considerable work.)

10 Paul and Barnabas returned to the port city of ***Attalia***, 14:24,25.

11 From Attalia, they sailed back to ***Antioch*** in Syria (14:21–23) and reported to the church there, 14:26–28.

Although the cities Paul and Barnabas visited tended to be insignificant, the work they carried out in those cities was effective. The people were particularly impressed by the healings and exorcisms, 14:3ff.,8ff. Although both Jews and proselytes were converted, the mission was more successful among the Gentiles. Paul and Barnabas deliberately turned to the latter because of violent opposition by some Jews, 13:45,50; 14:2,19ff. After returning to Antioch, the team summed up the outcome of the venture with "God has opened a door of faith for the Gentiles," 14:27. *The Gospel had been effectively presented to Gentiles outside Palestine.*

The Apostolic Council

Acts 15

1 The first missionary journey brought results, but also problems. It raised the burning issue of the relation of the new Gentile Christians to the older Jewish converts. Are the Gentiles to be circumcised? Must they observe the Mosaic Law? Should they adhere to Pharisaic dietary customs?

2 Shortly after the conclusion of the first missionary journey, the Galatian churches (Antioch, Iconium, Lystra, and Derbe) were troubled by Christians (whether they were *Jewish* Christians from Jerusalem or *Gentile* Christians is debated) who insisted that circumcision and the observance of the Mosaic Law were obligatory for all Christians. They claimed that Paul had taught the Galatian churches a false concept of freedom and that Paul was not a true apostle. It is possible that Paul wrote his Letter to the Galatians about this time. In it, he stated with a passion that to insist on circumcision is to destroy God's Gospel of grace!

3 Pharisaic Christians went from Jerusalem to Antioch to discuss the issue of circumcision and make the rite obligatory for all Christians. Dissension followed. Finally, the church at Antioch decided to send Paul, Barnabas, and others to Jerusalem to settle the question, ch. 15. The Apostolic Council took place there. The main item on the agenda was, "Does salvation depend on faith in Jesus *alone*, or on faith *plus* circumcision and other observances of the Mosaic Law?" Converted Pharisees insisted that circumcision and the observance of the Mosaic Law were necessary. Peter opposed this. Paul and Barnabas stated their position. James agreed with them, but suggested that, although the Gentiles were not to be troubled with circumcision and the ritual requirements of the Mosaic Law, they should abstain from making and worshiping idols, unchastity, eating what is strangled, and blood (details contained in the commandments of Noah). A decree to this effect was drawn up and sent to the churches of Antioch, Syria, and Cilicia.

4 Paul's position had been endorsed. The young church had been freed from its Jewish roots, and the acceptance of Gentiles into the church could proceed unhindered. The way was now wide open for the development of Gentile Christianity.

5 Paul's visits to Jerusalem after his conversion raise questions of chronology. Is Paul's visit to Jerusalem outlined in Galatians 2:1–10 to be identified with Acts 11:27–30 (the famine collection) or with ch. 15 (the Apostolic Council)? Some link the Galatians 2 visit with Acts ch. 11; others link it with ch. 15. Problems of interpretation result whichever view one accepts.

6 Significantly, Paul makes no reference in Galatians to the letter that James issued after the Apostolic Council. It would have been to Paul's advantage to do so had James' letter been in existence when he wrote. This suggests that Galatians was written *before* the Apostolic Council. Some scholars point to 21:25, and suggest that Paul did not even know about the existence of James' letter until he returned to Jerusalem after the third missionary journey. They suggest that a copy was sent to Antioch after Paul and Silas had already set out on the second missionary journey.

7 Galatians 2:11–14 describes a confrontation between Paul and Peter in Antioch. Apparently, Jewish and Gentile Christians had been eating together there on an equal basis. When Peter visited them, he joined in the practice. However, "certain people from James" (Galatians 2:12) objected to it, with the result that Peter withdrew from table fellowship with the Gentile Christians. Paul confronted Peter about the matter and accused him of hypocrisy, Galatians 2:14. The question is: Did Peter's visit take place before or after the Apostolic Council? Scholars argue in support of both alternatives. The question of the relationship between Jewish and Gentile Christians was an agonizing one during this early period, and the problem persisted beyond the meeting of the Apostolic Council.

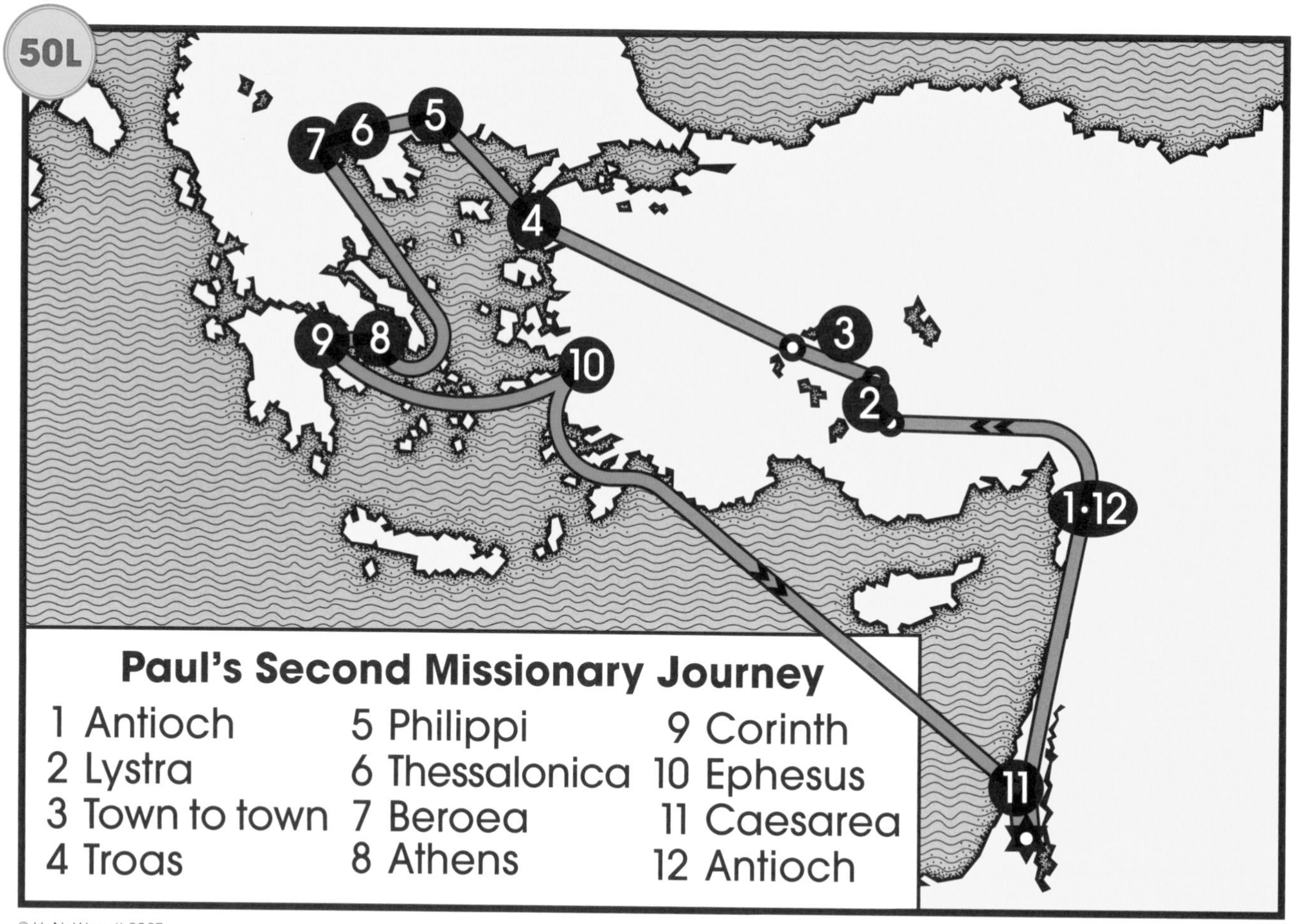

50L

7 6 5 4 3 2 1·12 9 8 10 11

Paul's Second Missionary Journey

1 Antioch	5 Philippi	9 Corinth
2 Lystra	6 Thessalonica	10 Ephesus
3 Town to town	7 Beroea	11 Caesarea
4 Troas	8 Athens	12 Antioch

Paul's Second Missionary Journey

Acts 15:36–18:22

ILLUSTRATION 50L depicts Paul's second missionary journey. The numbers below correspond to those on the illustration; texts quoted are from Acts.

1. Paul and Silvanus set out from Syrian ***Antioch*** to visit the churches Paul had established during his first missionary journey. Barnabas, who had accompanied Paul on his previous journey, traveled to Cyprus in the company of John Mark, 15:36–41.

2. In ***Lystra***, Paul and Silvanus were joined by Timothy, 16:1–3.

3. As they traveled from ***town to town***, the apostles shared with the new believers the decrees of the Apostolic Council (see Acts 15), 16:4,5.

4. At ***Troas***, God spoke to Paul through a vision, instructing him to cross over to Macedonia, 16:6–10.

5. In ***Philippi***, Lydia came to faith, 16:11–15. Lydia was engaged in the dyeing business; the dyes were obtained from the fluid of shellfish collected on the coast of Phoenicia. After Paul exorcised a spirit of divination from a slave-girl, her owners resented the resultant loss of income and dragged Paul and Silas before the local magistrates. Paul and Silas were imprisoned (16:16–24), but used the situation to witness to their jailer and were then miraculously released, 16:25–40. Philippi became the site of

the first Christian church in Europe. Luke begins to use the pronoun "we" at this point (16:10–17), suggesting that he has now joined the group.

6 After the apostles worked successfully in ***Thessalonica***, some Jewish opponents created an uproar that made it necessary for the apostles to move on to Beroea, 17:1–10.

7 Although the work in ***Beroea*** bore fruit, those who had caused the uproar in Thessalonica stirred up opposition also in Beroea, with the result that Paul was forced to move on to Athens, although Silas and Timothy remained behind. Paul gave instructions that Silas and Timothy were to rejoin him in Athens as soon as possible, 17:10–15.

8 Because of ***Athens***' income from commercial enterprises during the days of the Greek empire, magnificent public buildings (such as the Parthenon) were erected within the city. It became a university town to which prominent Roman citizens sent their sons to be educated. Although Paul's ministry in Athens proved to be a rather frustrating affair, it did bear some fruit. While there, he preached on the Areopagus about the "unknown god" and bore witness to the coming resurrection and judgment, 17:16–34. Although some listened with interest to what Paul said, others ridiculed him and said that they would hear him some other time, 17:32.

9 From Athens, Paul moved on to ***Corinth*** where he worked for eighteen months. Corinth was the administrative center of the Roman province of Achaia and was controlled by the Roman senate. While working in that city, Paul stayed with Aquila and Priscilla who had come to Corinth after the Roman Emperor Claudius issued an edict banishing Jews from Rome. He worked with Aquila and Priscilla, and preached in the Jewish synagogue. Once again the Jews stirred up trouble and brought Paul before the proconsul Gallio. Gallio dismissed the affair as an argument about words and refused to get involved. Eventually, Silas and Timothy joined him there. As more opposition developed, Paul left the synagogue and continued his work in the house of Titius Justus, a Gentile believer. A synagogue official, Crispus, came to faith—together with all his household and many others. After Jewish opponents again stirred up trouble and tried to involve the proconsul Gallio in their schemes, Paul set sail for Syria with Aquila and Priscilla, 18:1–17.

10 After reaching ***Ephesus***, Paul held discussions with the leaders of the synagogue there, who asked him to stay longer. Although Paul declined the invitation, he promised to return at a later date. He left Aquila and Priscilla in Ephesus, 18:1–22.

11 After landing in ***Caesarea***, Paul went to Jerusalem where he greeted the church, 18:22.

12 From Jerusalem, Paul traveled north to ***Antioch*** where he spent some time before setting out on his third missionary journey, 18:23.

Several incidents that took place during this second missionary journey show the pains Paul took to avoid offending the Jews. He circumcised Timothy, whose father was a Greek. Paul cut his hair after taking a temporary vow, 18:18. He observed the Jewish Law and expected other Jewish Christians to do the same. Even so, although some prominent individuals were converted during this journey (18:7,8), the Jews continued to offer strong opposition, 17:5,13; 18:6ff. They sought Roman support by suggesting that the missionaries were revolutionaries who aimed to establish another kingdom.

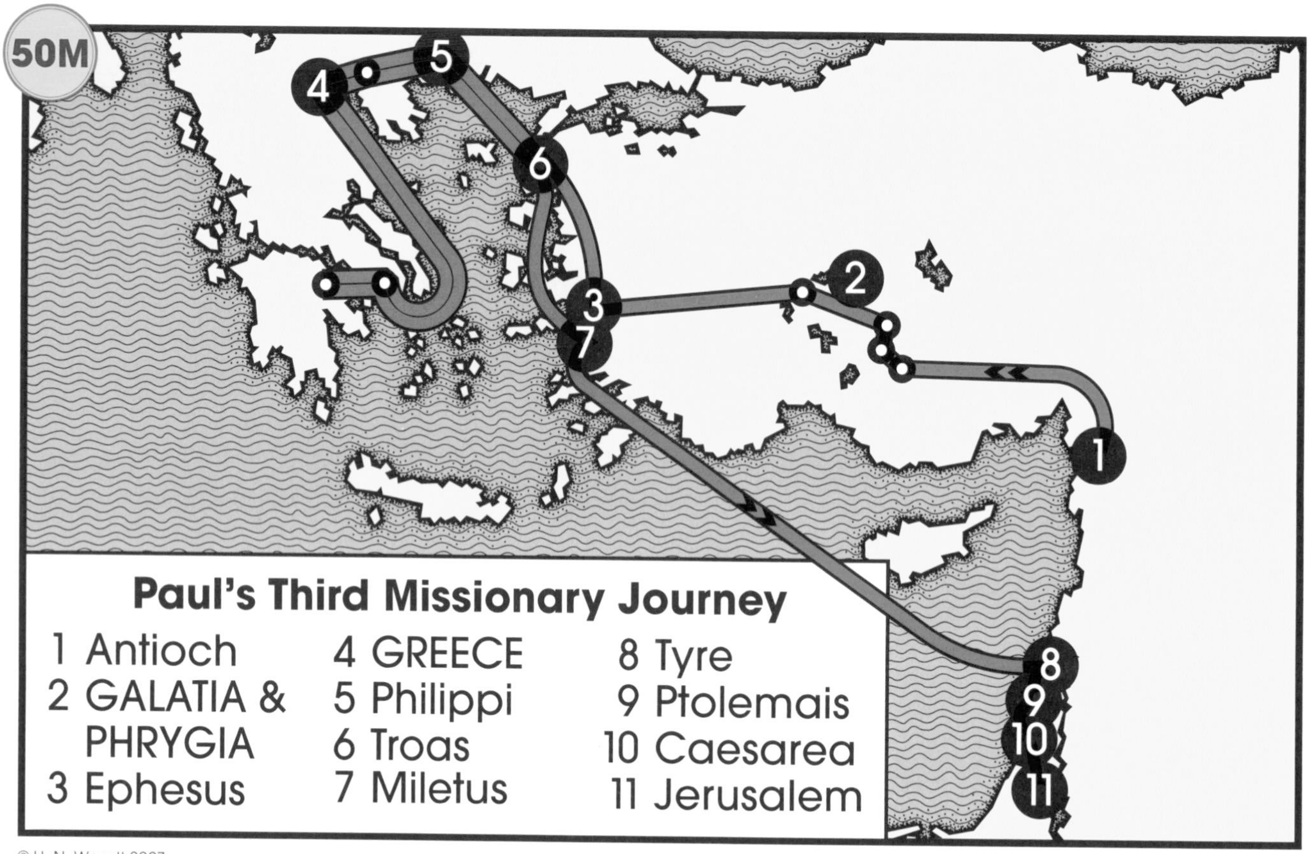

50M

Paul's Third Missionary Journey

1 Antioch
2 GALATIA & PHRYGIA
3 Ephesus
4 GREECE
5 Philippi
6 Troas
7 Miletus
8 Tyre
9 Ptolemais
10 Caesarea
11 Jerusalem

Paul's Third Missionary Journey

Acts 18:23–21:17

ILLUSTRATION 50M outlines Paul's third missionary journey. The numbers correspond to those on the illustration. The texts quoted are from Acts.

1 Paul set out on his third missionary journey from Syrian ***Antioch***, 18:23.

2 He began by strengthening the new believers in ***GALATIA*** and ***PHRYGIA***, 18:23.

3 Paul then made ***Ephesus*** his base for a period of time. Ephesus was the fourth largest city in the Roman empire—prosperous, with streets lined by colonnades, and a temple dedicated to Artemis (also known as Diana) who was revered because of her fertility powers. The temple in which Artemis was worshiped was made of marble, and was one of the seven wonders of the world. Miniatures of Artemis were sold by silversmiths. After teaching for three months in the synagogue in Ephesus, Paul moved into the lecture hall of Tyrannus for another two years. Having resolved to work in Macedonia and Achaia, he sent Timothy and Erastus on ahead. After a riot broke out among these silversmiths who feared for their livelihood if Paul's preaching was successful, Paul moved on to Macedonia and Greece, 19:1–20:3.

4 Paul then worked for three months in ***GREECE***, 20:3.

5 Although Paul had decided to return to Syria by sea, he changed his plans after discovering that some Jews were making a plot against him, and decided to travel back through Macedonia. Eventually, he sailed from ***Philippi***...

6 ...to ***Troas*** where a number of his co-workers were waiting for him and where he spent seven days, 20:3–6. On the night before Paul left Troas, a young man fell asleep while listening to Paul and tumbled down from his place in a window to the street three floors below. Although the young man appeared to be dead, Paul restored him to life, 20:7–12.

7 Paul's co-workers sailed from Troas to Assos, where Paul joined them, and the group then proceeded to Mitylene and ***Miletus***. During the stopover in Miletus, elders from the church in Ephesus met with Paul, 20:13–38.

8 After arriving in ***Tyre***, Paul visited for seven days with some disciples who warned Paul not to go to Jerusalem, 21:1–6.

9 After leaving Tyre, Paul sailed on to ***Ptolemais*** where he spent a day in fellowship with believers, 21:7.

10 Next stop, ***Caesarea***—where Paul stayed with Philip the evangelist and his four unmarried daughters, 8:26–40. Although Agabus, a prophet from Judea, warned Paul of dangers awaiting him in Jerusalem, the apostle elected to proceed to Jerusalem, 21:8–14.

11 Paul received a warm welcome in ***Jerusalem*** and reported to the leaders there what had taken place during his third journey.

After arriving in Jerusalem, Paul paid his respects to James, the brother of Jesus, in the presence of the elders of the Jerusalem church, 21:18. His report of the work done among the Gentiles was well received, 21:20. James, realizing that Paul's presence would cause a stir among the Jews, advised him to join four men in a ceremony involving a vow, and to pay their expenses as a gesture of goodwill to the Jewish Christians in Jerusalem. Paul agreed.

However, when the ritual seven-day period was nearly over, Jews from the province of Asia saw Paul in the Temple area. They accused him of advocating violation of the Mosaic Law and of defiling the Temple by bringing a Greek into it. A mob attacked Paul, dragged him from the Temple, and tried to kill him. Roman soldiers intervened to save Paul's life and placed him under protective arrest. They then gave Paul permission to address the mob. Paul's speech created a furor.

The Roman tribune ordered that he be taken into the barracks and examined under scourging. Paul's appeal to his Roman citizenship saved him from that painful experience. The following day, the tribune brought him before the Sanhedrin. Further violence resulted. Some of the Jews took an oath to refrain from food and drink until they killed Paul. However, news of the plot reached the ears of a son of Paul's sister, who reported the matter to Paul. After Paul informed the Roman tribune of the plot, Paul was transferred to Caesarea. (Read 21:17–23:35.)

After Paul's arrival in Caesarea, Felix, the Roman governor, read the tribune's letter concerning Paul's case. Felix placed Paul under guard in Herod's Praetorium until his accusers arrived from Jerusalem. After they arrived, Tertullus, their spokesman, brought their case before Felix. Paul was permitted to respond. Felix dismissed the Jerusalem delegation, saying that he would decide the case when the tribune himself came to Caesarea. In the meantime, Paul was to remain in protective custody. His friends were permitted access to him. Apparently Felix hoped Paul would bribe him—a hope quite in character with what Roman historians wrote about Felix, 24:26. The Roman historian, Tacitus, wrote of Felix, "Practicing every kind of cruelty and lust, he wielded power with the instincts of a slave."

When Porcius Festus took over the governorship from Felix, Paul was kept in prison out of consideration for the Jews. During a visit Festus made to Jerusalem three days after his arrival in Judea, a Jewish delegation requested that Paul be tried in Jerusalem; the plan was to kill Paul on his way there. Festus refused the request. He insisted that complaints against Paul be heard in Caesarea. After Festus returned to Caesarea, he summoned Paul before him. A Jewish delegation was present to press charges. When Festus asked Paul if he should be tried in Jerusalem, the apostle rejected the suggestion and appealed to the Emperor. Festus conferred with his council about the matter and acceded to Paul's request.

Some time later, King Herod Agrippa II (who ruled parts of Palestine) and his sister Bernice visited Caesarea to welcome Festus to his new post. During their stay, Festus discussed Paul's case with his visitor and arranged for Paul to address Herod Agrippa and Bernice. Festus found Paul's speech hard to take (26:24), and Herod Agrippa would not let himself be cornered by it, 26:28. However, between themselves they agreed that Paul had done nothing deserving imprisonment and, had he not appealed to Caesar, he could have been set free. (Read 24:1–26:32.)

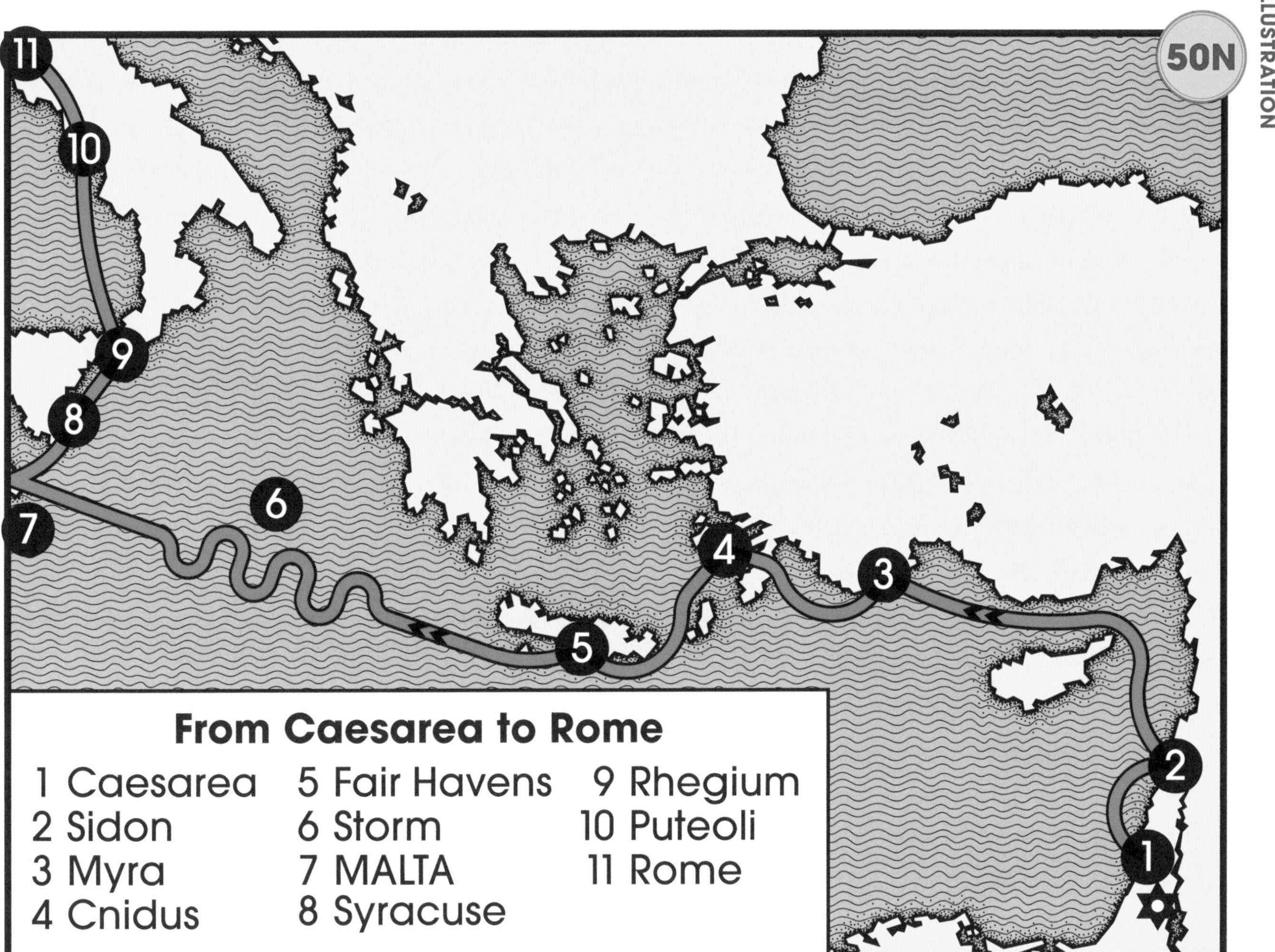

From Caesarea to Rome 50N

Acts 27,28

ILLUSTRATION 50N depicts the journey that took Paul from imprisonment in Caesarea to imprisonment in Rome. The numbers below correspond to those on the illustration; texts quoted are from Acts.

1 While in custody in ***Caesarea***, Paul appealed to the Roman emperor and was eventually taken on board a ship heading for Rome, 27:1,2.

2 The first port-of-call was ***Sidon***. Julius, the centurion in charge of Paul and other prisoners on board, allowed Paul to visit with friends there, 27:3.

3 At the next stopping place, ***Myra*** in Lycia, the company changed ships, boarding an Alexandrian vessel bound for Italy, 27:4–6.

4 From Myra, the group sailed with difficulty to ***Cnidus***, 27:7.

5 From Cnidus, the ship sailed under the lee of Crete to ***Fair Havens*** on the island's southern coast. Although Paul warned against proceeding further, the majority voted to continue the journey, hoping to spend the winter at Phoenix—a more secure Cretan harbor further to the west, 27:8–12.

6 However, soon after setting sail from Fair Havens, the ship was caught in a violent ***storm***, 27:13–38.

7 Finally, the ship ran aground on ***MALTA*** where Paul was able to carry out a remarkable healing ministry, 27:39–28:10.

8 After a three-month stay on Malta, the group set sail once again. This time, the first port-of-call was ***Syracuse*** in Sicily, where the travelers stayed for three days, 28:11,12.

9 Next came a one-day stop at ***Rhegium*** on Italy's west coast, 28:13.

10 Two days later, the ship put in at ***Puteoli***. After spending seven days with believers there, Paul's party set out for Rome, 28:13,14.

11 When believers in ***Rome*** heard of Paul's impending arrival, they went south to the Forum of Appius and Three Taverns (about halfway between Puteoli and Rome) to meet Paul and accompany him on the final leg of the journey, 28:14–16. While in Rome, Paul was allowed to live by himself, although under the guard of a Roman soldier. During the two years that followed, Paul sought to proclaim the message entrusted to him to any who would listen, 28:17–31. He lost little time in making contact with the local Jewish leaders, 28:17. They seemed to know little about him or his teaching, 28:21,22. When he expounded his faith to them, some accepted what he had to say, but others rejected it. Paul continued to welcome all who came to him and witnessed to them about the One he had met on the road to Damascus.

Acts finishes its account at this point, for Luke has accomplished his purpose: to outline the series of events that took the message of the Gospel from Jerusalem to the ends of the earth, 1:8. Paul's ministry continued after the Roman imprisonment. The Pastoral Letters (1 and 2 Timothy and Titus) and tradition give glimpses of Paul's subsequent life. Some traditions suggest that he worked in Spain. The Pastorals suggest that he revisited Ephesus, Macedonia, and Greece. Possibly he was arrested a second time at Troas (2 Timothy 4:13), and executed in Rome during the Neronian persecution. No doubt when his last day on earth came, he met it with joy. Second Timothy 4:6–8 speaks of Paul's attitude in relation to his approaching death:

> *The time of my departure has come. I have fought the good fight, I have finished the race, I have kept the faith. From now on there is reserved for me the crown of righteousness, which the Lord, the righteous judge, will give me on that day, and not only to me but also to all who have longed for his appearing.*

SUMMARY

50A Only Luke (in his Gospel and Acts) reports events associated with Jesus' ascension. Jesus has completed His saving work; the period of being a disciple ("student") is over for His followers. The period of being an apostle ("sent one") begins. There is a world to be won for Jesus the Messiah!

50B Those present in Jerusalem for the great Pentecost described in Acts 2 are *Jews and converts to Judaism*. They come from countries to the east, west, and south of Jerusalem. (The *Gentile* Pentecost is reported in Acts 10:1–11:18.) Events associated with the first Pentecost reflect those that took place when God gathered His people around His presence at Mt. Sinai.

50C Luke's Gospel tells us what Jesus *began* to do. Acts tells us what Jesus *continued* to do through His Holy Spirit. It depicts Christianity spreading in ever-wider circles from Jerusalem, the capital of the Jewish world, to Rome, the capital of the Gentile world.

50D As the apostles proclaimed God's Good News in ever-wider circles, they had to deal with opposition from Jews, Hellenizers, and the Roman elite. The Roman emperor referred to himself as Lord, the savior of the world, the one who proclaims good news, the one who brings peace. However, his method of achieving his goals involved the use of Roman swords.

50E Although the narrative in Acts refers to the work of Peter, James (the brother of Jesus), and John, most of it focuses on the work of Paul. Approximately one-third of Acts is made up of speeches: some by Peter, one by Stephen, and many speeches and sermons by Paul.

50F The work of witness begins in Jerusalem, spreads first to Samaria, then to Gentiles living in Caesarea and Antioch, then to an increasing series of Gentile regions, and finally to Rome itself.

50G Saul of Tarsus (later, Paul of Tarsus), a one-time student of Gamaliel, first bitterly opposed the Christian mission and approved of the stoning to death of Stephen. He then set out for Damascus to capture Christian converts to bring them back to Jerusalem—for trial and possible execution.

50H The Risen Jesus confronted Paul while he was on his way to Damascus—and involved Paul in a mission to make Him known to the ends of the earth.

50I There is good reason to believe that Paul did a lot of thinking, studying, and self-examination during the years immediately following his meeting with Jesus.

50J When carrying out his first missionary journey, Paul worked in cities in the center of the region known today as Turkey.

50K Acts speaks of Paul participating in what is referred to as an "Apostolic Council" in which decisions are made about what is required of Jewish and Gentile converts to Christianity in relation to observing traditional Jewish practices.

50L Paul and his fellow workers then undertake a second missionary journey—this time traveling further west to witness in Greece.

50M In his third missionary journey, Paul revisits many of the places where he worked during his previous journey.

50N After Paul returns to Jerusalem, he is threatened by Jewish leaders, imprisoned by the Romans in Caesarea, and finally taken by ship to Rome to appear before the emperor. Acts makes no mention of what eventually took place in relation to Paul's trial.